Defining Memory

AMERICAN ASSOCIATION FOR STATE AND LOCAL HISTORY BOOK SERIES

ABOUT THE SERIES

The American Association for State and Local History Book Series publishes technical and professional information for those who practice and support history, and addresses issues critical to the field of state and local history. To submit a proposal or manuscript to the series, please request proposal guidelines from AASLH headquarters: AASLH Book Series, 1717 Church St., Nashville, Tennessee 37203. Telephone: (615) 320-3203. Fax: (615) 327-9013. Web site: www.aaslh.org.

ABOUT THE ORGANIZATION

The American Association for State and Local History (AASLH) is a nonprofit educational organization dedicated to advancing knowledge, understanding, and appreciation of local history in the United States and Canada. In addition to sponsorship of this book series, the Association publishes the periodical History News, a newsletter, technical leaflets and reports, and other materials; confers prizes and awards in recognition of outstanding achievement in the field; and supports a broad education program and other activities designed to help members work more effectively. To join the organization, contact: Membership Director, AASLH, 1717 Church St., Nashville, Tennessee 37203.

Defining Memory

Local Museums and the Construction of History in America's Changing Communities

EDITED BY AMY K. LEVIN

A Division of
ROWMAN & LITTLEFIELD PUBLISHERS, INC.
Lanham • New York • Toronto • Plymouth, UK

AltaMira Press
A division of Rowman & Littlefield Publishers, Inc.
A wholly owned subsidiary of The Rowman & Littlefield Publishing Group, Inc.
4501 Forbes Boulevard, Suite 200, Lanham, MD 20706
www.altamirapress.com

Estover Road, Plymouth PL6 7PY, United Kingdom

British Library Cataloguing in Publication Information Available

Library of Congress Cataloging-in-Publication Data

Defining memory : local museums and the construction of history in America's changing communities / edited by Amy K. Levin.
p. cm. — (American Association for State and Local History book series)
Includes bibliographical references and index.
ISBN-13: 978-0-7591-1049-6 (cloth : alk. paper)
ISBN-10: 0-7591-1049-2 (cloth : alk. paper)
ISBN-13: 978-0-7591-1050-2 (paper : alk. paper)
ISBN-10: 0-7591-1050-6 (paper : alk. paper)
1. Historical museums—United States. 2. Historic buildings—United States. 3. Historic sites—United States. 4. Museums—Social aspects—United States. 5. Museums—United States—Management. 6. United States—History, Local. 7. Public history—United States. 8. Memory—Social aspects—United States. 9. Community life—United States. I. Levin, Amy K., 1957-

E172.D44 2007
973.075--dc22

2006100277

Printed in the United States of America

∞™ The paper used in this publication meets the minimum requirements of American National Standard for Information Sciences—Permanence of Paper for Printed Library Materials, ANSI/NISO Z39.48-1992.

Contents

Acknowledgments

First, I wish to express my thanks to the authors of the articles in this book for their perseverance through various revisions and delays not of their own making. Their continuing commitment to this project was heartwarming.

Second, my thanks to Martin Johnson, formerly of Northern Illinois University Press, for his enthusiasm about publishing this work. I was assisted at various stages in the process by current and former Northern Illinois University graduate students Erika Mann, Kai Zhang, and Lise Schlosser, all of whom helped with organizational tasks and ensuring the correctness of the manuscript's documentation. The Graduate School and the College of Liberal Arts and Sciences of the university provided travel funds for my research on New York museums in 2000 and 2004.

Chapter 5 by Richard Handler and Eric Gable was originally published in *Ethnos*, volume 65, number 2 (2000): 237–52. Eric Sandweiss's article, "Cities, Museums, and City Museums," is based on a short article that appeared in *Exhibitionist* 18.1 (Spring 1999): 45–47; portions of that piece are reproduced with permission from the National Association for Museum Exhibition.

Finally, this book is dedicated to Charles Lugo, together with Samantha, Gerald, and Melissa Crane, for their patience while I worked on this manuscript. I hope that some day they will enjoy museums as much as I do.

Foreword

In the past half century, American culture has become ever more standardized. Corporate brands, retail franchises, and look-alike shopping malls stretch from coast to coast, homogenizing the consumption of fashion, decorative arts, and material goods. Broadcasters, publishers, and cinema distributors convey the same information, entertainment, and ideas to audiences throughout the country. Regional differences in dress, diet, and even language fade as patterns of commerce and communication are universalized. One notable exception to this pattern of increasing uniformity has been the preservation of local culture and distinctive identity in America's vast number of small and local museums.

America's justly admired best-known museums are among its largest. From New York's Metropolitan Museum of Art, Museum of Natural History, and Museum of Modern Art to Washington's Smithsonian Institution and National Gallery of Art to Chicago's Art Institute and Field Museum of Natural History to Los Angeles's Getty and Huntington Museums as well as their only slightly smaller counterparts in Boston, Philadelphia, Cleveland, and a few other cities, these museums are among the world's finest. They tend, unfortunately, to overshadow thousands of smaller local museums spread across the

United States that not only are significant in their own right but also bring the museum-going experience within reach of a much larger public.

People visit museums for a variety of reasons, often overlapping ones. Many are eager to gain knowledge about some aspect of the past or some specific objects. Some, frankly, go from a sense of obligation, whether to validate their own social identity or add their support to a well-regarded institution. Others go on their own or are taken by parents, teachers, or others for the purpose of learning something about a place or topic. Still others, indeed perhaps most, find their way to museums to be entertained by the beautiful, the bizarre, the rare, and the captivating.

Reasons for visiting museums are often strongly linked to a sense of place, whether one's own community or one that sparks curiosity. The desire to connect to a locale, to understand it, identify with it, or simply enjoy its distinctiveness is a common impulse that a close-by museum serves to satisfy. Museums are the community's attic, the storage site for artifacts once created there or brought to that place for one reason or another. We may seldom visit the attic and, when we do, may find it difficult to sort through what has been preserved there, but nevertheless that is where we know to look for tangible evidence of our past. Those repositories, whether we call them attics or museums, allow us to connect somehow to a time, a place, or a phenomenon we desire to revisit in our mind or visit for the first time.

Beyond the few extraordinary ones already mentioned, the American museums that people visit are as varied as their reasons for making the effort. Proud local residents bring out-of-town visitors to see the High Desert Museum in Bend, Oregon, and the Gilcrease Museum in Tulsa, Oklahoma, to show off the sophistication of the area as well as offer an introduction to its history. An Eau Claire, Wisconsin, teacher takes a class through the Chippewa Valley Museum to make vivid to students through artifacts on display the region's long-gone lumbering economy. Her counterpart in Staunton, Virginia, leads students on a tour of the Woodrow Wilson Birthplace Museum to help them connect to their community's most famous son and thereby to the national and international stage on which he stood. Residents of Muskegon, Michigan, and Youngstown, Ohio, visit local museums to enjoy small but extraordinary art collections assembled by hometown robber barons. To renew ties to an immigrant heritage, upper Midwesterners of Scandinavian background find their way to the Norwegian-American Historical Museum in Decorah, Iowa, while Jews from the New York City area and beyond flock to the Jewish Museum in Manhattan. Museum visitation, whatever propels it, offers a wide range of rewards.

This collection of essays edited by Amy Levin illuminates the rich diversity of America's lesser-known local museums. Levin and her colleagues provide rich descriptions of a remarkable diversity of institutions, many of them unfamiliar outside a limited area or community of interest. Their selections reflect the wide variety of museums spread across the land and ranging from professionally to haphazardly administered, from well to precariously supported, and from broadly representative to highly unusual in content. More important, the authors raise significant questions about the functions of museums and the way in which they should be organized, employed, and explained. By offering such an extraordinary mix of examples, Levin and company force readers to think about what to expect from museums, what to demand, what to enjoy, and what might be best not to encounter.

An underlying theme of these essays is the relationship of museums to their locale. In some cases, the linkage is direct and essential, in others apparently tangential, and in a few instances so subtle as to seem nonexistent. Yet in every case, a specific place has provided the environment that has nurtured, or occasionally stunted, the museum's development. The more evident the nature of the bond, the greater the value of the museum for revealing the identity and idiosyncrasies of a particular place. In nearly every case, however, the museum reflects something about the nearby community.

The past remains ever present within and around a community and is reflected in its museums. It has always been vital to an understanding of a locale as well as generally of great interest to the residents of that place and occasionally to outsiders also. Years ago I began referring to this close-at-hand past as nearby history, though the standard term of reference continues to be local history. Whatever it is called, however, the past that is up close and personal has great value to those in its midst.

Whether passed on in the form of oral tradition, publications, or collections of objects, the localized past is a vital component of the identity of a place. It holds interest for both residents and those visiting the place for the first time. When, as often happens, people talk of their "roots," they are referring to a personal identity that sinks deep into the soil of a place. Local museums often serve to distill the identity of the community with which people identify, and whether they do it well or badly will affect attitudes toward the locale in question.

The understanding of a place and its history is always subject to selections of evidence from the myriad of possibilities, choices of focus, and interpretations made by persons long after the fact. As they seek to understand an earlier era, they of necessity view the past through the prism of their own situation and conception of how the world works. As experience accumulates, comprehension of what is significant about the past under consideration necessarily undergoes revision. In other words, history is not the past itself but a later generation's perception of that past. In the ongoing process of coming to terms with the past, museums, as collections of the physical remains of earlier times, can provide something of a reality check as well as reminders of what is believed, what remains a mystery, and what would be useful to investigate further.

The extent to which a museum should mediate its visitors' encounters with the past is in constant dispute. The view of most scholars and museum professionals has long been that those equipped with extensive knowledge of context and specialized skill in evaluating available evidence and linking it to other knowledge are best suited to interpret the past for those who come with curiosity and enthusiasm but little else. This approach finds little place for the anomalous, the freakish, the unrepresentative, or the merely redundant. A contrary view, at once older and more recent, is that anyone who visits a museum should be free to examine the full range of objects preserved there and make whatever connections and interpretations they wish. Examples and variations of each approach are described and commented upon in this collection of essays. Each account serves to raise important questions about preferable museum practices and approaches to enhancing historical knowledge.

Amy Levin's collection is valuable because it describes the reality of diverse approaches to museum presentation rather than offering a didactic guide to best practices. As such, the essays do more to stimulate reflection on what a museum should strive to achieve than merely set standards. Old Cowtown and the Freakatorium, two museums vividly described is this book, both stray from the ideals articulated by the American Association of Museums and yet both tell us something about the environment they inhabit. Even the most highly trained museum professionals can profit from a consideration of what exists as well as what might be ideal.

The essays in this book offer insights to readers thinking about how to design or reconstruct a local museum or whether to donate objects or funds to one. The book also has value for museum consumers who wish to strengthen their critical faculties for judging whether the museum they visit is providing as satisfying an experience as it might. Finally, the book speaks to the larger community of historians, self-propelled as well as professional, engaged in any effort to understand a community's distinctiveness. Evaluating the nature of the museums that have arisen as well as the artifacts they have preserved and presented as traces of the past can illuminate the assumptions and beliefs of a community over time. Thus, those interested in a nearby past will find themselves constantly intrigued, frequently amused, occasionally astonished, repeatedly enlightened, and, above all, amply rewarded by the work of Amy Levin and her colleagues.

David E. Kyvig
Distinguished Research Professor
and Professor of History
Northern Illinois University

I

FRAMEWORKS

Visitors impatient with the heavy traffic along I-70 about an hour west of St. Louis might take a detour onto one of the frontage roads at Wright City. This detour contains a remarkable site, the Elvis is Alive Museum, owned by Bill Beeny. It would take a stretch of the imagination to consider me a great Elvis fan, but like so many human beings, I have a more than "passing" interest in immortality and therefore incorporated this site into one of my trips. The museum is in fact little more than a '50s café with an annex full of Elvis memorabilia. All the publicity about Elvis serves as an attraction. The entire café has a shrine-like aura. Visitors have the opportunity to examine replicas of Elvis's funeral paraphernalia and studies "proving" that DNA evidence shows that Elvis survived. Punch a button on a cassette player, and you can hear the King's voice reaching out from beyond the grave, marred only by the blurriness of tapes that have been played a few times too often.

I was in for another treat as well. At a table nearby were several individuals discussing Elvis and the cassette tape. They were arguing intently among themselves about the veracity of Beeny's assertion that the real Lisa Marie was hidden in Europe and a stand-in was taking her place in public. The conversation was carried on with all the seriousness and intensity of a scholarly debate on the location of the Holy Grail.

This incident delighted me, but it served a more serious purpose as well, reminding me that for millions of Americans, museums—even the smallest roadside "shrines"—carry a certain authority and authenticity. For habitués of such sites, local museums *are* America. International tourists are more likely to visit major museums such as the Smithsonian, but local museums show us our smaller curiosities, dreams, and failures. Elvis Presley is an iconic figure in our culture, and it is no wonder that he is honored in a shrine so far from Graceland.

This book presents a bouquet of local small and medium-sized museums, offering an opportunity for visitors to learn about them and to reflect on their roles in culture. It is intended for connoisseur and amateur alike, scholar and tourist. Because varied audiences are likely to approach the book with distinct backgrounds, the next two chapters introduce and contextualize the topic of local museums.

The first chapter outlines some defining features of local museums, explaining why such institutions are important even though renowned critics such as Kenneth Hudson have refused to label them "museums of influence."[1] This section of the book traces the unique history of small and medium-sized museums in America, indicating why our nation has developed such an abundance of local institutions. In addition, this essay summarizes the themes to be discussed in the rest of this book.

The second chapter, by Elizabeth Vallance, offers frameworks for talking about and understanding the contributions of local museums. Vallance, a museum educator, is accustomed to introducing galleries to everyone from scholars to children. She has considerable experience in training museum employees as well. Her article therefore provides a clear guide to the variety of features that affect learning in museums, ranging from the physical setting to the values transmitted to viewers. These frameworks are intended to guide readers to make their own conclusions about collections, both those described in the following articles as well as those in museums they might visit on their own.

This collection of articles itself, then, may be considered a shrine to the living museum, as opposed to the living Elvis, a space where readers can hear the voices of scholars and museum staff about the ways in which local institutions shape our communities and our culture to render them distinctively American.

NOTE

1. Kenneth Hudson, *Museums of Influence* (Cambridge: Cambridge University Press, 1987), vii.

1

Why Local Museums Matter

Amy K. Levin

America's amazing array of small museums dedicated to everything from mourning to sex reflects not only the nation's often bizarre obsessions, but also its distinctiveness. No other nation boasts such a diverse range of institutions. The historical roots of this circumstance are complex, but they include the American cult of individualism in which every person is seen as capable of owning something unique to display and the expansion of the highway system in the fifties, rendering even small hamlets accessible to tourists. The plethora of local museums is also attributable to what we do not have. France, for instance, developed a network of regional museums with items from national collections during the nineteenth century.[1] These centrally supported institutions in some ways mitigated against the spread of neighborhood enterprises. The involvement of private individuals instead of the government in many small and medium-sized American institutions also facilitated their success. Even though they lacked funds from the central government, the institutions could rely on local entrepreneurs and were not bound to a rigid set of national museum standards.

DEFINITIONS

Today, our community institutions follow a variety of models. In defining local museums, I decided to take the term *local* literally, as defining the primary emphasis of the museum's collection or delineating the museum's main audience. This first part of the criteria allows for the inclusion of historic society collections, homes of famous citizens, historic sites, and exhibits devoted to an area's industry. Everything from Williamsburg to the Wheaton (Illinois) History Museum would qualify. The definition incorporates exhibits and collections that may claim to be "halls of fame" or "national museums" of quirky or odd objects, because they draw local audiences and offer a social outlet for citizens of the communities. Most of these museums are also facing challenges in their efforts to represent their communities in a time of rapid change. They attract tourists, but mainly those whose primary reason for visiting an area is other than seeing the museum. For instance, the Museum of American Financial History is unlikely to be someone's main reason for visiting lower Manhattan, but might be included in a sightseer's activities, just as the Spam Museum might make an amusing stop when driving across Minnesota on I-90, but would rarely be a final destination for a vacationer. And the Jell-O Museum in LeRoy, New York, at once offers a humorous stopping-off place and draws attention to local history. Not surprisingly, the institutions described in this book are also generally smaller than America's world-famous museums.

Many of these institutions lack accreditation from the American Association of Museums (AAM). Many are held back by the AAM requirement that they have an annual operating budget of at least $25,000. Other institutions fail to meet the AAM's definition of a museum because the professional organization stipulates that a museum must employ at least one full-time professional, while local exhibits may rely entirely on part-time or volunteer labor.[2] Yet clearly, these institutions *are* museums, and a major purpose of this book is to argue for a distinct category of local museums, whether they are tiny or medium sized. Another popular standard used to classify museums also excludes local institutions—Kenneth Hudson's 1987 pronouncement that certain major institutions were "museums of influence," relegating others to wings (the fact that all natural history museums were excluded from this category offered some consolation).[3] While Hudson's presumption provided useful shorthand for referring to major museums, its implicit valuing reified a traditional hierarchical conception of museums and their uses. Moreover, it revealed a neglect and misunderstanding of the importance of local institutions.

This devaluing is evident in the nature of recent publications on museums, too. The last fifteen years have seen the burgeoning of books on museum theory and criticism, ranging from works focusing on cultural difference such as Ivan Karp and Steven Levine's well-known collection, *Exhibiting Cultures: The Poetics and Politics of Museum Display*, to Tony Bennett's more philosophical

The Birth of the Museum, which draws on Foucault's research on the history of institutions, Marxist theory, and deconstruction. Very few of these serious works focus explicitly on local sites. *Museums and Communities: The Politics of Public Culture*, Karp and Lavine's second volume, edited together with Christine Mullen Kreamer, concentrates explicitly on the importance of communities to museums, but only some of the articles describe American museums. Other books, like Lawrence Wechsler's *Mr. Wilson's Cabinet of Wonder*,[4] present insights into individual museums but offer few options for comparative study. To this day, guidebooks remain the best sources for information on museums devoted to distinctive aspects of their communities, although these texts contain little or no critical analysis of the collections.

The neglect of local institutions in definitions of museums, accompanied by the gap in the body of published works, renders this book and an attempt at defining local museums especially necessary. The smaller, less famous institutions that occupy the writers of this book do influence communities and their citizens. The ubiquity of the automobile has rendered them more accessible to the average American citizen, and even though such institutions are often in financial peril, they manage to survive through donations of time and objects. The American Association of Museums reports that immediately after the September 11, 2001, terrorist attacks on the East Coast, many well-known museums experienced a precipitous decrease in visits from tourists, who were hesitant to travel significant distances to museums of influence.[5] In a time of vulnerability, local citizens more highly valued the importance of community and family, so they found the kinds of exhibits available at smaller, locally focused museums appealing. Museums had to become more conscious of their role in defining communities, as well as of the importance of inclusiveness. According to Ron Chew, "Since Sept, 11, small museums, especially those that have thrived on strong grassroots ties, have become natural focal points for community groups struggling with issues of cross-cultural tolerance and seeking healing and reflection."[6] Many institutions rushed to initiate panels and dialogues; others offered free days; others created exhibits relating to diverse aspects of the community. Thus, museums began to reassert their importance within their home communities.

RECENT HISTORY AND LOCAL MUSEUMS

The challenges faced by local museums are the challenges faced by America today. While the terrorist attacks increased museum attendance by community members, they also affected the level of funding available to small and middle-sized institutions, as donors attended to the needs of survivors, and many others who might have donated suffered financially as a result of the plunge in the economy. Such consequences demonstrate the extent to which museums remain vulnerable to the vagaries of the economy and national priorities. Moreover, the failure of major corporations such as Enron diminished the donations available to museums from private and corporate donors, rendering their abilities to meet the public's needs more limited. These issues will surface repeatedly in the chapters that follow.

But the shock following the dramatic assault on the United States was not limited to a nesting instinct and financial loss; it forced many Americans to question why and how it came to be that a religious minority could hate them so much and to realize the very grave consequences of not understanding the experiences of those from various cultures, religions, races, and ethnicities. The hollowness of lip service and hand wringing about minorities were exposed.

There were plenty of both to be exposed. In 1997, I noted that for the most part, smaller museums advertised in brochures and travel guides continued to offer pictures of a white middle class endlessly absorbed in its cultural products.[7] Even when these museums attempted to be inclusive, they tended to reflect mainstream cultural prejudices and reinforce popular stereotypes, creating another set of problems. An excellent example would be the way that African Americans were mostly presented as servants in historic houses, which continued to focus on the lives of wealthy European Americans. Similarly, Eric Gable, co-author of an article in this volume, has written a study of the difficulties of incorporating African-American history in tour scripts for Williamsburg titled, "Maintaining Boundaries, or 'mainstreaming' black history in a white museum."[8]

One complicating factor in the trend to render local museums more multicultural has been the Native American Graves Protection Act, or NAGPRA, which mandates the return of certain cultural artifacts and funerary remains to their original Native American peoples, without appropriating adequate funds for this process. This act has led to the involvement of the federal government in a number of community and regional museums, and it has stretched their limited resources. More importantly, it has forced such museums to review their holdings of Native American artifacts and to re-assess their value as important parts of their cultural heritage. As minorities and members of the working classes clamor more and more insistently for representation in museum narratives of their communities, the institutions must move from a "lifestyles of the rich and famous" approach to a more inclusive manner of display. At times, a museum's desire to diversify itself throws it into contradiction. Changes may threaten certain traditionally powerful groups within its community, yet local museums must appeal to the groups that support them. A museum celebrating Mormon pioneers and depicting Utah history is unlikely to present the Church of Latter-day Saints in a negative light or blatantly to oppose its views regarding women and minorities.

While local museums often concentrate on the experiences of those who succeed in conventional terms, they have also turned for audiences to depicting the lives of those who are notorious in their communities, and who are not necessarily venerated by citizens, such as criminal John Dillinger. Such subjects can be tricky because of their controversial natures. While the stories of these individuals create dramatic displays, museum staff must beware of creating hagiographies or of supporting values that the dominant public does not endorse, such as criminal behavior. Thus, in the end, many of these small and medium-sized museums continue to support the aims of late nineteenth-century galleries for members of the working class—to educate the poor and thus act as a means of social control.[9]

Museums also reflect the spirit of the times. History museums that have existed in communities for decades constantly revise their narratives to reflect the experiences of those who move to or away from the area as well as shifting ideologies about the importance of minorities and women. To be successful, museums must adopt the technology and display methods that will most attract visitors at a given time. The meticulously hand-written index cards characteristic of a nineteenth-century collection may seem charming today, but the public finds computer-generated labels more professional and hence authoritative. In fact, throughout the world of these museums, an imperative toward professionalism as opposed to volunteer or amateur staff is evident.

Museums change so rapidly, in fact, that some of the institutions in later chapters will have changed format or location by the time this book is published. We have continued to include these museums regardless, because the discussions are intended as case studies, and in that context, they remain useful. In the interests of accuracy, however, we have indicated whenever possible that a museum was likely to have changed or moved by the time the book reaches our readers.

Finally, local museums, as defined in this book, face distinct opportunities and constraints because of their locations. Since many of these museums occupy historic buildings, their ability to expand may be limited, and they may face costly repairs. Keeping old buildings up to code presents continual challenges. Furthermore, many of these institutions have become linked to regional promotions and therefore can only present their communities in positive ways. How various institutions deal with these challenges is a central focus of this volume.

COMMON THEMES

In addition to the challenges of local museums described above, there are several distinct themes that characterize such institutions and render them important participants in the creation of American history. Many museums exemplify several of these themes, but in the chapters that follow, I have grouped the museums according to the themes they illustrate best. This chapter and the next one are coupled in a section titled "Frameworks," because they offer readers ways of looking at and thinking about the museums in the rest of the book. The title "Frameworks" also indicates that local museums serve as frames for understanding larger visions about America. For example, the importance of pedagogy to museums led to my selection of the next article in this collection. As former director of education at the St. Louis Art Museum, former head of Northern Illinois University's Museum Studies program, and member of the art education faculty at the University of Indiana, Elizabeth Vallance is able to blend educational theory with practical experience. Vallance's essay, "Local History, 'Old Things to Look At,' and a Sculptor's Vision: Exploring Local Museums through Curriculum Theory," offers a more in-depth definition of local museums, together with structures for studying them. First, she presents a schema developed by Joseph Schwab for discussing the different aspects of an educational experience. She explains a second schema, proposed by Dwayne Huebner, for categorizing museums' rationales. These theories enable Vallance to analyze three very different institutions—the Geneva History Center in Geneva, Illinois; the Martin Home Place, formerly the Louisiana Art and Folk Festival Museum in Columbia, Louisiana; and the now closed Continental Sculpture Hall in Portis, Kansas. The Geneva History Center is a fairly typical historic society collection. The folk art collection at the Martin Home Place represents the type of institution that provided "old things to look at" without offering a picture of the real diversity of the community. And the Continental Sculpture Hall reflected the idiosyncrasies of a small museum based on the collection and tastes of a single individual. As Vallance argues, the application of the theoretical models shows readers and visitors "how to document and quantify the unique impact they [local museums] make in their communities."

The second section of this book, "The Rebirth of a Nation," examines museums that depict early American history. In each site, the nation is continually "reborn" as tour narratives shift to incorporate recent interpretations of history, particularly those that are more inclusive of diversity, and as visitors create their own memories of their experiences with the artifacts. The museums demonstrate, too, that one of the ways the nation may continually be renascent is through the mediation of contemporary technologies. In "Public History, Private Memory: Notes from the Ethnography of Colonial Williamsburg, Virginia, USA," Eric Gable and Richard Handler suggest that a historic site may impose a "regime of knowledge" on visitors. This darker view of Vallance's educational mission of local museums is more consistent with Langford's opinion of the early days of Dickson Mounds Museum detailed later in the book. The authors of this article focus on a site with a national reputation, one that may defy the definition of a small museum but not the descriptor of "local museum." They show how supporting the reconstruction of colonial Williamsburg allowed John D. Rockefeller, Jr., to disassociate himself from "new money" and industrialism in order to link himself to an idealized vision of an American past.

While the varying origin stories of the site suited individual agendas, the narrative of a colonial past shifted between competing staff missions: the goal of presenting a local history as "authoritative" as textbook history written by academics and the need to render the site a popular destination. For many members of the public, the latter part of the mission has prevailed, and Williamsburg has become important not so much as a historical site but as the location of personal memories. These memories supersede learning about colonial America, even though the institution is predicated on the notion of using "real" objects and places to teach about this subject. The issue of what visitors remember is central to any analysis of the role of local museums in the United States, because museums' educational goals are as important to their survival as their functions as bearers of cultural prestige, places for community celebrations, and contributors to the local economy.

Tami Christopher's chapter, "The House of the Seven Gables: A House Museum's Adaptation to Changing Societal Expectations since 1910," reprises Handler and Gable's concerns regarding the nature of private memory and public history. Christopher focuses on the House of the Seven Gables in Massachusetts, showing how local mythology, public history, and private memory have shaped different scripts for tours of the historic house. Christopher's analysis is particularly helpful in its treatment of the complexity of the conflations of the actual history of the house and its inhabitants and of their representation in Nathaniel Hawthorne's eponymous novel. Not only does she show how individuals' visits to the site are influenced by their memories of previous visits, community lore, and documented history, but she indicates how interpretations of the exhibitions in the house are affected by events in Hawthorne's novel. For example, in some tour scripts, rooms are referred to as belonging to characters in the novel. Other scripts indicate—incorrectly—that Hawthorne himself lived in the house. To complicate matters, scripts are also influenced by the interests of individual guides. This analysis underlines the idea that local museums present more than academic history, that their narratives reflect multiple voices and agendas and are shaped by shifting social needs. For example, while earlier scripts focused on the house as an icon of an idealized Yankee New England, later scripts referred to the house's place in the Underground Railroad. Finally, Christopher explains how the tours have focused increasingly on the commercial nature of the house, on the gift store and its restaurant. This discussion of a museum's importance in generating business in localities prepares for similar analyses in later chapters.

J. Daniel d'Oney's chapter, which follows Christopher's, focuses on another local and regional icon—the Old State Capitol Museum in Baton Rouge, Louisiana. While Christopher is primarily concerned with shifting views of the past, d'Oney concentrates primarily on the current state of a museum, using the Old State Capitol as an example of an institution with some consciousness of the constructed nature of history and the ease with which local myths may be enshrined. Specifically, d'Oney points out how easily the museum could have turned an exhibit on Huey Long into a martyr's shrine, the accompanying narrative a hagiography. However, through signs carefully distinguishing between the myth and the man, the museum staff has been able to maintain some balance. A display on Louisiana's other governors avoids a common trap for historic museums—focusing on the lifestyles of the rich and famous—by emphasizing the way Louisiana's governors have represented the diversity of the common people of the state.

Another exhibit at the Old State Capitol, "We the People," is designed specifically for fourth graders and thus exemplifies especially well the commonplaces of education delineated by Elizabeth Vallance in chapter 2. The display's use of its setting and emphasis on its audience are particularly important, even as this is the part of the museum in which a particular set of values are especially evident. The exhibit, designed to teach schoolchildren democratic values through interactive displays about politics and the voting system, is perhaps less balanced than others in the institution. For example, if a student gives a wrong answer while going through a maze of questions, she is pulled out of the "democratic" process. As d'Oney indicates, the direction of the exhibit is conveyed subtly: "No judgments are made in the exhibit about those who choose not to vote, but thoughtful visitors leave the room knowing that plenty of others lived and died for the right they now choose to exercise . . . or not to exercise."

This museum's claim to a place in the nation's self-definition as a cradle of democracy is a common way for a smaller museum to justify its own importance. Such claims are not only linked to notions of nationhood, however; they are also essential to another central theme of the articles in this text, that local museums depend on a certain kind of nostalgia, and that this nostalgia functions as a way of structuring knowledge. The chapters in the section titled "Nostalgia as Epistemology" refer not only to shifts in museum narratives, but also expose how such narratives rely on nostalgia for a fictive past.

Jay Price's article on Old Cowtown reveals how film myths and popular stereotypes of the Old West contribute to a museum's representation of early Wichita. Price explains in fascinating detail how the living history site creates a version of the past that does not reflect the reality of Wichita's history. According to Price, Wichita never was a small, rural town as it is depicted at the site; instead, the construction is more typical of the surrounding county. This museum differs from those previously discussed in its lesser concern for authenticity, and, therefore, the article provides new insights into how visitor expectations which are not based on collective memory can affect tours and the educational message conveyed by an institution.

Even though Old Cowtown is in many ways a creation of an elite composed first of local patrons and later of museum professionals, the museum is also constrained by its own institutional history and location. Price argues, "Features that scholars might conclude represent ideological positions might actually be more the result of 'making do' with what was available." The representation of old Wichita cannot be fully authentic because the site is too confined to hold urban buildings of several stories. Instead, it includes old buildings that became available at the site as well as structures small enough to be moved easily or reconstructed.

While Wichita (re)creates a certain vision of the West, Arthurdale offers a reconstruction of a New Deal community with its own inhabitants acting as living history interpreters of the town's earliest days. Arthurdale was first built as a model colony of subsistence homesteads in a region of the Appalachians that had suffered from poverty among coal miners. Despite the town's early democratic ideals, it was originally a restricted community, excluding most immigrants and all African Americans. Moreover, its farming experiment, though successful, did not provide enough food for the town's residents, and the land soon became privately owned. In the 1980s, community members began to buy back and restore the original buildings of the town under the umbrella of a new nonprofit organization, Arthurdale Heritage.

What is interesting about Arthurdale Heritage is that many of the citizens essentially perform themselves in the restoration, and instead of celebrating the New Deal concept of subsistence farming, they emphasize the ideal of community (one certainly timelier when Americans everywhere are struggling with notions of diversity). Moreover, as at Williamsburg and Old Cowtown, nostalgia pervades the restoration, so that, as Patterson asserts, the museum's task is one of "re-inventing the past, rather than simply re-imagining it." Clearly, then, even when museums attempt to represent relatively recent historic eras, they run into some of the political and ethical difficulties that are pertinent to displays of earlier artifacts.

The following article, Heather Perry's "History Lessons: Selling the John Dillinger Museum," discusses an institution that focused on a different part of Depression era life in the United States. Perry describes the changing history of the Dillinger Museum in Indiana, which told the story of one of the country's most notorious bank robbers and murderers. Whereas Patterson and Christopher are concerned with the shifting focuses of history exhibits that remain essentially in one place, Perry describes how the Dillinger Museum changed or had to be "sold" to the public when it moved from rural Indiana to the Hammond area. In its original site, the museum in some ways presented a nostalgic view of Dillinger as a folk hero taking from greedy bankers during the Dust Bowl years. But when the museum relocated, it received a cold response from local law enforcement officers and individual citizens who worked hard to combat stereotypes of the area as a center for crime and gangs. These people did not welcome a museum celebrating a criminal in the vicinity; consequently, the museum had to be recast so that its message was that crime did not pay. In the transformation, the institution's focus shifted to depicting the history of law enforcement. Multimedia and interactive displays forced visitors to participate in the process of judgment and law enforcement. To the extent that the museum drew on nostalgia, it relied on a nostalgia for a time when law and order (might have) ruled. The museum became an arm of the state, reinforcing mainstream ideologies. It is not surprising, then, that controversies involving the Dillinger family and the marketing of the site led to litigation and the museum's closing.

The Dillinger article is important not only because it describes the history and changing message of the museum, but also because it focuses on the marketing of the museum and nostalgia to its neighbors. Perry indicates, for instance, how a design firm played an important role in creating the new exhibits and explains how media campaigns minimized the folk hero image of Dillinger by always portraying him in shackles. In essence, one type of nostalgia —for the gangster hero—was replaced by another—for a time when law and order prevailed. Ironically, both of kinds of nostalgia were based in part on myths of the past.

While nostalgia offers a way of structuring knowledge and conveying a message in the Dillinger museum, certain other local institutions are best characterized by their precarious status and, at times, the very question of their survival. Many lack structure or organization. Such museums resemble community attics or storehouses, and they can be repositories of everything from old newspapers to false teeth and a good many oddities in between. Visitors may consider these dusty collections among the least progressive museums. However, in an odd sort of way, these museums are modernist, for they celebrate the fragmentary and the encyclopedic, the elusory desire to find a single perfect representation of an idea and the willingness to include every possible example of the same idea. The lack of a coherent narrative and sometimes the absence of any narrative at all (as at the Louisiana museum described by Elizabeth Vallance) parallel the unsettling of authority in modern texts as well.

Other museums may be in a precarious situation or have negotiated changes to ensure their survival because of political issues surrounding their collections or their communities. In particular, shifting perspectives on the inclusion of objects created by minority groups create many dilemmas for museums, as do changes in communities' self-images. Donna Langford's article on the Dickson Mounds Museum illustrates how a local collection of fossils and early human remains offers glimpses not only into the distant past but also into twentieth-century views of prehistory. Langford's narrative begins in the 1920s and continues into the present. She traces the importance of early remains in establishing the value of a community, and she shows how popular boosterism and patronage spurred the creation of the Dickson Mounds Museum. Moving forward in time, Langford focuses on contemporary political dilemmas surrounding the ownership and exhibition of Native American burial remains. She explains how the institution at Dickson Mounds faced a crisis before the passage of the Native American Graves Protection and Repatriation Act and how a compromise was negotiated, one that moved the museum from local patronage to state control, from representing European-American views of Native Americans to incorporating indigenous peoples' self-perceptions, from an amateur's collection to a professional exhibition. While the original burial objects can no longer be displayed, the museum retained its educational mission and broadened its constituency.

In contrast to the Dillinger hall of fame, the museums discussed by Jessie Embry and Mauri Liljenquist Nelson in "'Such is Our Heritage': Daughters of Utah Pioneers Museums" have deliberately eschewed multimedia innovations, didactic exhibits, and heavy tourist marketing. Their futures, too, remain uncertain. As with many other small museums, their exhibition strategies are determined by their independence (the Dillinger Museum was operated by a county visitors' bureau) and their limited funds. Their history is critical as well. Originally opened as "relic halls" or repositories for artifacts pertaining to the first Mormon pioneers to Utah, the museums were founded by an organization of an elite local group, the Daughters of the Utah Pioneers (DUP). Now, many of the museums have their own buildings, but the DUP museums as a group remain distinctive, too.

Embry and Nelson emphasize repeatedly that these institutions "reflect little or no attention to modern museum theory, updated conservation methods, or new exhibition techniques." Many of the objects on display are accompanied simply by handwritten cards prepared by the objects' previous owners, and displays tend to be encyclopedic rather than representative. Instead of selecting one or two particularly fine samples of Utah silk, DUP volunteers might mount several cases containing every pair of silk gloves donated to them. Obviously, this strategy is designed in part to gratify donors, but, as the authors indicate, it is also a function of the institutions' limited resources and minimally trained staffs. This seemingly antiquated museum methodology affects the number of visitors to the displays. The severely limited signage allows visitors to create their own narratives about the exhibits in a way that would have been virtually impossible at the Dillinger Museum, but does not permit them to learn more factual information about the objects. The meanings of the exhibits may also be unclear because the staff makes little effort to select objects.

Ironically, the unwitting or accidental modernism of the DUP museums exists in constant tension with the more contemporary methodology of another local museum, one run by the Church of Latter-day Saints. DUP museum visitors are more likely to be descendants and friends of the families of Utah pioneers than they are to be tourists. The items on display focus almost entirely on a small portion of the state's population, with little attention to diversity. With the aging of many members of the DUP and the increase in the number of working women, the DUP museums struggle to find volunteers, and the lack of funds for conservation has led to the deterioration of some of the collections. But the organizations are independent of the Mormon Church. In contrast, the LDS church museum attracts international visitors and is characterized by exhibits that tend to be more representative, didactic, and scripted. The professionalism and global scope of the LDS museum further challenges the DUP halls to the extent that the latter are facing major dilemmas pertaining to their very survival. Ultimately, then, the DUP exhibit halls are also important as indicators of the future of other local museums that are endangered by the very community ties which initially gave them reason to exist.

The U.S. Army Medical Museum described in Rhode and Connor's article, like the DUP museums, has faced challenges to its survival. The medical museum, now called the National Museum of Health and Medicine, was instituted during the Civil War as a research collection, with displays as open storage—accumulations of objects without interpretation were on exhibit. Medical specimens were juxtaposed seemingly randomly; no narrative connected them as it might in a contemporary museum. Nevertheless, the institution gained some prominence and had exhibits at the World's Columbian Exposition in 1892. After its peak, the museum declined as pathology specimens became used for increasingly specialized research projects, and the other kinds of medical exhibitions came to be seen primarily as places for popular amusement and education rather than for scholarly pursuits. Some specimens were de-accessioned; tools were kept for their antiquarian value; and the institution came to be seen as a small, local institution, part of Walter Reed Medical Hospital, rather than serving a major national mission. The medical museum resembles the DUP galleries in that it has lost some of its connection to its original mission, and some of its display methods may seem antiquated. However, it deserves a chapter of its own because it addresses issues particular to institutions that have displayed human remains (like Dickson Mounds) and to those that originally had visions of national prominence. Moreover, the display methods embody a kind of modernism with their focus on the fragmentary and disconnected, one that subverts scientific narratives of universality and logic.

The medical museum's collections have a certain public appeal because of their oddity or gruesomeness (for example, a leg with elephantiasis). The institutions discussed in the next section of this book also attract visitors because of their reliance on oddities. In their emphasis on the unusual, freakish, or bizarre, these institutions hark back to the early days of American museums, and especially to P. T. Barnum's American Museum, a nineteenth-century collection that displayed sideshow marvels among other things. At the same time, these institutions undercut the orderly categories and tasteful displays commonly found in contemporary museums, throwing into question the very definition of a museum.

Lucian Gomoll's article on the New York Freakatorium addresses these issues directly. Situated in lower Manhattan, the Freakatorium displays such oddities as two-headed cows and penis bones of various sizes. The dizzying array of oddities, seemingly jumbled together, challenges the categorical ordering of major museums while raising questions about the authenticity of objects in museums. Even more, such displays force viewers to confront the ways in which museum displays confer authority on objects that might not seem important or interesting in other settings, as well as the ways in which museum narratives confer interpretations on collections. Finally, this institution leads visitors to think about their humanity when faced with images of freaks.

"Cities, Museums, and City Museums," by Eric Sandweiss, portrays another urban institution, the City Museum of St. Louis, which raises similar questions, though it displays primarily urban artifacts instead of parts of or representations of humans and animals. City Museum is characterized by the author as a "funhouse of industrial proportions" instead of as an entirely serious historical gallery organized by topic or chronology. Sandweiss traces the roots of this institution to the early museums of the American republic, designed to entertain and instruct. Yet while the entertainment in an exhibit such as the one on voting at the Old State Capitol in Baton Rouge might come from innovative technology, here the humor arises from the oddness of many of the objects (for instance, the world's largest pair of underpants); the idiosyncratic nature of many of the labels; the mixture of architectural and industrial salvage; objects recycled into "art"; and temporary exhibits on subjects ranging from architect Louis Sullivan to the humble corn dog. Sandweiss compares this museum to the National Architectural Arts Center, a collection which is not currently open to the public and which takes a more reverent approach to the city's architecture.

Whereas attendance at the unmediated exhibits in DUP museums may be sparse, the City Museum is a popular attraction for city residents, suburbanites, and tourists. The somewhat tongue-in-cheek approach puts into question the definition of a museum, while its location in the city center draws attention to industry, social class, and other urban realities in a way that an art museum in a park cannot. The carnivalesque nature of this museum and the Freakatorium further reflects the excitement of the city's disorder, so that in a modern way, their methods of presentation come to reflect both the content and message. Significantly, the rise of the City Museum has been linked to an urban revival in its neighborhood, reminding citizens of the way museums can affect the very communities they represent.

The urban renewal in the neighborhood of the St. Louis City Museum brings us to a final theme of local museums—their connections to business. The three museums I discuss in my article, "Business as Usual," are also connected to city revivals. The growth of the New York City Police Museum, the Museum of American Financial History, and the Heye Center of the National Museum of the American Indian accompanied the recasting of lower Manhattan as a tourist site in the 1990s. While the latter two institutions call themselves "national" and "American," the embeddedness of their themes in local history and culture renders them appropriate for inclusion in this book. This circumstance was evident when, on September 11, 2001, the World Trade Center towers, blocks from the institutions, fell to terrorist attacks, and the chapter—completed weeks earlier—had to be revised in light of the changing significance of the neighborhood within American national consciousness and the lives of local citizens.

My analysis of the New York Police Museum before 9/11 begins by echoing concerns expressed in Heather Perry's discussion of the transformation of the Dillinger Museum in Indiana. Like the Dillinger Museum, the New York Police Museum in its former site was largely dedicated to glorifying the importance of those in law enforcement and to demonstrating that crime does not pay. These messages were conveyed effectively because the museum used many of the pedagogical strategies outlined by Elizabeth Vallance in the first chapter of this work. But the focus of my piece is on how business and individual sponsorships of the New York institution raised questions that might have countered or clouded the didactic message about crime. In the end, what the museum might have displayed best was the inextricability of social and political power from police presence.

The American Museum of Financial History, too, was very much about business and power prior to 9/11. The museum's collection and temporary exhibits focused on major business successes, such as J. P. Morgan, as well as on educating the public about the functions of the stock market, bonds, and other investments. Its pedagogical content was designed to educate visitors about the importance of capitalism, so its values were explicit. Of the three institutions discussed in this chapter, this museum was perhaps most appropriate to its setting in the heart of Manhattan's finance district.

While the financial history museum glorified an elite group, with special exhibits on such characters as J. P. Morgan, the Heye Center of the National Museum of the American Indian then and now focuses on a population that has been largely marginalized or excluded from other institutions' accounts of U.S. history. This site reminds us at once of the original sale of Manhattan Island and of the hordes of immigrants and business people that came through the building when it was a U.S. Customs House. Now, the building is important because it participates in a shift *away* from commercial ventures toward valuing the creations of Native Americans for their aesthetic qualities. Native American works were first classified as ethnographic artifacts to be collected and sold to museums and collectors; later, Native American art was viewed as industrial or tourist art. At the Heye Center, exhibits are especially good at illustrating American diversity and in giving voice to a range of peoples, despite the irony that Heye himself was a white collector. I offer a discussion of this institution as a counter to some of the difficulties described when other museums, including those in my own article and in earlier chapters, attempt to deal with business and diversity.

The concluding article of this book examines how these three museums were affected by the terrorist attacks of 2001. It focuses particularly on how exhibits changed to reflect the terrible events and the attitudinal shifts following them. While history will link the three sites inextricably to business as a result of their closeness to the World Trade Center, their new incarnations are also dramatic examples of the use of showmanship in imagining a new America.

It is my contention, then—supported by the authors of the following articles, who are museum staff, historians, and other academics—that far from playing a minor role in the creation of contemporary America, and far from being footnotes to history, local museums are central to understanding the forces that create communities in the United States. For us, local museums are museums of influence, deserving critical and public attention, because they may ultimately tell scholars more about contemporary life than all the branches of the Smithsonian put together. All museums tell narratives about culture—no matter how quirky, or dusty, or unprofessional they might seem. Local museums offer us glimpses at the contradictions and dilemmas evident in any effort to present or represent culture. With these points in mind, we offer this book as witness and as tribute to the value of these institutions.

NOTES

1. Daniel Sherman, *Worthy Monuments: Art Museums and the Politics of Culture in Nineteenth-Century France* (Cambridge: Harvard University Press, 1989), 126–32.

2. American Association of Museums, "Museum Accreditation: Criteria and Concerns," www.aam-us.org/programs/accreditation/webc&c.cfn (accessed June 27, 2006).

3. Kenneth Hudson, *Museums of Influence* (Cambridge, England: Cambridge University Press, 1987), vii.

4. Ivan Karp and Steven Lavine, eds., *Exhibiting Cultures: The Poetics and Politics of Museum Display* (Washington: Smithsonian Institution Press, 1991); Tony Bennett, *The Birth of the Museum* (New York: Routledge, 1995); Ivan Karp, Christine Mullen Kreamer, and Steven D. Lavine, eds., *Museums and Communities: The Politics of Public Culture* (Washington: Smithsonian Institution Press, 1992); Lawrence Wechsler, *Mr. Wilson's Cabinet of Wonders* (New York: Vintage, 1996).

5. "Attendance, Finances Become Post-September 11 Concerns," *Aviso* (Nov. 2001): 1–2.

6. Ron Chew, "In Praise of the Small Museum," *Museum News* 81, no. 2 (March/April 2002): 41.

7. Amy Levin, "The Family Camping Hall of Fame and Other Wonders: Local Museums and Local History," *Studies in Popular Culture* 29, no. 3 (1997): 77–90.

8. Eric Gable, "Maintaining Boundaries, or 'Mainstreaming' Black History into a White Museum," in *Museum Theory*, ed. Sharon Macdonald and Gordon Fyfe, 177–202 (Oxford: Blackwell, 1996).

9. Seth Koven, "The Whitechapel Picture Exhibitions and the Politics of Seeing," in *Museum Culture: Histories, Discourses, Spectacles*, ed. Daniel Sherman and Irit Rogoff, 22–48 (Minneapolis: University of Minnesota Press, 1994).

2

Local History, "Old Things to Look At," and a Sculptor's Vision

Exploring Local Museums through Curriculum Theory

ELIZABETH VALLANCE

There are over 8,000 museums in the United States, and by one count about three-quarters of them are "small," defined by the American Association of Museums (AAM) as those with budgets under $250,000.[1] We can all think of many kinds of museums that seem to be "small," regardless of budget, floor space, staff size, or other criteria. There are museums that occupy single rooms of municipal buildings (or former municipal buildings), such as the new history museum in Sycamore, llinois, housed in the former hospital, which now also includes the Chamber of Commerce and a nonprofit community art school. Recently, this one-room museum displayed military memorabilia, newspaper clippings, old photos, and staff desks. House museums in communities across the country offer microcosms of life at a given point in time—often the lives of the rich (and their servants) around 1900, as at Campbell House in St. Louis. Some house museums celebrate their architects. Frank Lloyd Wright homes, restored and maintained by area organizations in Illinois and Michigan, probably exceed the AAM's budgetary definition but still offer experiences that differ from those offered by larger, more comprehensive museums. The City Museum in St. Louis—not especially small, but definitely quirky, and treated in Eric Sandweiss's chapter later in this book—was created by a visionary local sculptor. It fills several floors of an abandoned factory downtown with fanciful interactive installations made of recycled materials as well as with occasional exhibits (architectural fragments, objects from an old garbage dump, and odd things from artists' collections). County historical societies operate museums documenting the pasts of their local regions: the one in Empire, Michigan, operates in a former grocery store, while the one in Manhattan, Kansas, is in a lovely modern building built for the purpose. And there are the many museums advertised on billboards on our back roads and interstates, odd self-styled museums housing idiosyncratic collections. For example, in this chapter, we will visit the Continental Sculpture Museum in Portis, Kansas, the private domain of a sculptor who carved Kansas limestone into likenesses of Jesus and Abraham Lincoln under special instructions from God. While there are many small museums in cities, benefiting from the tourism and regular traffic of the urban setting, there are thousands more in small communities and rural locations, and these local resources merit special consideration here.

Little museums in small towns and rural communities merit attention for many reasons, as the essays in this book will attest. At a meeting of the National Trust for Historic Preservation in the mid-1980s, James Michener spoke eloquently of the importance of the local collections (his specific example was the Buffalo Bill Museum in Cody, Wyoming) in the communities where he was researching for his books. Without people preserving the records of the distant and recent past, our national memory and Michener's books would be much thinner. Many small museums are the only museums in their communities, the only place where time can stand still. These museums may be the only places where people have the chance to view special or once-ordinary objects in new contexts that can place a special spin on their meaning. A community museum may be the only place in town where visitors can see the artifacts of traditions that make the town distinct. By implication, local museums may also raise questions about how and why the town is different today from the vision being celebrated in the artifacts on display. And it is my experience—anecdotal only, but suggesting a line of later research—that most community history museums celebrate their pasts without critically scrutinizing them. These local museums collect and display documents of a past that is looked back on fondly, wistfully, or proudly, and whose story is told straightforwardly without overtly revealing that anyone's special narratives[2] are being omitted. They can raise questions of insider/outsider relationships and old and new power structures within the population. (How important is it these days in Geneva, Illinois, to be of Swedish descent? How does an African-American visitor to the Geneva History Center connect to the town's history?). Finally, small museums of any kind are a part of the social structure of the community: they may be a locus for genealogists, for aspiring artists, for the power elite of board members and volunteers, or for teachers. They may have quite different and equally important values for various parts of the community.

For these and many other reasons, it is worth looking carefully at the educational nature of local museums. Small museums can, and arguably do, educate (although the data on what visitors actually learn from museums are incomplete).[3] Museums' dynamics are different from those of schools, but it is instructive to analyze museums in terms congruent with our traditional definitions and expectations of educational institutions. The similarities and differences between museums and schools are both evident and surprisingly complex; the special case of the local museum suggests criteria that can shape our notions of educational theory in general and enlighten our uses of these special educational settings in particular. This chapter presents two traditional models from the field of curriculum theory and analyzes three local museums through these powerful lenses.

THE "COMMONPLACES OF SCHOOLING": AN INTRODUCTION

In the late 1960s, Joseph Schwab, a science educator and curriculum theorist from the University of Chicago, proposed a framework for thinking about curricular decisions. He called it the "commonplaces of schooling."[4] Curriculum theorists have used this model as a guide for talking about change, settings, and innovations in education. It is an astonishing formulation, for I have never been able to find an educational situation which cannot be described in terms of the commonplaces, although the various commonplaces assign distinct values to diverse educational programs.

Schwab posits that there are four elements to any educational moment: education happens in a setting of some kind (he called it "milieu," and he had in mind variations on the traditional classroom), with a subject matter to be taught, by a teacher, to students. The archetypical example of an educational situation describable in these terms would be a history teacher presenting the Industrial Revolution to tenth graders in a public school. In a traditional classroom setting, we can know and control each of the commonplaces: schools are created to address specific grade levels and subjects, they hire teachers with specified qualifications, and they know who their students are. Progression through subject matter can be tracked through the formal curriculum, and subject matter mastery can be measured by tests. The model describes the curricular life of schools, and it provides convenient and common-sense dimensions for comparing schools, curricula, the impact of teacher training, and other variables.

Beyond traditional schooling, any teaching/learning situation can be described in terms of the commonplaces, although the values of the commonplaces may slide along different scales in various settings. Students working in a computer lab learning Photoshop may be in a traditional school setting with a definition of the subject matter to be mastered, but the instruction may be less by a live teacher than by the instruction manual and the Photoshop program screens themselves. Adults meeting regularly in a book club can be considered students in a nontraditional setting where the students teach themselves.

Some years ago, I spent time analyzing the setting and programs of the large public art museum where I worked, using Schwab's commonplaces as the gauge.[5] The model works, but the differences in applying it to a school setting and a museum are instructive. Consider, for example, the subject matter of the large art museum: it includes art objects, decorative arts pieces such as furniture and porcelain, and ceremonial or religious objects from a range of cultures and historic periods, distributed among many galleries. The subject matter is vast. No "student" could cover the whole subject in a single visit (and most museum visitors are occasional, not regular visitors).[6] Visitors pick and choose their curriculum (literally, the course they run) on the basis of criteria the staff can never fully know, and no two visitors will select the same curriculum. We know from visitors' comments at the Information Center, from their remarks to each other, and from earlier focus group work that the setting itself conveys messages and expectations to visitors. First-time visitors can be overwhelmed by the choices available (a hundred galleries on three floors), think they must speak in hushed voices, display an awareness that they are in the presence of unseen experts who have decided what is and isn't art, and believe that the physical amenities of the setting affect where they go and what they see. The preferences of the students are, within very loose boundaries, almost completely unpredictable for the museum staff, although they know that a certain percentage will be out-of-town visitors, a certain percentage will be school groups, and such. Visitors walk in on no set schedule, may or may not get past the main floor, may or may not have an agenda for the day's visit. Planning a curriculum is the unceasingly challenging task of museum educators. The teachers in this setting are many. Explicitly, they are the docents leading tours, gallery lecturers, speakers in lecture series, and museum educators teaching hands-on classes. Tacitly, however, the teachers in a museum also include the curators, whom visitors almost never see, because they select and arrange objects to display, write labels, and create other interpretive materials. As a result, the curriculum followed by any one visitor on any given day is a complex experience reflecting the visitor's choices (of directions to turn, galleries to view, labels to read, conversations to have with comrades) within the content provided by curators and programs developed by educators. Any large museum's exhibitions cover a vast number of contingent choices, and no two visitors will follow the same curriculum. As Falk and Dierking and others have pointed out, visitors' psychosocial backgrounds shape their experiences even if they follow the same route over the same period of time.[7]

Schwab's commonplaces help us to see the ways in which the teaching and learning experience can be understood in a large museum. The commonplaces don't make it easy to know what the visitors' museum experiences actually are, but they offer a common terminology for describing and comparing available options.

WAYS OF VALUING EDUCATION

Also in the late 1960s, a curriculum theorist at Columbia University's Teachers College proposed a model for understanding the way we value education. Dwayne Huebner posited five criteria for valuing a teaching/learning experience.[8] He called these "rationales," or what we might call arguments, for education. They are more usefully thought of as criteria for assessing educational moments and include: the technical (did it work? Did students respond as we had hoped? Did they learn anything?), the scientific (what did educators learn about teaching or learning, from this lesson?), the political (what is the value of this curriculum, school, unit, for the power structure of the community or the political weight of the school?), the aesthetic (was this lesson artfully done? Did it hold together in its own terms?), and the ethical (was the relationship between student and teacher a respectful one? Did the lesson respect the integrity of the child?).

Huebner's criteria can be applied to assessing any experiences in museums and, as such, function as the defining qualities of the museum experience.

Indeed, large museums undertake data collection for marketing and evaluation purposes and tout the technical success of exhibitions through the attendance figures and happy crowds generating big revenues. A museum can bask in the political capital gained by providing the community with a popular or well-targeted exhibition (a museum in a large African-American community, for example, may win political points with exhibitions of African-American artists or history), while board members and volunteers may be selected to increase the museum's political value, or, in turn, these individuals may acquire political cachet from their involvement in a museum. Museums routinely use aesthetic criteria. Curators design and judge the effectiveness of their exhibitions on aesthetic grounds, and the staff knows when an exhibition is "beautiful," a lecture is "excellent," or an audio tour is "terrific." Assessment of aesthetic qualities strongly guides the planning and self-critique of exhibitions and programs by museum staffs. Less pervasive as an assessment strategy is the scientific rationale: museums rarely know from rigorous study what visitors really learned or what contributed most to their learning, although there is a growing interest in audience evaluation. But—to return to Schwab's commonplaces for a moment—it may be that those designing exhibitions and programs rely more on their own knowledge of the content and on assumptions about students' characteristics than they do on scientific understandings of the impact of their own previous programs. Finally, most museums do have a special feeling for their visitors and are attentive to the ethical dimensions of how visitors (and volunteers) are greeted, assisted, guided, and solicited for memberships or donations. The results of ethically good relationships with visitors may emerge in technical or political terms (ever-increasing memberships or a stronger political base in the community), but most museums, dependent on goodwill and visitors' comfort, are generally more attentive to this criterion than traditional public schools have been.

Huebner's five criteria, then, show that museums emphasize a different mix of qualities in their evaluations than do traditional educational institutions. It is arguable that museums lag behind schools and educational research in understanding why what works works, because some very large museums have evaluation or research departments to study visitors' learning experiences.

SMALL MUSEUMS: THREE BRIEF CASE STUDIES

Let's look at local museums through the lenses provided by Schwab and Huebner. These small museums, which may have staffs of as few as one full-time professional, or even be run by volunteers, may have a room or two for displaying artifacts, restricted budgets, no departments dedicated to publicity or fundraising, and specialized audiences. Three local museums, none of them listed in the American Association of Museums' directory, are cases in point. Analysis of all three requires the past tense: the Geneva History Center in Geneva, Illinois, moved to a new downtown location after this chapter was written, remaining a strong presence in its community; the Louisiana Art and Folk Festival Museum in Columbia, Louisiana, made the opposite move, from a downtown location where I knew it best to a farm outside of town, where it has been renamed the Martin Home Place; and the very quirky, and now defunct, Continental Sculpture Hall in Portis, Kansas. The first is a long-standing community history museum with a full-time paid staff including a director, curator, and educator, located initially in a city park, with free admission, and with an annual attendance of about 6,000 that may increase tenfold now that it has moved a few blocks to a downtown location; its collections are organized into exhibitions that tell stories. The second museum is run almost entirely by elderly female volunteers in the parish (county) seat, a town of about 400. Its idiosyncratic collection consists of local household and farming items arranged roughly in subject order. The third museum was a highly idiosyncratic private preserve, owned by an elderly sculptor, Inez Marshall, who created and displayed her own limestone creations in a converted gas station in a town of 150. A cutout of a full-figure photograph of the sculptor greeted the visitor, as did the legend from the Bible, "On Christ, the solid rock, I stand, all other ground is shifting sand." Ms. Marshall herself served as tour guide. The Continental Sculpture Hall as a separate entity depended on its eccentric owner, although at her death the collection became part of the Kansas Grassroots Art Museum not far away in Lucas, Kansas.

The Geneva History Center packs a remarkable amount of story into a small space. It has moved from its home in a city park building to a more professionally designed space downtown, but this chapter addresses its original, more homemade, venue (in the past tense) and design as well as its ongoing mission. Its exhibition area consisted of two rooms totaling about 2,000 square feet. Its director, a professionally trained historian with a graduate degree in historical administration, is committed to the museum's mission: to tell Geneva's history. This mission guides the accession policy and shapes the use of the permanent collection. At the times I visited, the main entry gallery was devoted to a timeline exhibition, "Geneva 1900: As the Century Turned."

The timeline headed the exhibit panels and took the visitor clockwise around the room through a display rich in text (newspaper articles and extended labels) and photographs, with occasional objects (dresses, luggage, implements). Grouped within the timeline arrangement, although not clearly tied to any particular time within the century, were topical displays devoted to aspects of Geneva's history, such as the civic improvement association, schools, family farming, as well as local writers and artists. At twenty-two points along the way, small red triangles reminded the visitor to ask a standard question of "Nettie," the telephone operator featured in one of the topical displays: "How is Geneva the same? How is it different?" A small booklet responded to these questions with clues that the visitor could use to explore the issues raised. There was a narrative here, and it was one that longtime Genevans knew and newcomers might welcome: this thriving, mostly upscale community has deep roots and long traditions (for example, the Swedish heritage). The second room had more objects and less text, and it portrayed in topical groupings, without a chronological structure, the history of the various businesses that have operated in Geneva: a Styrofoam Pillsbury Doughboy, for example, was a symbol of an industry active in Geneva today.

The opportunities for learning in this small space were many. The director and volunteers gave tours. There was a reading table with binders of information gathered by the volunteer historians who researched and developed the "1900" exhibition. Vast quantities of information were presented in printed form in the clippings and exhibition labels. There were objects to touch in the second gallery and an interactive computer station in the main gallery. The local archives held in the storage area of the Geneva History Center were substantial and well organized, and they were increasingly used by genealogists and others. (Indeed, the new downtown museum has a much-improved area for genealogical research, giving this purpose greater visibility than before.) The staff was fundraising for the move to a renovated historic building downtown, now completed. Although the Geneva History Center receives no public funding, this community resource collects artifacts that tell the town's story, and this mission guides the museum's acquisitions policy—if an object is not from Geneva, or fails to fit into a story about the town, it is not accepted. It was and is a model of a local museum.

The self-styled Louisiana Art and Folk Festival Museum (not an official state museum) was a delightful anomaly. Located in an old frame building downtown near the river, just off the main road that runs through Columbia,

Louisiana (seat of Caldwell Parish), it recently moved to a house outside of town and was renamed the Martin Home Place. In its original incarnation, it had little "art" in it. The museum was a single vast room with an upstairs loft, with displays along the walls and down the center, and a small side room containing kitchen implements. The collection was an array of homey artifacts: dishes, measuring cups, quilts, medical equipment, a dentist's or barber's chair, wedding dresses, tools, butter churns, photographs, toys, and other items. What labels existed were handwritten in fading ink on paper strips or on little tags with strings, with information such as "Old Waffle Iron" or "Quilt, 1930s." The objects at the Louisiana Art and Folk Festival Museum were typical of local historical society museums all over the country, with two exceptions: everything could be handled and some items were for sale. New folk art was for sale near the entrance (cornhusk dolls, for instance, or local jellies), but the line between museum, museum shop, and antique shop was not entirely clear.

The museum was a project dear to a few old women who were proud that school groups came and were told about long-ago days through these objects. Yet this is the Deep South, an area that has grown cotton for over two centuries. Much of the African-American population in the area remains impoverished. None of their social history was evident at the museum. In fact, it seems fair to say that no real history was being told. What this museum did best was simple: it provided old things to look at. Visitors might recognize these objects, and they might connect them to their own personal stories, but the museum did not really tell the history of the area except by implication (there were farms, a long time ago, and so forth). And while it did not explicitly avoid narratives such as those of the African-American population, neither did it proclaim any particular narrative that it assumed all visitors shared.

In this environment, the museum was a source of pride for a small core of volunteers. This was not a museum that invited visitors to act as historians by testing hypotheses against questions and evidence as some museums do (including the Geneva History Center). It did not teach visitors or schoolchildren analytical skills to critique the history on display or to see what narratives might be missing. Yet despite the many gaps in the social and professional structure of this small museum, I appreciated its courage in the face of limited resources, and ultimately its community value. Someone was preserving the artifacts and, to some extent, documenting their provenance, and someone was trying to show a view of this town through objects left behind.

This museum came into being when the town was redeveloping its downtown with a riverfront walk and refurbished storefronts in an effort to attract tourists. Future James Micheners may depend on just this sort of museum. Such collections may also be children's first—maybe only—contact with the concept of a "museum," with learning from objects. These odd unofficial museums are treasures.

Finally, before we return to the big theories that opened this chapter, a few words about the quirky Continental Sculpture Hall, "the only one of its kind in the world," according to its brochure, and the creation of "Inez Marshall, Sculptress," according to her business card. A postcard sold at the museum featured a carved limestone Model T; its back described the museum as featuring "10,000 Pounds . . . Over 450 Pieces—Hand Carved Limestone," all the work of one sculptor. Inez Marshall was a former truck driver who began carving (a limestone squirrel, using her father's knife) while in her twenties and recovering from a broken back. She saw sculpting as a God-given talent and made it her life's work, taking instructions from God to create a collection that she claimed numbered 450, although when it was inventoried after she suffered a stroke at 77, the pieces totaled 68. The museum, housed in a former service station in a prairie town of 150, miles from anywhere, housed her whole collection and at least one work in progress (the wheel for a life-sized Harley-Davidson motorcycle). The staff consisted of Ms. Marshall and her companion, Beulah Smith, who collected the $1.50 entrance fee. The sculptor gave the tours herself. Objects included a small diorama of Jesus and the twelve disciples at the Last Supper; a pioneer couple driving a Conestoga wagon; and Abraham Lincoln's whole family in a room with a table, chairs, lamps, and dishes. The brochure said that "everything is done freehand; she never knows what it is going to look like until it is finished. Everything is done under inspiration," with "no electric tools whatsoever," and layers of thick paint. The Continental Sculpture Hall was a testimonial to one person's unusual mission, to the rewards of solitary labor, and to the basic human impulse to create things beyond the functional.

APPLYING THE BIG THEORIES

The Geneva History Center, the Louisiana Art and Folk Festival Museum, and the Continental Sculpture Hall take on different characters when explored through the lenses of Schwab's commonplaces of education and Huebner's ways of valuing educational experiences. Applying these curriculum models suggests questions that can be asked of local museums to assess their value, their impact, and their potential as community resources.

The Geneva History Center is a case where Schwab's four commonplaces are distinct, made especially so by its clear mission to "tell Geneva's history." The subject matter is the story of this single town—the social, cultural, educational, business, and religious histories of current and past inhabitants. The subject matter is a narrative that can be documented through archives, well-researched objects, oral histories, photographs, and other artifacts. The immediate setting of the museum was a comfortable low old building in a city park, now relocated to a restored commercial building downtown. The history of Geneva was told in this space; the broader setting was and is the town itself, reflected in microcosm in the Center's collections. The students were the museum visitors, disproportionately graying but also including school groups and tourists; these self-selected students came voluntarily, and they were not a microcosm of the town's population. But the museum director seemed clearly to see his potential students as all Geneva residents, newcomers seeking background on the community, and other visitors interested in local history or with specific questions about areas of the collection. The teachers included the professionals who used the collection to tell stories and create educational programs, the volunteers who developed the "Geneva 1900" exhibition and its accompanying binders, the objects themselves, which carry their own meanings for those who recognize them, and the information in labels and text. The Geneva History Center was (and remains) a classic case of a museum with a clearly defined subject matter, taught through carefully designed installations and programmatic offerings to a population that could be fairly accurately predicted in terms of number, demographics, and interests. It was and is a small museum whose educational focus has been clear.

How do the four commonplaces apply to the Louisiana Art and Folk Festival Museum? This is an interesting challenge. The setting was clear—a building adapted for this special collection and designated as a museum that welcomed locals and strangers. The subject matter was problematic: ostensibly, it was the history of the area as seen in its folk art, loosely defined. The content consisted of artifacts reflecting the history of this community, but since the objects were arranged in a non-narrative way with no clear story line, the subject of this museum was not really clear. What did a person learn from a visit to the Louisiana Art and Folk Festival Museum? No data are available to document this, but the arrangement suggested that the content was more about nostalgia than about any particular story. Although we can describe the students as likely to have been older persons, with some school groups, the absence of clear subject matter makes it difficult to deduce the students' educational goals. Were the older visitors seeking a reconnection with their memories? Were they seeking to fill gaps in the community or family narratives? Were they coming to socialize? What did schoolchildren learn beyond how some old tools worked (which may in fact have value in some curricula)? While we often don't know the educational motivation of museum visitors, more structured museums present their curricula clearly. Although we can tentatively identify some teachers (the tour guides and their objects), the real teaching value of this museum may lie in community pride that there is a museum at all. This sort of heroic museum occupies a special niche in its community and in the museum world. The niche may be less educational than those of more traditionally structured museums, and it may require other descriptive models altogether to account for its special role. Huebner's five rationales apply better here than do Schwab's commonplaces of schooling.

The Continental Sculpture Hall was a case unto itself, but there are many such places in this country – all the odd little roadside museums proclaimed on faded billboards share much with this preserve of an individual driven by her own private mission. Again, the setting was a space converted from another use to house a subject matter entirely created by its teacher. What, then, was the real content? Sculpture? Stone? Lonely creativity? Undaunted determination? Abraham Lincoln and other heroes? God? The brochure addressed the sculptures and the process of their creation, and they were indeed what was available to be seen and learned, for I recall no extended labels or explanatory wall texts other than the titles. Isolated in Portis, Kansas, were there really any students beyond the occasional community arts scholar or bus trip by grassroots art aficionados? Did students even matter in this situation? Somehow I doubt it. Visitors might occasionally validate the sculptor's calling from God, but this remarkable woman, who was both teacher and subject matter in this museum, didn't really need or respond to visitor interest. Her museum was simply what she had to do. This "art for its own sake"[9] attitude characterizes many so-called grassroots or outsider artists: we see this lonely burning determination to create in such marvels as the Watts Towers in Los Angeles or backyard installations of pinwheels. Inez Marshall took this impulse further and made a museum that challenged many definitions of museums.

Huebner's five qualities of education may help to assess local museums. Again, the Geneva History Center, a small but traditional and clearly focused museum, was a case in point. It could readily assess its success in technical terms (attendance, fundraising, donations), and with a little effort could determine whether its exhibitions "worked" in a scientific sense (the staff do care about how children can develop better skills in analyzing historic artifacts, and they use pedagogical principles in creating exhibitions). Its political value in the community remains a clear criterion for success of which staff members are aware as they plan exhibitions, programs, and fundraising campaigns. Although the political rationale is not the overt mission of the Center, it is undeniable and probably quite measurable. Likewise, this museum is in a perfect position to cultivate its ethical ties to the community, since the fairness with which segments of the community are treated will affect the Center's community standing and ultimately its political and technical effectiveness with those on whom it depends for funding. Finally, the aesthetic dimension strongly guides assessments by staff and visitors. Lacking regular visitor surveys or exit interviews, staff know the exhibitions are good in aesthetic terms, tempered by their appreciation, as historians, of the value of objects. For example, the "Geneva 1900" exhibition succeeded or failed to the degree that it was visually engaging, moved easily from introduction to conclusion, compelled the visitor to stop and explore key objects, and left the visitor with a sense of an experience that was whole and satisfying.[10] Thus, the Geneva History Center demonstrates how Huebner's five rationales can work as evaluative criteria for local museums.

The Louisiana Art and Folk Festival Museum may be richly, though differently, understood in Huebner's scheme. If its mission is to elicit nostalgic recognition rather than to teach historical narrative or historical methods, then this museum's technical rationale would "work" if visitors expressed pleased astonishment X number of times in the course of a visit. If attendance grew over time, that would be "technical" evidence of success, as would an increasing diversification of the audience. The scientific rationale does not apply here: its exhibits are not oriented toward teaching identifiable concepts and reflect no concern with how people learn. The political value of this museum is highly individualized and personal. The museum keeps elderly volunteers involved in the community, and as such it makes a valuable, if subtle, contribution to the life of the town. The Louisiana Art and Folk Festival Museum might also evaluate its success in aesthetic terms, but again in a highly focused way. Little attention is given to creating visually compelling exhibitions, but volunteers and visitors respond strongly to the aesthetic qualities of individual objects. Volunteers may also have a general sense of the completeness of the collection as it grows to cover more aspects of bygone days. This is, of course, true of any museum displaying artifacts, and of any curator's, educator's, or visitor's reaction to them, but in a local museum without a clear narrative, sheer delight in the visual design and craftsmanship of the objects becomes especially important. The ethical dimensions of this museum are complex. I might never have known of the museum's existence without a friend's involvement, for its presence was not highly visible through signage or advertisements. It told no particular story, so the museum cannot be faulted for explicitly favoring any single narrative or leaving out any of the narratives that Roberts encourages exhibition designers to include. [11] However, in allowing objects to speak for themselves, the museum raises ethical issues of whether and how to present objects out of context, as if in an antique shop, without providing interpretive materials to help visitors make informed judgments about their meaning. A Huebnerian assessment of the Louisiana Art and Folk Festival Museum might question the ethical neutrality it evinces by omission; at the same time, this might stimulate discussions about how the museum could connect to all parts of its community through the stories its objects could tell.

The Continental Sculpture Hall is an extreme case that tests all of Huebner's ways of valuing an educational resource, and yet it is in Huebner's terms that this odd museum is most interesting. Who would know whether and on what terms this museum succeeded in a technical sense? Did attendance numbers matter? There was no fundraising aside from the $1.50 entrance fee. The museum seemed to have no mission against which anyone besides its owner could assess what she did with it. Politically, this museum was a lonely anomaly; it carried no practical political value (no board of influential people, no prestige in being a docent there), but it was fiercely valued by the tiny Kansas Grassroots Art Association (KGAA), which included it in annual bus tours, and valued by others in the far-flung Kansas arts community for being a wonderful and courageous creation. Ultimately this loose confederation of distant admirers managed to save the sculptures and move them to the KGAA's museum in Lucas, some miles distant. And why did these strangers come to value the museum so? First, its charm was in its aesthetic impact: in the middle of the Kansas prairie, in a worn-out building, were stone carvings made by a single old woman, proudly displayed in a setting with a grand name, humble and roughhewn, colorful with glossy paint—a stone world of forty-five years' making that no one would visit without knowing about it in advance. The place was memorable for its ethical impact on those who came to love it: it invited the visitor to respect the eccentricity of this unusual and isolated sculptor and appreciate her for what she demonstrated of the human spirit. The Continental Sculpture Hall reminded visitors that political entities such as the National Endowment for the Arts—which had nothing to do with any of these three museums, to my knowledge—and school art programs generally, are crucial for the contact with art they give to people in all kinds of communities, urban or rural, and that we need to support these chances for people to discover the work that loners like Inez Marshall undertake. The commitment that the few visitors made in coming there was a clear statement of what it means ethically to respect the unexpected in people.

CONCLUSION

Local museums offer an instructive test of traditional educational curriculum theory, and in turn this traditional theory can inform our judgments about what works and what puzzles us about the unique resources that local museums offer. This chapter has illustrated how three small museums—one solidly traditional community museum, one eccentric collection of uninterpreted objects styling itself as a museum, and one unusual artist's private and remote domain—can be assessed in these terms. Each of the nine dimensions suggested by Schwab's commonplaces and Huebner's qualities could itself become the basis of a formal evaluation of any museum's collections, exhibitions, or programs, and many of the judgments suggested in these pages could be tested through rigorous visitor studies, interviews, comment books, observations, and other methods. We might learn that each museum has a different definition of technical effectiveness, or that the political underpinnings of some museums drive them more than we can see on an occasional visit, or that ethical issues of narrative building could completely reorient how a local museum might use its collections. This chapter suggests how these dimensions of curriculum theory can help us understand what makes small, local museums—and larger, quirkier museums such as St. Louis's City Museum—so memorable. Further research using these theories may show exactly how small, local museums differ from large and traditional ones, and how to document and quantify their community impact. We who love museums have always enjoyed these unusual places, but perhaps with these tools borrowed from traditional curriculum theory we can better learn to characterize and understand why we do.

NOTES

1. Ron Chew, "In Praise of the Small Museum," *Museum News* 81, no. 2 (March/April 2002): 36–41.

2. An especially rich discussion of narrative possibilities in museum exhibitions appears in Lisa Roberts, *From Knowledge to Narrative: Educators and the Changing Museum* (Washington, D.C.: Smithsonian Institution Press, 1997), 131–52.

3. John Falk and Lynne Dierking, *The Museum Experience* (Washington, D.C.: Whalesback Books, 1992).

4. Joseph Schwab, "The Practical: A Language for Curriculum," *School Review* 78, no.1 (November 1969): 1–23.

5. Elizabeth Vallance, "The Public Curriculum of Orderly Images," *Educational Researcher* 24, no. 2 (March 1995): 4–13; Elizabeth Vallance, "The Lively Non-Curriculum of the Museum Curriculum," invited address at a seminar on learning in museums sponsored by the American Association of Museums, Chicago, Ill. (November 1995).

6. Falk and Dierking, *The Museum Experience,* 11–24, explore demographics and behavior patterns of museum visitors, including data on museum visiting as a leisure experience.

7. Falk and Dierking, *The Museum Experience,* passim.

8. Dwayne Huebner, "Curricular Language and Classroom Meanings," in *Language and Meaning,* ed. J. B. Macdonald and R. R. Leeper, 8–26 (Washington, D.C.: Association for Supervision and Curriculum Development, 1966).

9. Elizabeth Vallance, "Art for Its Own Sake: The Lonely, Whimsical Creations of Grassroots Artists," invited lecture for the First Thursday Program, Friends of the Saint Louis Art Museum (February 1986).

10. Philip Jackson's *John Dewey and the Lessons of Art* (New York and London: Yale University Press, 1998) offers a book-length summary of John Dewey's concept of aesthetic experience, with an unusually clear framework for valuing individual experiences of all kinds.

11. Roberts, *From Knowledge to Narrative: Educators and the Changing Museum,* 131–52. Roberts builds an argument throughout the book that visitors make their own narratives and concludes in chapter five with a strong case for museums deliberately facilitating the process of developing narratives.

II

THE REBIRTH OF A NATION

The United States is reborn in museums all the time. Exhibits about the nation's origins and early days are cast and recast to take advantage of new display technologies, incorporate recent knowledge about the past, and reshape narratives to suit our times. The Peabody-Essex Museum in Salem, Massachusetts, for example, completed a new building in 2003 to house its collection of New England historical objects and artifacts from around the world. At the new site, parts of the collection are on display for the first time in the museum's two-hundred-year history; it was founded by merchants in 1799. Twenty-four architectural properties are arrayed on spacious grounds. For the new building, curators have "transformed"[1] the exhibits, allotting more space to the large collection of New England decorative arts, firmly reminding visitors of the institution's roots in the young republic—a transformation that, in Huebner's terms, resulted in aesthetically changed exhibitions.

At the same time, the museum engages both Huebner's political and ethical rationales. Museum staff members consciously present global acquisitions in terms that reflect contemporary museum theory about the importance of incorporating diverse viewpoints. In a press release, Don Monroe, the museum's executive director and chief executive officer, comments, "Museums can present art and objects in ways that create dialogue rather than support a singular worldview."[2] In his own institution, objects that were brought back by New England merchants as trade goods or souvenirs of travel to the "exotic" climes of Asia or Africa can now be viewed through a lens that emphasizes their original cultures as well as the lives of the eighteenth-century merchants. According to Ross Atkin of the *Christian Science Monitor*, the institution thus "walks a fine line in trying to remain both global and local in outlook."[3]

Finally, the Peabody-Essex Museum puts individuals in touch with a variety of materials through the use of contemporary technologies. These technologies consist of state of the art lighting and display cases, computer displays and a web page allowing people to access information, as well as modern methods of conservation and preservation. Technology mediates between the viewer and the collection. Yet the museum also consistently touts its ability to create direct visitor experiences, similar to a living history museum. The top of its web page section on visiting bears the tags: "art culture experience" and "Journey to a World of Art and Culture."[4] According to the museum's deputy director of special projects, John Grimes, museums like the Peabody-Essex "are increasingly going to be touchstones of real experience. . . . They will affirm that it's not just a virtual world out there, with pictures and words on the internet. It's a place where you can stand in front of the original document or inspect what someone created with their . . . hands hundreds of years ago, far, far away."[5] There appears to be little awareness of the irony that the "real experience" of the museum is in fact delivered with the help of "pictures and words on the internet."

These three features of the Peabody-Essex Museum—its claim to a place in narratives of the origins of our nation, the changing rhetoric surrounding its exhibits, and the role of technology in bringing us the past—are also essential to the three museums featured in this section. While the latter two features are to some extent apparent at all history museums, they are brought into unique relief in local museums that lay claim to a place in national history. Colonial Williamsburg, the House of Seven Gables, and the Old State Capitol Museum in Baton Rouge are important because they are sites where our nation is perpetually reborn, its history refracted through local lenses.

In each of the three museums discussed in the following chapters, the shifts in the museums' narratives have followed recent social trends toward inclusiveness, especially in terms of race and class. In Gable and Handler's article on Williamsburg, we learn how part of the original purpose of the institution was to make the Rockefellers' new money look old. Since then, the roles of teachers and the content or history lessons to be taught have shifted. Tour scripts have moved from referring to African Americans as servants to referring to them more accurately as slaves. At the House of the Seven Gables, tour scripts now include references to the Underground Railroad and to the home's association with a settlement house. And at the Old State Capitol, curators emphasize that from the time the Louisiana Purchase brought the state into the union, Louisiana's culture has been a blend or *gombo* of cultures. Tours contain a section on the democratic process and a room devoted to populist politician Huey Long, while the governors' room emphasizes the roles of African-American and lower class governors as well as of the Bourbon aristocracy. In each institution, these shifts are part of the museum's efforts to become a local icon of democratic ideals. The combination of early national history and an appeal to the masses appears to be a winning one when it comes to drawing audiences, and it situates places outside Washington and Boston on the nation's colonial map.

All three sites are also in some ways places where history—the content—is turned into experience. Williamsburg, most obviously, is a living history museum, a site which the authors indicate mediates between the extremes of scholarly history in books and theme parks full of technical marvels. As Handler and Gable show, Williamsburg is a place where public history may be transformed into collective memory as visitors come to remember the experience of visiting the site rather than "pure" history. This, in turn, creates visitor demands for constant novelty on return visits. At the House of the Seven Gables, most of the changes are evident in the tour scripts, and the site is marketed in part through its popular restaurant and gift shop. A change made possible by contemporary technology is the move of another home to the vicinity, thus giving visitors more to see and learn. At the Old State Capitol, youngsters have opportunities to pretend they are politicians giving speeches, to develop a simulated state budget, and to use interactive media to learn about famous figures in Louisiana history. They visit copies of the French and American versions of the Louisiana Purchase enshrined in a semi-dark room, these precious documents given an aura of extreme importance through the technology that secures and conserves them, keeping visitors at a safe distance.

Significantly, the historic properties in this section, all in the East, market themselves as popular sites. In their selling of democracy as an educational value, they sometimes romanticize the past or create near hagiographies of such celebrated figures as Nathaniel Hawthorne and Huey Long. At times they may idealize or romanticize the nation's early days, but even so, their scripts reflect current ideologies: as politically inspired moves, perhaps, these shifting interpretations also raise ethical questions as to who is telling whose story, and for which audiences of "students." As Gaynor Kavanaugh has noted in her book *History Curatorship*, "Inevitably, the past becomes a contemporary construction built out of present-day interests with the materials that immediately come to hand. This holds risks. History can become many things: a political tool, an escape route from present realities or the key to liberation."[6]

NOTES

1. "Transformed Peabody-Essex Museum Opened to International Acclaim," Peabody-Essex Museum Press Release, 21 June 2003 (<http://www.pem.org/press/index/.php?id=14> (accessed June 28, 2006).

2. "Transformed Peabody-Essex Museum Opened to International Acclaim."

3. Ross Atkin, "Museum Makeover," *Christian Science Monitor*, March 10, 2000.

4. Peabody-Essex Museum Website, www.pem.org/visit (accessed 28 June 2006).

5. "Transformed Peabody-Essex Museum Opened to International Acclaim."

6. Gaynor Kavanaugh, *History Curatorship* (Leicester: Leicester University Press, 1990), 4.

3

Public History, Private Memory

Notes from the Ethnography of Colonial Williamsburg, Virginia, U.S.A.

Eric Gable and Richard Handler

Colonial Williamsburg is the reconstructed capital of the colony of Virginia at the dawn of the American Revolution.[1] It is one of the largest national heritage sites in the United States, and it is among the largest and most visited of the many similar twentieth-century recreations of the past that are by now a taken for granted, one might even say quintessential, element of the landscape of modernity.[2] Like other similar sites, Colonial Williamsburg not only bills itself as a mimetic representation—an "authentic" replication—of an era in which diverse peoples were "becoming Americans,"[3] it also claims that it is a place where contemporary citizens of the nation-state can reexperience a kind of personal identification with a national identity. Americans visit Colonial Williamsburg, immerse themselves in what the town has to offer, and emerge as somehow more American as a result.

As such, Colonial Williamsburg asserts that it turns "official history" into "collective memory"—to use the current terms of an increasingly interdisciplinary scholarly discourse. Yet, in many ways, the managers of the site treat personal memory as if it were anathema to history as they conceive it. People's memories—of how the site "used to be," of what they "know" about eighteenth-century America and its founding fathers—often get in the way of the site's pedagogical mission. By the same token, those in charge of Colonial Williamsburg encourage their public to make a visit to the site a personally memorable experience. They do so, in part, because museum pedagogy grounded in what Huebner refers to as an ethical rationale demands a certain affective identification between the visitor and the site's regime of knowledge. They do so, also, because they assume that visitors with fond memories of Colonial Williamsburg will become loyal customers—a vital constituency in the site's ongoing efforts to maintain market share in the heritage and tourist industry.

The result, as we argue in the present chapter, is that Colonial Williamsburg tends to transform public history into private memory by collapsing the distance between the reconstructed past (the museum's history lesson) and the visitor's touristic or familial experience on the site. Visitors indeed remember their visits to Colonial Williamsburg, but their specific memories (as we sketch them below) would seem to have little to contribute to any "collective memory" of a "national history."

Although one goal of this chapter is to challenge the terms of the conventional dichotomy between "history" and "memory," let us begin by using the terms as they are often used. In conventional scholarly usage, "history" refers to the results of the work of professional historians, distinguished from "memory," the layperson's recounting of personally experienced events that historians may or may not come to consider "historical." Elaborating on that distinction, we would say that history is for the most part not based on personal experience but on "data" derived above all from written sources, and further, that history is a narrative account of some past sequence of events constructed by a historian located at some considerable distance—a distance both personal and temporal—from the events or epoch being narrativized. Memory, by contrast, suggests a personal and direct connection between the person who remembers and the remembered events. Almost by definition, memory requires temporal absence combined with an imaging of personal presence. With memory, a person in the here and now remembers his or her participation in some past, there-and-then scene or event. That is, with memory, a rememberer represents him- or herself as a figure or an actor or a character in a scene that is understood by the rememberer to be both temporally distanced (located in the past) and phenomenologically real (it "truly happened" and "I was there"). A final point of contrast between the two terms is that history is primarily associated with written evidence (so-called primary documents) and written results (history as book, as scholarly essay), while memory is thought of most frequently as an oral accounting.

In what follows, an outline of an ethnography of memory at Colonial Williamsburg, we explore memory making on the ground at Colonial Williamsburg. In doing so, we will discover the many (often unacknowledged) ways that individual memories become entangled with the site's explicitly acknowledged project, one that echoes Schwab's commonplaces of schooling: to teach an American history (based on a thorough reading of the best available documentation) to an American public. The entanglement of history and memory, as revealed in the ethnography, will lead to some final speculations about the problematic distinction between the two terms.

MEMORY AND THE MAKING OF COLONIAL WILLIAMSBURG

One of the most intriguing and significant features of Colonial Williamsburg is that it tells three stories about the past simultaneously. For us to write that Colonial Williamsburg "tells stories" is not to make an inadvertent analogy between what the site does as a purveyor of official history, on the one hand, and orality, on the other. With its hundreds of reconstructed and restored buildings filled with artifacts arranged in *tableaux vivants*, and its unending production of visual images (brochures, newsletters, glossy advertisements, coffee table books), Colonial Williamsburg is above all a stage upon which costumed employees talk to visitors about the eighteenth-century capital, about the twentieth-century reconstruction of the capital, and about history itself as a regime of knowledge. This talk—a blurred chorus of guided tours (with their more or less staged scripts), informal conversations, and formal lectures and performances—is what we refer to when we say the site tells stories. That oral storytelling is more often associated with memory than with history is only the first of the many entanglements we will discuss.

The featured story at Colonial Williamsburg is, of course, the official history lesson—that is, the information the museum conveys about eighteenth-century Williamsburg and, by extension, America's colonial era. But there are two other stories at least as important as the first to our discussion of memory making. First, there is the story Colonial Williamsburg tells its public about its own founding. In the site's origin story, early-twentieth-century Williamsburg is portrayed as a forgotten backwater—a casualty of modern capitalism, of the automobile, of transregional mobility. The once illustrious town's drift into oblivion prompts a local but well-connected Episcopalian minister, the Reverend W. A. R. Goodwin, to cajole, without success, Henry Ford, and later, more successfully, John D. Rockefeller, Jr., to bankroll the town's architectural resurrection.[4] Goodwin's conversion of Rockefeller to his cause is assimilated into a larger counter-modern or romantic critique of industrial civilization: a good, even golden, past paved over by modernity's juggernaut needs to be restored so as not to be forgotten, irretrievably lost.

In for-public-consumption versions of this origin story, Rockefeller's motives are portrayed as intrinsically altruistic: the patron was a philanthropist whose financial contributions count as a farsighted patriotic sacrifice to the common good, even as a twentieth-century extension of the patriotism of Colonial Williamsburg's revolutionary inhabitants. But Rockefeller's various biographers suggest other motives on the part of the man who not only paid for the restoration but came to inhabit one of the town's antebellum plantation households. In their analyses we get a sense of one of America's plutocrats concerned with erasing popular memories—those of his family's plebeian origins and of the taint "new money" had at the time of crude and brutal exploitation of American workers and the American public.[5]

Another crucial story the site tells concerns the nature of history itself. Here the primary images are of a place using cutting-edge research continuously to edit itself, to prune from its landscape inaccuracies and anachronisms, and to replace them with more accurate and truthful historical representations. Reconstructed pleasure gardens, researched and designed in the 1930s, are discovered in the 1970s to be rather more "colonial revival" than colonial, and they are then either ripped out and replanted or, at least, "interpreted" to the public as being inaccurate. Picket fences and "outbuildings," well maintained since their construction in the 1930s, are determined in the 1980s to be too neat for the reality of eighteenth-century backyards, and their surfaces are subsequently less frequently painted to give the town a more accurate appearance. Another kind of anachronism has been apparent in the town's inhabitants. From its beginnings, Colonial Williamsburg hired "hostesses"—tour guides—from among the local white gentry. These people, who cherished familial memories of an antebellum, slave-holding aristocracy, an aristocracy more closely tied to the South of the "lost cause" than to the continental United States, had to be taught to forget their personal connections to the site in favor of a more distanced historical understanding of eighteenth-century Williamsburg as a cradle of American nationhood.[6] In addition, Colonial Williamsburg made often unsuccessful efforts to convince the local African-American community that the site's urge to depict "servants" (in fact, they were slaves) for segregation-era white audiences would not cater to white prejudice.

In large measure, the site's interactions with these local constituencies reveal its dominant orientation toward popular memory. In the beginning, both black and white local memories got in the way of the site's pedagogical mission. Indeed, to this day, Colonial Williamsburg's historical interpreters and managers constantly complain about the ("misguided") resistance they face from public memory as they work to make the site more accurate, more true to the past. When they decide to change furnishings or wallpaper or paint color in several of the museum's well-appointed exhibition buildings, visitors complain that they remember the houses differently, that the new colors are too bright and therefore not authentically old. Conversely, when the site tries to rusticate itself, to apply a patina of poverty or realistic sloppiness to exterior surfaces, visitors again complain because they remember a tidier and more bucolic village.

If historians at Colonial Williamsburg feel compelled to struggle against the recalcitrant memories of the site's various publics, the institution's marketing staff has generally encouraged the paying public to think of their sojourn at the site as memorable. Marketers recognize that Colonial Williamsburg depends on creating and maintaining a following—visitors who will return time and again, visitors who will instill in their children a taste for Colonial Williamsburg, visitors who, as they age and their incomes grow, remember the museum fondly and donate to it. For these reasons, when marketers communicate to this public, they are constantly using the word "memory" in interesting ways. Here, for example, is a letter (dated May 17, 1999) we received reminding us that our annual pass was about to expire. The letter begins, "Some of your fondest memories of the past year may have actually occurred in 1775—because last summer, you visited Colonial Williamsburg and immersed yourself in the 18th century." After listing what we might enjoy, were we to visit in the upcoming summer, the letter stresses, "It will be a year to remember. *So remember to renew now.*"

In contrast to the historians, the marketers who wrote this promotional text celebrate and promote visitors' memories. However, the content of memory—what is to be remembered—is left up to the imagination. "Memory" is simply another term for "experience," the experience visitors have when they come to an attraction where, as is constantly repeated, history (whatever that may be) comes alive. In sum, Colonial Williamsburg's marketers work at cross purposes to its historians. By packaging history as experience, they encourage precisely the kinds of anachronistic expectations the historians find so irksome. These historians, in turn, respond to such memories in ways typical of official or academic history. For many historians, memory is not to be trusted. It stands between the present and the past. In many ways, the job of historians is to destroy or at least transcend memory by creating history. This work, this duty, is a function of a pedagogical mission. It is also, as we now suggest, a function of the way Colonial Williamsburg legitimates itself in the educational tourism industry.

HISTORY AND THE LEGITIMIZATION OF COLONIAL WILLIAMSBURG

The institutionally mandated pedagogical mission of a museum like Colonial Williamsburg is to teach history. A museum's connection to history, its possession of history, is crucial to the authority and prestige it wants to claim in relation to other types of institutions against which it must compete. Two of the most important of those competing institutions (from the perspective of those who work at and manage Colonial Williamsburg) are the university and the theme park. The theme park—epitomized by the sites of the Disney corporation—is both feared and admired by museums like Colonial Williamsburg. Theme parks are feared because they are aggressive and successful competitors for market share. That is, museums must compete for their audiences against all sorts of institutions which seek to entice the public to visit and thus to spend its leisure time—and the dollars that finance leisure time—within their premises. Competing in this market, history museums rely on the prestige that their possession of "real" history and their scholarly authority can generate. At Colonial Williamsburg, employees told us repeatedly that theme parks are not "real"—that the scenes and landscapes they construct are not factual because Disney and its ilk are not bound by any scientific rules of evidence or by historiographic standards of accuracy and documentation. Colonial Williamsburg and other history museums thus appeal to the public by saying, in effect, "our product differs from the products of Disney as fact differs from fantasy, history from myth. If you want the real thing instead of fakery, visit us, not Disney."

Flanked on one side by theme parks, history museums are flanked on the other side by the university. In our research at Colonial Williamsburg, we found that historians working in history museums feel themselves to be looked down upon by historians in universities, and that such feelings are not unfounded. From the perspective of many scholars in the university, history museums are far too much like theme parks. That is, academic historians often see history museums at best as adjuncts to the "real" work of "serious" history ongoing in the academy, and at worst as popularizers, vulgarizers who have borrowed so much from Disney that they have become little more than theme parks.

History museums fight such prejudices and their own feeling of status inferiority by emphasizing the advantages of pedagogy based on artifacts that are either not used or not available, for the most part, in university teaching. As we have seen, to distinguish themselves from Disney, history museums claim possession of the "real thing," with the emphasis on the word "real." By contrast, to distinguish themselves from universities, history museums like Colonial Williamsburg claim possession of the "real thing" with the emphasis on the word "thing." In a curiously anti-intellectual argument, they claim that museums specialize in an experiential, object-based kind of curriculum that is in some ways superior to learning processes based solely upon reading. "Come to the museum," they say to potential visitors, "and experience history, three-dimensionally, personally, as you cannot experience it in schoolbooks."

Let us note, provisionally, that within the frame of reference provided by the conventional definitions of history and memory, the idea of a three-dimensional, experiential approach to history is problematic. As we have seen, history is usually understood to be not personal experience but a distanced and considered recounting of past events based on ongoing scholarship. Constructing landscapes—"museumscapes"—intended to recreate, mimetically, a past historical scene collapses the distance between history and personal experience. Or, to put this another way, it leads visitors to such scenes to conflate their own experiences in the museum with historical experience or historical knowledge, as these are conventionally defined.

Despite the fact that history museums like Colonial Williamsburg stress to the public the three-dimensional, experiential aspects of the learning they offer, these museums insist that the knowledge they convey is, in fact, "historical" knowledge. That is, even though they claim that their medium of instruction is unique, they would not claim *not* to be doing history; rather, they say that they are doing good and legitimate history in a new way or in a way that differs pedagogically from the way history is done or taught in the academy. Moreover, much of the research that professional historians working in museums conduct is no different from the research that university-based scholars conduct: it is text-based. Thus much of the research that underpins the exhibits of a museum like Colonial Williamsburg involves archival research and the use of the data thus amassed to write historical narratives. Those narratives are then imposed on the tableaux of the public museum so that museum scenes and artifacts are used to tell the story historians have written (this statement must be modified in relation to archaeological research within museums, but that is not our topic here).

Thus historians at Colonial Williamsburg and other museums like it do not talk much about "memory" in the rhetoric they elaborate about their institutions. Colonial Williamsburg, in its own eyes, is a history museum, and both words, "history" and "museum," are routinely used by the institution to describe itself. Indeed, its toll-free telephone number, established for the convenience of visitors and potential visitors, is 1-800-HISTORY. But if "memory" is all but absent from the stories Colonial Williamsburg tells about itself, it is central, as we shall see, to its marketing and the stories visitors tell abut the site.

VISITORS MAKING MEMORIES AT COLONIAL WILLIAMSBURG

As anyone who has studied museums on the ground knows, and as Elizabeth Vallance has indicated in an earlier chapter, it is notoriously difficult to learn about visitor responses to their museum experiences. At Colonial Williamsburg, our research focused on the institutional structure of the museum and on the relationship of that structure to the process of history making. Visitors were not our main concern, but we still found time to interview many dozens of visitors. To write this essay, we reviewed our visitor interview materials and found that they are full of memories, statements about memories, and interpretations of present-day museum visits ("present" referring to the moment of the interview) in terms of memories of past visits. There are also many assertions in these visitor interviews concerning the importance and meaning of "history." Yet, on balance, we might argue that "memory" is more important in visitor responses than "history," as the following examples suggest.

Often people's memories of family visits to Colonial Williamsburg were explicitly associated with cherished objects purchased literally as souvenirs or remembrances. Sometimes they told us of objects they had purchased for themselves, objects that marked a memorable earlier period in their lives and thus accrued meaning over the years by connecting the rememberer to that past state of self:

> I think it was the King's Arms [Tavern] at that time, too. And I was so intrigued with this little saltcellar. So we went to one of the gift shops. And . . . we were very poor, so we scraped our pennies together so I could buy my saltcellar and my pepper shaker. And of course I treasure them. Since then, I've come back,

> and I have [bought] a lot of things—but nothing as meaningful as the little salt-cellar and the pepper shaker.

Here, in what is one of the paradigmatic touring patterns at sites like Colonial Williamsburg (and one that such museums depend on and exploit), this woman is entranced by a museum object on display, then finds her way to the gift shop where, despite her poverty, she buys a replica of the displayed object. In other cases, treasured objects were given by elders to visitors when they were children. One woman told us, "My folks bought me this bracelet I don't know how many years ago." Such objects can trigger memories of deceased relatives and past relationships as well as of prior family trips to Colonial Williamsburg. Thus, through the objects it sells, the museum becomes a site of family memory.

Even without reference to purchased objects, many visitors experienced Colonial Williamsburg in terms of remembered family visits to the site—visits understood to be connected together as a series ("our first visit ten years ago" or "the last time we visited") that might span three generations. Listen to "Bob," an elderly teacher, explaining to us why he returned many times over the years to Colonial Williamsburg:

> I'm not sure it's history. Although in my case, my dad lived in Rochester [New York, the home of Eastman Kodak]. And he was fascinated by travel and by this place as it grew up . . . So it's been a part of the family, in that sense. George Eastman and Mr. Rockefeller and Mr. Ford and those kinds of folks were part of the vocabulary—not the friendships or contacts, but in Rochester, with George Eastman, we had to watch what he was doing every day.

This is an unusually "dense" memory because it suggests not merely a family history of interest in and visits to Colonial Williamsburg, but a familial connectedness to some of the most famous of American plutocratic families. Many other visitors remembered their families' connections to the museum, though without any explicit mention of people like the Rockefellers. The following statement is typical: "I've loved this place ever since my parents brought me down here when I was a young boy . . . This is the kind of a place that seems to draw me back, the history of it and so forth." Here "history" is almost an afterthought—an idea to which we will return.

If many visitors mentioned having been taken to Colonial Williamsburg by their parents or others, parents with children in tow talked about their visit to the museum in terms of providing their children with memories. They might say, for example, that they had brought their children to Colonial Williamsburg when the children were very young and that now, several years later, they were bringing them again to reinforce and add to the children's memories from previous visits as well as to introduce them to history lessons that the children had been too young to assimilate on prior visits. One couple explained to us that they were visiting the museum explicitly to encourage their daughter to remember history lessons she'd learned but forgotten!

> Mother: She [her thirteen-year-old daughter] has been here [before], it's been about four years now, and so she's seeing things she doesn't remember at all. And she did her social studies project this year on Williamsburg.
>
> Daughter: Mom, that was last year.
>
> Mother: Yes, it was last year.
>
> Interviewer: What did you write about?
>
> Father: It was mostly—I don't mean to answer for her—but it was mostly pictures . . . We had some 8 x 10s made so that they could be seen . . . and pamphlets from Colonial Williamsburg.
>
> Mother: And of course she's forgotten a lot of what she even did in the report now, and so we're trying to point out: *This* is what you talked about!

Note how thoroughly history and memory are entwined here. The parents are concerned not simply that their daughter learn history; they seem to want to reconnect her to knowledge she once possessed but later forgot. They want her to remember what she once knew, perhaps as a way to reestablish a legitimate claim to the historical knowledge Colonial Williamsburg can convey—or, more generally, because they want to ensure the continuity of their fashioning of her as a culturally respectable person. The parents' desires have the strength of Huebner's ethical rationale. Another kind of remembered connection to the past, as mediated by the museum, concerns the association of Colonial Williamsburg scenes with a past understood in terms of biographical or familial time. In such cases, people use the museum to remember their own childhood or that of their ancestors. For example, we had a long conversation with the father and grandfather of a three-generation family that was touring the site. Their encounter with a museum interpreter playing the role of a slave led, as we questioned them, to a spirited, thoughtful disagreement between the younger and older man. Both men rejected slavery, but the younger man went on to mount a moral critique of colonial society and of the American founding fathers. The older man, by contrast, defended the founders' reliance on slavery by saying that it was a necessary evil—necessary, that is, to the creation of a greater good, the country that became the United States of America. Significantly, the older man responded to the slaves' misery in terms of his own remembered experience of childhood during the Great Depression:

> When I was a kid growing up, I knew nothing but depressions . . . so I can relate to her [the slave] in many ways. . . . In the fall, she said she did certain things—I did certain things in the fall; I remember I used to go out and pick these wild grapes, which we made jelly from . . . I related to that big fire going [i.e., at the site where the slave spoke to them]. Let's put some more wood . . . on it. So in many, many ways, I lived, I'm sure not as bad as they did, but I can compare—there's a comparison there.

In this case, an elderly visitor compares his own childhood experiences directly to the experience of slavery portrayed at Colonial Williamsburg. We frequently spoke to younger people, especially children, who related Colonial Williamsburg scenes to the way they imagined the childhoods of their parents or grandparents. For example, a thirteen-year-old boy on a formal school visit to the museum explained, in the face of our persistent questioning, that the history taught at Colonial Williamsburg allowed him to understand stories his parents had told him about their childhood: "because you hear your parents saying, back then, I had to walk fifteen miles to school—so it's interesting to . . . see what we were like . . . back then, before modern technology."

Without sketching further examples, we might begin to elaborate a typology of memory experiences and memory narratives at Colonial Williamsburg and museums like it. We might note, for instance, the presence or absence of memorialized consumer objects (of a personal or domestic nature), or we might chart the span and "direction" of memories (elders remembering their own past, elders bestowing memories on children, children remembering their elders' past). But given limitations of space, we turn instead to a consideration of the entanglement of history and memory and its significance for the history/memory distinction we sketched at the outset.

MEMORIES OF CONSUMER DESIRE

Because "memory" is a central preoccupation in both vernacular discourse and scholarly studies, it must be critically scrutinized rather than unreflectively exported as a social science model.[7] In writing this ethnographic sketch we are assuming that studies of the production of "memory" at sites such as Colonial Williamsburg are good places from which to begin such a critique. At the risk of oversimplifying the explosion of writing on the topic of "memory" as it relates to "history," we would like to note an ongoing tendency to contrast the two terms in a specific way. Memory is associated with the popular and plebeian, history with the elite and official. In this conception, memory either lends itself to a certain academic populism or to academic elitism—that is, memory can be romanticized as a form of resistance against official historical discourses, or it can be exposed as misguided and naive.[8]

Our work at Colonial Williamsburg leads us to argue that the two terms, memory and history, are less easily dichotomized than standard usage suggests. For one thing, and here we are following Michael Lambek,[9] both history and memory are culturally particular terms that refer to culturally particular genres.[10] This means, first, that historical stories and memory stories are *both* narratives and, as such, one is not necessarily more objective than the other since both are shaped by certain generic conventions. This apparently banal observation has, we feel, several less-than-banal implications. For example, against those who argue that memory is the more subjective, and history the more objective, genre, we can counter that historians' subjectivities are not at all irrelevant in the making of history, as anyone knows who has studied the ways cultural positioning and ideological inclinations influence historians' professional work. On the other hand, to those who might see the subjective sources of memory—its "I was there" aspect—as a guarantor of a certain privileged objectivity, we can respond that memory is by definition always a *retelling*. It is a story or account in which the storyteller tells about herself or himself, but it is a story nonetheless, and thus, as many strands of twentieth-century psychology have argued, it is at once more than and less than "the whole story" or the objective truth. All of which is to say that although it may be useful to maintain a distinction between memory and history, that distinction ought not to be articulated as one of objectivism versus subjectivism.

We can make similar suggestions with respect to the oral/written distinction, a distinction publicly emphasized at history museums and one, moreover, which often maps one to one onto the memory/history distinction. As we mentioned briefly at the outset, sites like Colonial Williamsburg present a confusing picture of the relationship between oral and written knowledge and their transmission. To legitimate itself as a producer of historical knowledge, the site stresses the written, above all in the form of "documented" evidence. On the other hand, much—in fact, probably the far greater part—of teaching and learning occurs in an oral medium at the museum: frontline interpreters study historical documents and secondary sources, but they are largely "trained" in oral sessions by in-house staff; and those interpreters then teach the public almost exclusively via oral presentations. In pointing this out, we are not criticizing the museum's reliance on orally transmitted knowledge. Rather, we are emphasizing the discrepancy between that all-pervasive reliance on the oral and the site's public relations erasure of the oral in favor of written history.[11]

The memories of Colonial Williamsburg visitors suggest other ways to question any simple distinction between the oral and the written and between memory and history. For example, visitors to the museum may interpret the history presented there in terms of their memories of childhood or in terms of their parents' storytelling about their own childhood. Or visitors may interpret the site in terms of what they can remember of a history they learned (probably with much oral, classroom transmission) as schoolchildren. We might even argue that the museum's presentations unintentionally but nonetheless consistently collapse the distance between history and memory—a distance it otherwise seeks to preserve—precisely because its "product," the three-dimensional "experiencing" of history, encourages the public to "remember" history as personal experience.

What, finally, of this museum's, and most history museums', claim to create collective memory and thus to serve a vital function in democratic societies? Is so-called collective memory a fair exchange for the local memories destroyed, as we suggested at the outset, when nonprofit corporations or government agencies take over historic buildings and districts and remake them as museums? An easy, obvious, yet not trivial response to such a question is that we are not at all sure what the phrase "collective memory" might mean. Strictly speaking, collectivities do not remember. If by the term we mean to indicate institutionally sanctioned and transmitted histories, histories that have enough social clout to reach masses of people, then we are talking about a phenomenon that is surely a hybrid one from the perspective of any neat history/memory distinction. For whatever it may be, collective memory (at least in the contemporary world) is fostered in socially complex interactions involving written documents and orally transmitted stories, occurring in a variety of contexts, from a sole individual reading a text, to a school group listening to a teacher tell historical stories, to a group of tourists experiencing three-dimensional but nonetheless documented history at places like Colonial Williamsburg and then telling stories about those experiences.

But putting aside such questions, and accepting "collective memory" as a useful term, it is still worth noting that neither the currently fashionable romanticization of memory against history, nor the more conventional dismissal of memory in favor of history, account for the types of memories we found among visitors on the ground at Colonial Williamsburg. With respect, in particular, to the romanticization of memory, it is often taken for granted that the antithesis of memory is not just history but "official" history. Official history is the photograph, as Milan Kundera notes[12] out of which the purged politico has been inexpertly airbrushed. Official history erases messy or unpleasant truths in order to make useful propaganda out of the past. Memory, by contrast, is the weed that grows through the cracks in a public monument's foundations. Memory is the joke people tell behind the bureaucrat's back or while the politician is making his speech. Memory is what lies beneath the hastily covered over patch of earth. Memory contests and resists official history. And this is one reason why it has become so fascinating to current scholarship. Memory is what we can recover in order to give voice to the disenfranchised, the oppressed, and the silenced.

Yet in this essay we have suggested that memory, collective or individual, at Colonial Williamsburg is an unlikely candidate for such romanticization. Indeed, the memories people related to us were above all memories of consumer desire or memories of family history experienced as a comparative accounting of lifestyles.

Nevertheless, it might be said that such memories contest the site's official mission and its official history, albeit in ironic ways. Thus such memories seem to be unaffected by the project of shaping collective memory that Colonial Williamsburg announces in its promotional rhetoric. In this rhetoric, Colonial Williamsburg is "a brick-and-timber embodiment of a revolution in the rights of man," where visitors can "stride in step with patriots" and "walk in freedom's footfalls." This rhetoric, which usually borrows from the incandescent language of high Protestantism and links it to high-minded patriotism, justifies the existence of Colonial Williamsburg as a pilgrimage site in an American civil religion, the kind Robert Bellah so aptly described.[13] By its own accounting, Colonial Williamsburg is a patriotic shrine. And its visitors should reflect on profound moral principles, renew their dedication to them, and leave the shrine better citizens. If nothing else, then, the kind of individual memorializing visitors do at Colonial Williamsburg suggests that the site's claims about its capacity to shape public memory in predictable ways is an exaggeration.

Visitors' memories call into question whatever claim the site can make that it has succeeded in its pedagogical mission to teach a history that is to some degree disruptive of complacency. Visitors tend if anything to domesticate the site when they turn it into a memorial. But the gap between the site's claims and visitor memory is not because visitor memories are somehow separate from the site, somehow intrinsically intractable or at odds with official history. Rather, as we have suggested in this essay, such memories are as much a product of the site's own unexamined pedagogic routines as of anything else. Indeed, in privileging visitor "experience" as a necessary pedagogic medium, Colonial Williamsburg turns public history into private memory.

NOTES

1. The authors conducted twenty months of ethnographic fieldwork at Colonial Williamsburg between January 1990 and August 1991. Their research was supported by the Spencer Foundation, the National Endowment for the Humanities, and the University of Virginia. The results are reported in Handler and Gable, *The New History in an Old Museum* (London: Duke University Press, 1997).

Colonial Williamsburg, first opened to the public in 1932, is today run by the Colonial Williamsburg Foundation, a nonprofit corporation that includes a for-profit component that manages the site's hotels and restaurants. The museum itself occupies the restored portion of the city of Williamsburg, Virginia, a 173-acre "Historic Area" with over one hundred gardens, eighty-eight "original" buildings, an additional fifty major buildings, and a few hundred smaller "outbuildings" that have been reconstructed according to archaeological and documentary evidence. The foundation employs over three thousand people, and visitors number close to a million a year.

2. David Lowenthal, *The Past Is a Foreign Country* (Cambridge: Cambridge University Press, 1985).

3. Colonial Williamsburg, *Teaching History at Colonial Williamsburg* (Williamsburg, VA.: Colonial Williamsburg Foundation, 1985), 2.

4. Philip Kopper, *Colonial Williamsburg* (New York: Harry N. Abrams, 1986), 139–55.

5. Peter Dobkin Hall, "The Empty Tomb: The Making of Dynastic Identity," in *Lives in Trust: The Fortunes of Dynastic Families in Late Twentieth-Century America*, ed. George Marcus and Peter Dobkin Hall, 255–348 (Boulder: Westview Press, 1992).

6. Andrea Foster, "They're Turning the Town All Upside Down": The Community Identity of Williamsburg, Virginia, Before and After the Reconstruction (Ph.D. diss., George Washington University, 1993), 122–67.

7. Eric Gable, "Review of *How Societies Remember*, by Paul Connerton," *American Ethnologist* 19 (1992): 385–86; Marilyn Strathern, "Nostalgia and the New Genetics," in *Rhetorics of Self-Making*, ed. Deborah Battaglia, 109–13 (Berkeley: University of California Press, 1995).

8. There is a vast and growing literature on memory, both collective and individual. Although the present chapter concerns institutionalized history making and thus, to some extent, so-called collective memory, our primary ethnographic concern here is the personal memories of visitors to Colonial Williamsburg. In our analysis, we have drawn on the essays collected in Jonathan Boyarin, ed., *Remapping Memory: The Politics of TimeSpace* (Minneapolis: University of Minnesota Press, 1994) as well as in Paul Antze and Michael Lambek, eds., *Tense Past: Cultural Essays in Trauma and Memory* (New York: Routledge, 1996), though of course Freud is foundational (though perhaps unread these days) to any work on personal memory.

The literature on collective memory can be roughly divided among that which focuses on the invention of history and the politics of history making, on the one hand, and on memory as socially embedded. In the latter approach, typified by Paul Connerton in *How Societies Remember* (Cambridge: Cambridge University Press, 1989) and Maurice Halbwachs in *On Collective Memory* (Chicago: University of Chicago Press, 1994), the term "memory" seems to us to stand in for terms like "the social" and "culture." Indeed, we are suspicious of the way "memory" has become a fashionable term in the transdisciplinary world of cultural studies, broadly conceived. Studies that we found to mediate usefully between these various approaches to memory (and to history) include Thomas Abercrombie, *Pathways of Memory and Power: Ethnography and History Among an Andean People* (Madison: University of Wisconsin Press, 1998); Joanne Rappaport, *Cumbe Reborn: An Andean Ethnography of History* (Chicago: University of Chicago Press, 1994); Richard Terdiman, *Present Past: Modernity and the Memory Crisis* (Ithaca: Cornell University Press, 1993); and Richard Werbner, ed., *Memory and the Postcolony: African Anthropology and the Critique of Power* (London and New York: Zed Books, 1998).

9. Michael Lambek, "The Past Imperfect: Remembering as Moral Practice," in *Tense Past: Cultural Essays in Trauma and Memory*, ed. Paul Antze and Michael Lambek, 235–54.

10. Richard Parmentier, *The Sacred Remains: Myth, History, and Polity in Belau* (Chicago: University of Chicago Press, 1987), 4–10.

11. Richard Handler and Eric Gable, *The New History in an Old Museum: Creating the Past at Colonial Williamsburg* (Durham, NC: Duke University Press, 1997).

12. Milan Kundera, *The Book of Laughter and Forgetting*, trans. M. H. Hein (London: Penguin, 1981), 3.

13. Robert Bellah, *The Broken Covenant: American Civil Religion in Time of Trial*, 2nd ed. (Chicago: University of Chicago Press, 1992).

4

The House of the Seven Gables

A House Museum's Adaptation to Changing Societal Expectations since 1910

TAMI CHRISTOPHER

The House of the Seven Gables began its life as a historic house museum in 1910. Located in Salem, Massachusetts, the house is an important icon of the New England region for two reasons. Foremost, the House of the Seven Gables is representative of a New England shipbuilding community spanning from the colonial period through the late nineteenth century. Second, it boasts an affiliation with Nathaniel Hawthorne, who not only based the novel *The House of the Seven Gables* on various elements of the house, but also had relatives associated with the structure.

Tourists visiting any historic site are interested to some degree in learning about the past; therefore, the way in which the House of the Seven Gables presents New England history is essential to its success. Significantly, the manner in which the House of the Seven Gables has been presented to the public has changed drastically over the years, as evident in the eleven tour scripts dating from 1910 through 1999. Heritage tourists expect history museums both to reinforce and supplement their preconceived sense of place. As a result, the museum must adjust its "history" to meet the shifting needs and preferences of society. This is a common practice and concern of other historic sites in New England such as Lowell National Historic Park, where in "1935 [the] architects' report . . . explained that the restoration had to struggle against 'the visitor's preconception' of how the town should look."[1] As we have seen in the previous chapter, this changing perception of history is not exclusively a New England phenomenon. Handler and Gable discuss the importance of visitors' memories in shaping the views of the past on display at Williamsburg. Similarly, in *Possessed by the Past,* David Lowenthal analyzes the history of Colonial Williamsburg and how its presentation has changed over time. As an interpreter at Colonial Williamsburg commented, "The interpretation of history changes and [we] have to change along with it."[2] Concurrently, the image of New England as a region has evolved. How do we account for the changes in presenting history? Can history change?

There are two ways in which history has changed in relation to the House of the Seven Gables. Ongoing research helps to verify or nullify previous conceptions of history. These facts may be directly related to artifacts or more abstractly related to historical narratives. Second, history alters because the market for history changes. Society's needs for history change over time, and historic sites adjust to meet these societal needs. In *Everyman His Own Historian,* Carl Becker argues that "Each age reinterprets the past to suit its own purposes."[3] These changing preferences can be attributed to a variety of factors. A national focus on patriotism during a time of war, movements for civil rights, and advances in technology are just a few factors that can shape the public's preferences for a certain "brand" of history. In their book-length study of Williamsburg, *The New History in an Old Museum,* Richard Handler and Eric Gable note that history, or the content of the site, "is not treated as past actuality, but as present possibility—raw material to be shaped by contemporary exigencies."[4] In a discussion on the changing presentations of history, they state, "To say that history needs a theme that 'sets the agenda' is to recognize that history is more than just the facts. In this view, themes, agendas, paradigms, or conceptual frameworks guide historians to choose particular facts and to use them in particular ways. Themes and agendas also make it possible for historians to be unconcerned with facts that have no bearing on the issues that excite them, or even to overlook them altogether."[5]

In an attempt to present and exhibit history, historians and curators are, to a large extent, not only teachers but also the definers of history. Yet, as Roy Rosenzweig and David Thelen discovered, the public ranks the credibility of museum exhibits highly.[6] The public does not take into account how the presentation of history is manipulated by the selection of items to display and the context in which they are exhibited. The history exhibited is also dependent on the target audience, funding, collection scope, and research. These factors, combined with ethical and political rationales, come together to create a contemporary historical market.

Using the House of the Seven Gables as a case study, it is possible to study the evolution of exhibited "history" by analyzing the purposeful inclusion or exclusion of facts and how they are manipulated when the museum is presented to the public. The tour scripts of the House of the Seven Gables dating from 1910 to 1999 are a valuable resource that reveals the shifts in the house's presentation in accordance with society's historical preferences and needs. Some of the scripts emphasize antiquity and tradition as a response to immigration, patriotism and the importance of "history makers" as a response to civil rights, the power of common citizens and minorities as a response to globalization, and the museum as a money-making entity as a response to an evolving market for heritage tourism. By analyzing the tour scripts chronologically, it is possible to trace the development and presentation of history in correlation to these various social and political issues.

The first evidence of the relationship between the presentation of history and the marketing of history appears with the inception of the House of the Seven Gables as a museum. Caroline Emmerton, a wealthy Salem resident, purchased the House of the Seven Gables in 1908. After a two-year restoration process, the house opened to the public as a museum. As evident in the recreation of Williamsburg, it was common during this period for wealthy, upper-class East Coast Americans to be involved in the creation of historic museums. Michael Wallace, too, has commented that "Patricians discovered in their historical pedigrees a source of cultural and psychic self-confidence and took the lead in forming a host of new institutions."[7] Most often these patricians were those who traced their ancestry to individuals who fought or participated in the Revolutionary War; they considered themselves the "true" Americans and felt threatened by the increasing stream of immigrants. With the influx of immigrants from other countries, these affluent white individuals searched for ways to validate their historical importance to contemporary society. The original tour script is an example of these viewpoints and conceptions of New England history. As Michael Wallace argues, "the museum builders simply embedded in their efforts versions of history that were commonplaces of their class's culture."[8] In other words, those images of history that best reflected the image of the affluent white American were presented. In fact, Miss Emmerton actually sat in the dining room as the tours of the House of the Seven Gables were being conducted and oversaw the training of the guides.[9]

This premiere tour script focuses on the antiquary aspects of the house and New England traditions. At the time, names and dates were not believed to be as important to visitors as romantic images of the past and its customs. Therefore, in this script, artifacts are commonly referred to as "old fashioned" and people as "a Salem merchant" or "a Salem Sea Captain."[10] An excellent example of the romantic nature of this tour is a reference to a butter churn: "This churn may be the oldest in the United States. It belonged to a man whose great-grandfather owned a plantation in the state of Maine. He cut down the finest primeval [forests] and this churn was made out of some of the wood."[11] Notice the vagueness of the passage; the important aspect is the evocation of a time gone by. A secret staircase is said to be "a means of escape in witchcraft times."[12] The inclusion of this idea supports the romanticizing of the Salem witchcraft trials. No mention is made of the injustices that occurred during this period. Similarly, a passage located at the end of the script encourages the visitor to "bring to mind the day of Salem shipping," another nostalgic notion.[13] In reaction to an increasingly industrial New England, society was anxious for a past, seemingly simpler time. Miss Emmerton and others in her class were searching for a way to hold on to their heritage in the face of new cultures and lifestyles. The House of the Seven Gables delivered this with a tour idealizing the bygone era of a New England seacoast community.

Another prevalent theme of this tour script is Nathaniel Hawthorne's affiliation with the House of the Seven Gables. Hawthorne's second cousin, Susanna Ingersoll, lived there for the majority of her life, and he visited her often. The family papers contain evidence that many situations occurring in *The House of the Seven Gables* may have been connected to events that transpired in the house, and many architectural details are incorporated in the novel. Yet it is important to note that Nathaniel Hawthorne never lived in this house. His association with the structure would have been hard to avoid in a tour, however, since his novel was an important part of what made the house seem historic.

The original tour script lacks this background information, and the visitor is led to believe that Hawthorne did indeed reside in the House of the Seven Gables. For example, a line from the kitchen section of the script states, "From this old toaster Hawthorne had many a slice of toast."[14] The novel's narrative, rather than the events of real life, also serves as a basis for the house's history. The majority of the rooms are described in terms of the novel rather than the actual occupants of the house. Actions occurring in the novel are described as if they occurred in the house. Some of the rooms are named in terms of the characters in the book, such as "Phoebe's room" and "Clifford's room."[15] This is partly due to the fact that the common person's life was not regarded as historically significant during this time. Hawthorne's fame validated the museum's existence.

During this time period, New England history was described in terms of famous, patriotic, or affluent individuals. In *On Doing Local History*, Carol Kammen writes, "most of the records that were sought out and collected . . . stem from and document a community's elite—or its emerging elite; the commercially successful, the socially prominent, the upwardly mobile, those participating in community institutions. Most of the story is about the white upper classes."[16] Because no individual fitting this profile ever lived in the house, the tour focused on Hawthorne's novel and his visits to the home. The novel *The House of the Seven Gables* was seen as a historic event in itself. Hawthorne was an ideal historic figure because he embodied many aspects of the New England Yankee. Seen as hardworking, serious, and moral, he represented an archetype that many upper-class whites felt was increasingly lost in the influx of immigrants who had very different lifestyles and cultures. Using Hawthorne and his novel as the basis for the perceptions and descriptions of the house, the script met the cultural needs of the white upper- and middle-class Americans. They were allowed to experience and identify with an ideal social and cultural climate that they believed was rapidly disappearing.

Unfortunately, the next tour script is not dated; however, its estimated date is 1958 or shortly thereafter.[17] Even without a specific date, this script exemplifies an evolution in society's preferences for the dissemination of information on historical New England. In the face of the blossoming civil rights movement, the House of the Seven Gables again attempted to fill a cultural need. The idea that the past was something to be cherished and remembered was again portrayed in the face of cultural change.

A blatant creation of New England iconology occurs in the description of the top floor in this tour script: "This is the attic and it is furnished to represent an old Salem garret. There are spinning wheels, [a] blanket closet, [a] sea chest, [and a] trunk."[18] This area was created by the museum to foster a romantic notion of a lost New England. The objective of the tour was to freeze a particular time period for introspection and contemplation. It offered a stable history that individuals could look back upon when faced with the dramatic cultural changes of the 1960s.

Perhaps the most significant aspect of this script is its focus on the Settlement Society affiliated with the House of the Seven Gables. Caroline Emmerton, among others, founded the Settlement Society several years before opening the museum. Historically, settlement houses were facilitators of mainstream American values and culture. Created by affluent white Americans, they taught cooking, sewing, and other components of domestic life to immigrants. Settlement houses were created as a response to the vast influx of immigrants who brought their own customs and cultures to the United States; these social service agencies attempted to assimilate immigrants through their work. Immigrants were taught that the "American way" (as the promoters of the settlement houses saw it) was the right way and that old world customs and traditions should be abandoned in order that the immigrants become good Americans. The function of the settlement house, as described in this tour script, was to create "planned recreation for the young people in this section of the city" and support "over 500 hundred young people in this neighborhood."[19]

The original 1910 tour served some of the same purposes as the settlement houses. Attributes and qualities of mainstream Americans were highlighted, and cultural differences were not discussed. Settlement houses and historic house museums worked together; one attempted to "Americanize" immigrants while the other attempted to reinforce those ideals considered to be American. Why was it at this time—1958—that the history of the settlement house was considered relevant to the tour of the House of the Seven Gables? In the face of increasing social change, associating the museum with the settlement house inspired visions of community involvement. In the 1958 version, the tour does in fact portray the settlement house as an entirely positive, community-building organization: "In two of our adjoining buildings we have clubs and classes afternoons and evenings in cooking, sewing, arts and crafts, sports, dancing, and many other activities."[20] Promoting cooperation and community values would have addressed the cultural needs of middle class white Americans in the early 1960s.

This script also covers topics not mentioned in the original script, such as the background information on Hawthorne's affiliation with the house. In fact, by this point the museum had been actively acquiring Hawthorne family artifacts (including a bed and a desk) and exhibiting them in the House of the Seven Gables rather than at Hawthorne's birthplace, which had recently been moved to the site.[21] These acquisitions were indicative of a continuing societal need to present the history of important individuals in conjunction with

New England history. The successful presentation of history at this time still required that historic topics, ideas, or artifacts be linked to socially, politically, or economically significant individuals or families. The increased acquisition of Hawthorne-related artifacts represented the museum's ability to create a history that meshed with these cultural trends.

A secret staircase mentioned in the original script only in terms of the novel is now described more completely. It is interesting to note that the uses of this secret stairway do not include the possibility of concealing runaway slaves. The possibility of it being used for a hiding place from Indians, a storage area for smuggled goods, or a safe place during the witch hysteria are all introduced, but the underground railway is not suggested at this early date. New England history at this point still resisted the reality of slavery. This was not unusual in the South, which had many more ties to slavery but did not emphasize slavery in the presentation of history during this time period. For instance, in the 1930s, Colonial Williamsburg made "no reference to the fact that half of eighteenth-century Williamsburg's population had been black slaves."[22] The lack of focus on slavery during this era of museum presentation may be attributed to the strained race relations prevalent during the early 1960s.

The last note of considerable change evident in this script is the mention of a museum shop. The guides were instructed to mention to the visitors, "We have a copy of the novel *The House of the Seven Gables* for sale in the shop."[23] This is the first mention of the "business" of the museum, and thereafter it became a standard element of the tour. Again, selling history (or a novel) in this manner is common to many historic sites. In their book *The New History in an Old Museum*, Handler and Gable quote a contemporary interpreter at Colonial Williamsburg: "We have two divisions: we have the museum division, which is educational, and we have hotels, restaurants, and retail sales. And those are the people who help pay the bills."[24] The idea of history being marketed and sold as a commodity for tourists seeking memorable holidays has only increased over the years.

The third script in the chronology again lacks a specific date but can be placed between the years of 1958 and 1978. There are elements in this script that appear in the earlier scripts as well, implying that various cultural concerns were still being met by the previous methods of presenting history. For example, the reasons for the secret passageway remain the same, and references to the novel exist but not in as much depth as in the previous scripts. The "social service agency" (previously referred to as the settlement house) was mentioned as providing programs "for over 500 Salem residents a week."[25] At the conclusion of this tour, the guides were again instructed to direct visitors not only to the gift shop but also to a recently opened coffee shop.

Perhaps the most obvious alteration in this script is the amount of detailed information given about the artifacts on display in the house. This may reveal a shift in personnel from volunteers to a professional staff. As Wallace indicates in *Mickey Mouse History*, museums became more professional as the desire of historians "to work with wider constituencies" increased in a difficult academic job market.[26] Indeed, dates, markers, and detailed descriptions are given for many of the artifacts in the house. For example, descriptions such as "two 19th century Hitchcock side chairs . . . Sheraton Fancy arm chairs" and a "high Sheraton style bed has ball and bell posts (c. 1825)" occur throughout this script. What is the reason for this drastic change in the scripting style? The previous scripts rarely mentioned dates or detailed descriptions of artifacts and relied heavily on hearsay and ambiguous narrative. The representation of a more generalized past was necessary to portray a romantic past rather than lived experience. Perhaps an increase in research and study also contributed to this change, demonstrating how history changes with the discovery of new information. Another likely reason for the alterations in the descriptions is the public's increasing fascination with antique collecting and documentation. Catering to connoisseurs in this manner can be interpreted as a new form of elitism.

The next four scripts, the first dated 1978 and the last dated 1980, are very similar. They use a completely different format from their predecessors. Rather than focusing primarily on social and cultural needs, this group of scripts reflects an evolution in tourism and marketing, as well as the increasing professionalism of public history. This format stresses the idea that the tour guide is a salesperson of New England history and implies that the museum is a business to be marketed. Not only do the guides encourage visitors to spend money in the museum gift shop and café at the end of this tour, but they also stress the presence of other historical sites in the area (the significance of connections between museums and business is further discussed in chapter 14).

In addition to the Seven Gables tour script, the packet given to guides contains a script about Hawthorne's birthplace, a timeline, and a brief history of Salem. The guides have to meet various stipulations and follow certain rules. A guide's responsibility is to ensure "that the memory of their [visitor] is vivid and pleasant."[27] This mandate shows that the museum served as a consumer-sensitive business similar to Colonial Williamsburg. Rather than providing a specific historical education, the main goal of the museum at this time was to provide enjoyment, pleasant memories, and entertainment, helping to ensure the return of individuals and their tourism dollars.

In addition to the marketing package, the scripts themselves provide specific information about artifacts: "The sideboard is a Hepplewhiteone [sic]. On it is an English Sheffield silver tea service with a large urn and Canton china."[28] Perhaps this focus on the artifacts is due to a resurgence in collecting or the fact that reproduction artifacts and books about these artifacts are sold in the gift shop. These scripts, in essence the tour's curriculum, again tell the story of the house through characters in the novel rather than through the actual occupants of the house, as though the characters are more historically important than the people who actually lived there. This return to a focus on Hawthorne's text distinguishes the House of the Seven Gables from other house museums in the region. In a time of increasing competition from other museums, historic house museums increasingly find themselves trying to distinguish their homes' histories (essentially their product) in order to gain a larger share of the market.

In 1995, the format of the guide ("guide" more accurately describes the text, for it is no longer a script to be read) again took a drastic turn. Most notable are the changes in the elements focused on in the telling of New England history. This guide presents the museum not only in terms of the occupants of the house (rather than Hawthorne's characters) but also in terms of popular culture. It seems to be moving toward a more accepting and encompassing history. It exemplifies the common trend in historic sites whose focus was "formerly about grand monuments, unique treasures, and great heroes" and "now also touts the typical and evokes the vernacular."[29] The first mention of the triangular slave trade occurs in this guide in reference to John Turner, the original owner of the house. The fact that "Turner owned three black slaves who served the family as domestic servants" is also exposed.[30] This aspect of New England's participation in slavery is not typically included among its characteristics as a region, yet the museum exhibits its ability to broker the regional identity of New England by including this fact. This view of New England history is a reaction to an increase in regional studies as monolithic definitions of the nation are increasingly challenged. Previously, the climate was such that historic homes would never have alluded to New Englanders being involved in the slave trade. Now, the ethical and political rationales guiding the museum are different, allowing for the inclusion of this information.

Another enlightening component of this guide is its mention of the third John Turner (owner of the house during the Revolution) being loyal to the British during the war. This type of information was not disclosed to the public during the early years of the museum's operation, particularly in the original script. In fact, the museum was presented as if its history partook completely of American patriotism. It is also in this tour that the history of the women of the house is discussed. We learn that from the 1830s until the close of the Civil War, the secret passageway was used by Susannah Ingersoll to hide runaway slaves. According to the tour script, she was a stationmaster in the Underground Railroad.

In this particular case, New England was behind Colonial Williamsburg in the presentation of a history that involved slavery. In *The New History in an Old Museum*, Handler and Gable remark with irony that "finally, in the 1970s slavery was discovered at Williamsburg."[31] The idea of "history" increasingly shifted from a strict narrative of the affluent and powerful to the inclusion of stories of common lives. The change in tours at the House of the Seven Gables reflects this cultural shift.

The guide manuals from 1995 to the present have not changed drastically. The tour guide is presented with a list of rules and regulations, an inventory of artifacts, a list of important dates, and a few thematic sample tours to use as models. The structure of current tours at the House of the Seven Gables suggests that the museum is determined to give the public what it seeks. Guides are instructed to be prepared with basic facts and a theme but to let the visitors' questions and comments determine the content of the tour. Visitors thus seem to control and choose history. However, as one researcher for the museum pointed out, guides construct tours "using not only the basic facts, but also [their] own interests."[32] In this respect, the House of the Seven Gables is still presenting a history based on the interests of the guides, which undoubtedly leads to inconsistencies in the format and content of the tours. This problem is found in many house museums. Tour guides of the Wadsworth-Longfellow House in Portland, Maine (home of the poet Henry Wadsworth Longfellow), follow a similar protocol. Their docent training manual is "designed to provide . . . the basic core of knowledge. It includes factual information about the house and collections, an interpretive framework to facilitate the development of [the] tour, helpful hints on guiding, and some general reading material about historic interpretation."[33]

In a tour I recently attended at the House of the Seven Gables, the museum's affiliation with the novel was only briefly mentioned, suggesting the novel is no longer a primary literary landmark and that the history of the actual inhabitants of the house was considered of sufficient historical significance to merit a museum. The guide enthusiastically followed the lead of questions and comments from visitors. On at least three occasions, the guide stressed that Hawthorne did not live in the house. This emphasis suggested a concern not only for accuracy but also for consistency. The business aspect of the museum received heavy emphasis. Not only did the guide suggest a bite to eat at the café and some shopping in the gift store, but the admission ticket visitors were required to wear reminded them, "Visit Our Museum Store & Gables Garden Cafe."

Although most historic sites are part of nonprofit institutions, they are still businesses. They need to market themselves effectively and adapt to a volatile consumer environment. In a recent interview on the historic sites in Connecticut, Bruce Fraser of the State Department of Tourism commented that the people who visit heritage organizations are "looking for a sense of place. And this is the audience that the tourism people want most because the longer they stay, the more money they spend. They are the attractive upscale market for the tourism industry . . . heritage is business."[34] The success of New England historic sites depends on their ability to react to this audience's ever-changing perceptions of regional history and identity, and visitors' needs echo those described by Handler and Gable in the previous chapter. According to Steve Grant of the *Hartford Courant*, "They [historic sites] have to constantly be telling a new story. There has to be a reason for people to come back. 'Been there, seen that' is the death knell of these places."[35] Consumers of heritage tourism need to find a history that meets their cultural needs at the time.

The House of the Seven Gables is a museum that embodies the characteristics of New England. This important regional icon tells many stories of New England history from the slave trade to settlement houses, from the lives of common people to the fame of Nathaniel Hawthorne. Evidence of changing views of New England history and New England's regional identity are apparent in the ever-evolving content of the tour scripts of the House of the Seven Gables. Since its public debut in 1910, the museum has evolved from exhibiting selected and sometimes ambiguous aspects of New England history to providing a basic framework of facts and allowing tour guides and visitors to shape the tour experience.

These changes in the presentation of history can be accounted for in two ways which involve Huebner's rationales. Ongoing research continually uncovers new ideas, disproves previous conceptions and theories, and validates currently held notions of history. These new ideas, however, must be acceptable to the intended audiences and culturally relevant before they become incorporated in the presentation of the site's history. Secondly, it is apparent in the tour scripts of this museum that at different time periods the public expected and preferred to be exposed to particular presentations of the history of New England directly related to current events as well as the political and social climates. The continued success and expansion of the House of the Seven Gables prove this point.

This pattern of changing history's presentation applies to other successful museums as well. As we have seen, institutions such as Colonial Williamsburg thrive because they continue to pay attention to the public's demands. Organizations that remain stagnant in their presentation of history lose the opportunity for increased visitation and visibility. The Butler-McCook Homestead in Hartford, Connecticut, has recently completed a $1.3-million-dollar revitalization project. In order to increase visitation and community involvement, this house museum now boasts a "Main Street History Center," which taps into the current fascination with urban renewal and history.[36] The current trends in corporate-sponsored and mass-marketed history present themselves as perfect opportunities to evaluate an organization's ability to adapt to the public's changing expectations of the historic museum experience.

NOTES

1. Douglas DeNatale, "Federal and Neighborhood Notions of Place: Conflicts of Interest in Lowell, Massachusetts," in *Conserving Culture: A New Discourse on Heritage*, ed. Mary Hufford (Chicago: University of Illinois Press, 1994), 77.

2. Richard Handler and Eric Gable, *The New History in an Old Museum* (London: Duke University Press, 1997), 53.

3. Carl Becker, *Everyman His Own Historian* (Chicago: Quadrangle Paperback, 1966), 169.

4. Handler and Gable, *The New History in an Old Museum*, 51.

5. Handler and Gable, *The New History in an Old Museum*, 61.

6. Roy Rosenzweig and David Thelen, *The Presence of the Past: Popular Uses of History in American Life* (New York: Columbia University Press, 1998), 103.

7. Michael Wallace, "Visiting the Past: History Museums in the United States," in *Presenting the Past: Essays on History and the Public*, ed. Susan P. Benson, Stephen Brier, and Roy Rosenzweig (Philadelphia: Temple University Press, 1986), 141.

8. Michael Wallace, "Visiting the Past," 137.

9. Irene V. Axelrod, Head of Research, House of the Seven Gables, letter to author, 13 April 2000.

10. Tour script 1, 1–2.

11. Tour script 1, 2.

12. Tour script 1, 5.

13. Tour script 1, 5.

14. Tour script 1, 1.

15. Tour script 1, 5–6.

16. Carol Kammen, *On Doing Local History*, 2nd ed. (New York: AltaMira, 2003), 43.

17. This estimate is based on the mention of Nathaniel Hawthorne's birthplace having been recently moved to the site of the Seven Gables in the text of this script: "Perhaps you may have read recently in the newspapers that Nathaniel Hawthorne's birthplace . . . here in Salem was for sale. The House of the Seven Gables bought it, and it has joined the other old house here in the garden" (Tour script 1, 24). The house was moved in 1958 (Tour script 1, 59).

18. Tour script 2, 3.

19. Tour script 2, 4.

20. Tour script 2, 2.

21. Tour script 2, 5.

22. Wallace, "Visiting the Past," 148.

23. Tour script 2, 2.

24. Handler and Gable, *The New History in an Old Museum*, 53.

25. Tour script 3, 2.

26. Michael Wallace, *Mickey Mouse History and Other Essays on American Memory* (Philadelphia: Temple University Press), xii.

27. Tour script 4, 1.

28. Tour script 5, 1.

29. David Lowenthal, *Possessed by the Past: The Heritage Crusade and the Spoils of History* (New York: Free Press, 1996), 14.

30. Tour script 8, 18.

31. Handler and Gable, *The New History in an Old Museum*, 156.

32. Axelrod, letter to the author, 1.

33. *Wadsworth-Longfellow House Guide Training Manual* (Portland, Maine: Maine Center for History, 1999–2000), 1.

34. Steve Grant, "Wanted: More State Attention to Historical Tourist Sites," *Hartford Courant*, February 28, 2000.

35. Steve Grant, "Wanted."

36. The Butler Homestead is owned and operated by the Antiquarian and Landmarks Society.

5

Louisiana's Old State Capitol Museum

Castle on the Mississippi

J. DANIEL D'ONEY

Looking to the world like a Gothic cathedral picked up and placed in the Deep South by a playful giant, Louisiana's Old State Capitol Museum in Baton Rouge is unusual in appearance and focus. Burned in the Civil War so that only the outside walls remained, and rebuilt in 1882, the structure is one of two Gothic Revival statehouses in America. Combine this architectural distinctiveness with the museum's focus on Louisiana politics, a unique facet of American political history, and one has a museum unlike any other in the country. Still, there are certain similarities between this museum, the House of the Seven Gables, and many others. Foremost is the question of presenting realistic and encompassing political history in an arena where diverse political, social, and ethnic groups share common history, but not necessarily a common experience. Just as important is the issue of interpreting history, or histories, in a manner readily accessible to state natives, American tourists, and international visitors. Who owns these histories, and who determines the version to be told? How does one convey such a rich topic to the public? Is anyone excluded? Most importantly, by examining this museum's approach, I hope to illustrate themes inherent in all museums, as well as further applications of the frameworks for discussing museums introduced at the beginning of this book.

The mission statement of the Louisiana Old State Capitol emphasizes its political rationale, maintaining that the museum "provides a learning experience in Louisiana history and the democratic process through exhibitions, educational outreach and the arts. This historic and diverse facility advances the visitor's knowledge of our rich cultural heritage and vibrant political tradition." In reference to Kenneth Hudson's theories on museums of "influence," this mission statement would make the Old State Capitol *the* museum of influence in its field, as it is the only one in the world devoted exclusively to Louisiana politics. Having said that, the staff has taken its own stand in the debates over the ownership of culture. As Donna Langford will further explain in chapter 9, views on this subject tend to fall into three groups: those who believe that objects may be owned by individuals and institutions, those who hold that objects belong to everyone, and those who contend that objects cannot be owned. The staff of Louisiana's Old State Capital Museum maintains that there is no such thing as ownership of culture, political or otherwise. Individuals or museums might own objects, but it is impossible to own the experiences or beliefs these objects illustrate. Although many observers call the state America's first melting pot, Louisianans often refer to their culture as a *gombo*, and a brief glance at some of the state's ethnic groups illustrates why. Native Americans, Africans, French, and Spanish produced a Creole culture base, leavened by successive waves of Canadians, Irish, Germans, Acadians, Hungarians, English, Slavs, Canary Islanders, Koreans, assimilated Americans, and about every other group one can imagine. The northern part of the state is conservative and Protestant, while southern Louisiana is more liberal and Catholic. In a state so diverse in political, social, and ethnic groups, if this museum attempted to speak for all or present a single, unified history, it would quickly find itself mired in controversy. When dealing with thousands of visitors every year, the staff bears in mind that there are many stories, and that each is valid.[1] In other words, museum employees recognize the shifting, diverse nature of students and other visitors.

The Old State Capitol Museum staff draws upon as many avenues for interpretation as possible. A multimedia presentation and optional guides add perspective to the museum as a whole, but individual displays are interactive and can stand alone. Although thirteen of the museum's major rooms are devoted to permanent and rotating exhibits, only six exhibits will be examined in this article. They are chosen not only because they are the most popular in the building, but also because they illustrate major themes in museum theory and state history. The building itself serves as an artifact and exhibit reflecting Louisiana's political history; the Louisiana Purchase Room emphasizes the international roots of American politics; the "We the People" exhibit examines who is included or excluded in the political process; the Huey Long Assassination Room emphasizes detective work and the role of the individual in politics; the Governors of Louisiana exhibit illustrates how even those considered to be the elite represent diversity; and the Merci Train boxcar reflects modern ties with Louisiana's former mother country.

This belief that the museum structure and its history constitute an exhibit is central to the philosophy of the staff.[2] The history of the statehouse is also inherent in every exhibit and must therefore pervade any examination of the modern museum. Surveys of visitors show that the single most common reason they come to the museum is to learn about the history and architecture of the building. This survey data is supported by Marie Louise Prudhomme, the director of the Old State Capitol Museum: "We view the building as an artifact and exhibit in its own right, and we believe this view is shared by the majority of people who come as our guests. To paraphrase Sir Christopher Wren, if you want to learn about our history, look around you. We interpret the architecture and physical history of the building through film, tours, and exhibits. To understand the architecture and physical beauty of this statehouse is to understand Louisiana's political history. It would be most appropriate to view the statehouse as an exhibit housing smaller exhibits."[3]

The story of the Old State Capitol museum forefronts its political rationale, for the institution offers a microcosm of Louisiana politics, explained through film, interpreters, and exhibits. The original move to Baton Rouge illustrates the decline of French power in the state and the eclipse of New Orleans in politics, as well as the rise of the country parishes. The move from Baton Rouge corresponds with the Civil War, a seminal time in Louisiana political history, with the changes in status for slaves, free people of color, and whites. War changed the political structure of Louisiana and ushered in Reconstruction, during which time P. B. S. Pinchback, America's first African-American governor, served in office. The decision to move the capitol back to Baton Rouge in 1877 and the official statehouse opening in 1882 correspond with Bourbon restoration, an era characterized by attempts to return the state to the antebellum status quo. Huey Long's construction of the new statehouse and decommission of the old in 1932 reflect a sea change in Louisiana politics and the death of Bourbonism. Finally, the conversion of the Gothic Revival statehouse into a museum devoted to state politics in 1994 reflects a maturation of political thinking—politics recognized not just as a battlefield, but as a source of knowledge for better understanding who we are.

Of all the exhibits within the Old State Capitol Museum, the Louisiana Purchase Room is the most international in scope and the most detailed. It emphasizes politics but also raises issues of transportation, trade, and military activity. Using a chronological approach, the exhibit starts with the Spanish closing of New Orleans to Americans; nervous about American expansion, the Spanish decided an expedient move would be to exclude Americans from the colony unless they swore allegiance to Pope and King. The exhibit then illustrates how all American rivers west of the Alleghenies emptied into the Mississippi, which strangled national expansion. Signage details the secret treaty which allowed the French to revoke the colony from the Spanish, as well as the American delegation sent to buy the port of New Orleans, only to be told by Bonaparte that he would sell them all French possessions in North America for four cents an acre. Text further explains the economic machinations with Dutch and English banking houses which secured necessary funding, and the resulting attempt by East Coast states to derail the Purchase. Five countries were active players, and another four were minor players in the transaction. All are given equal representation in the display. Clearly, from the beginning, the state's history included different and often competing constituencies, which are reflected in the Louisiana Purchase Room. The overriding exhibit "curriculum" is how international events drove a transaction Americans associate with nationalism and individuality.

The designers created an exhibit which combines reminders of nineteenth-century American imperialism with the elegance of Napoleonic France. Placards with the look of vellum and old-fashioned writing hang below colorful flags representing France, America, and the fifteen states which came either whole or in part from the Purchase area. Mellow lighting reflecting off dark wood and tawny walls gives a golden, refined mood. Combined with handsome portraits of some major players in the Purchase, copies of antique maps, and the hanging flags, the displays and lighting give an impression of empire, elegance, and authenticity. This feeling is heightened by the room's centerpiece, a state of the art display case which held the American copy of the Louisiana Purchase borrowed from the National Archives when the museum opened and now contains copies of the French and American versions. These copies link visitors to the original document, illustrate that France was an equal partner in the transaction, and, with their wax seals and elaborate script, emphasize the feel of empire. Elegant as the exhibit design might be, visitors who actually read all the material draw the impression that the Purchase was anything but glamorous both in its cause and its transaction. As an example, the Spanish were terrified that godless Protestants would invade Spanish holdings and contaminate Catholic society; xenophobia led them to close their colony to all who did not swear to uphold their beliefs. Another example was Bonaparte's desire to rid himself of an unprofitable colony and thereby gain ready cash for his bloody military campaigns in St. Domingue and Europe. A last example was how Creoles in Louisiana were overjoyed to hear that they had been taken back by France, only to learn they had been sold to America, a nation whose population they viewed as being a mass of unwashed, lower-class, illiterate Protestants. A thoughtful visitor is left with the feeling that, as with most political activity, the Purchase negotiations involved hard work, hurt feelings, and several ruined careers, masked by a skillfully created aura of elegance and empire.

It is ironic that the exhibit has perhaps the most antique atmosphere of any in the museum, because the feel is possible only because of state of the art technology. The dark wood display case towers toward the ceiling like an ancient curio cabinet, yet humidity filters hidden in its joints treat the southern Louisiana air and early on ensured that the original Louisiana Purchase document was maintained in pristine form. When the document was lodged in the case, no direct lighting was allowed, and even today, hidden motion detectors bring up the lights only when a person enters the room. The glass of the case is unobtrusive, but a bulletproof barrier protects the document from casual contact or deliberate attempts to remove it. As intended, the visitor never notices the security measures, but the combination of grace and grim reality typifies the Louisiana Purchase transaction better than the aura of elegance the visitor invariably remembers.

While the exhibit on the Louisiana Purchase examines international themes, the "We the People" exhibit focuses on what it means to live in the American political system. All of Schwab's commonplaces are in evidence. Although geared toward fourth grade school groups, it raises adult issues and, of all the exhibits in the museum, stands out in its examination of national and regional political culture by emphasizing themes inherent to national, southern, and Louisiana politics. Housed in four rooms, its purpose is to teach children about the political process and involve them in voting. The underlying theme is that of inclusion versus exclusion. In the first room, one learns about the responsibilities of political officials by placing one's face in cutouts with mirrors, such as one finds in a fun house. When visitors look through the cutouts, mirrors reflect them as voters, senators, or other public officials. Viewers then read in the reflection what their responsibilities would be as each particular individual. Geared toward children, these mirrors teach that although politics is serious business, politicians are basically ordinary people, demystifying much of the political process. Visitors also use a computer to devise a $13.9 billion budget and then compare that to the actual state budget. The computer then informs them what will happen to various state agencies and the people they serve if too much money is spent by one particular agency. Visitors can change their priorities at will and see how their actions affect constituencies throughout the state.

In the second room, the visitor may use an electronic messaging system to contact an elected official's office and also learn about people who made a difference in Louisiana politics. Scattered among displays on politicians are sections on such "unknowns" as the first child to integrate the New Orleans school system, a nineteen-year-old city council member, and an environmental lobbyist.

In the third room, one learns about the various forms of media upon which a well-informed voter draws and the advantages and disadvantages of each. Visitors also devise their own political platforms and then see if their choices on issues such as taxation, spending, and the environment make them Republican, Democratic, or Independent "candidates." One activity that is very popular during the school year is a mock election in which students designate a peer "candidate." That student then speaks for the group, and everyone sees what is involved in making a political speech. This activity gives a sense of participation and empowerment few other exhibits in the museum can match.[4]

The displays in these rooms are constructed so the visitor cannot simply be a passive observer. In order to learn from the exhibits, one *must* join the "political process." To do otherwise means self-exclusion. In the final room, the political rationale—the issue of involvement versus self-exclusion—is most pronounced. Children walk through a maze in which they must answer questions about elections, such as, "Do you believe your vote counts?" and "Do you care who wins?" If they offer the "wrong" answer, they are pulled out of the process. Regardless of whether visitors make it to a final voting booth, they see displays about women, Native Americans, and African Americans and their struggles to gain the vote. Visitors examine the test given to African Americans in the South to discourage their voting in decades past and listen to oral histories of people involved in the Civil Rights movement. After passing these displays, visitors confront a final sign asking if those who excluded themselves from the simulated voting process would like to rethink their positions now that they know how many people struggled for that right. No judgments are made in the exhibit about those who choose not to vote, but thoughtful visitors leave the room knowing that plenty of others lived and died for the right they now choose to exercise . . . or not to exercise.

In contrast to the design of the other exhibits, "We the People" does not have a dramatic or antique feel. On the contrary, it appears very contemporary and streamlined. Part of this atmosphere stems from the exhibit being created by another designer several years after the other exhibits, but part of it stems from a desire to reach a particular target audience. Jenny Zehmer of Whirled Peas, Inc., a design firm centered in Birmingham, Alabama, geared the displays toward fourth graders. Although adults certainly learn from the exhibit, the age of the target audience dictated signage, design, display heights, and the atmosphere. Moreover, Zehmer chose to avoid drawing attention to the architecture and instead to focus on the displays. Clean white walls, bright rooms lit by tall Gothic windows, and an open plan combine with child-friendly displays to impart information with a deliberately light and non-threatening approach.

The "We the People" exhibit is powerful and raises concerns well beyond the scope of Louisiana politics. By doing so, it also raises a vital issue in museum theory today: how much museum educators can assume visitors know. During the school year, six hundred students a day might tour the building, to say nothing of the adults. Given the diversity of museum guests, can one assume that the visitor has a good working knowledge of the material in a particular exhibit, or is the museum required to "dumb down" the material so all can learn from it? The Louisiana Old State Capitol's Education Department deals with this question by sending to schools throughout the state a packet titled "Louisiana's Old State Capitol Classroom: A Teacher's Guide for Grades K-12." Offering lesson plans for students K-3 and 4-12, the packet trains teachers, who in turn educate their students before they arrive at the museum, and it also offers post-visit lesson plans. Once the students are in the building, the guide gears the tour to the particular age group. The packet provides information on all the exhibits and gives a general history of the building, but it focuses the most on the "We the People" exhibit. This packet has proven one of the most beneficial elements of the museum outreach program; not only is it a way of educating students so they appreciate the museum more upon their arrival, but many teachers around the state have incorporated the packet into their social studies lesson plans. Given the exhibit's design, visitors who have not had access to the packet still learn from the exhibit, but not as much as they would have with its materials. Adults in the museum are presumed, rightly or wrongly, to have a fair grasp of the American political system, but the fact that children will not have the same grasp of these issues necessitates the close partnership the museum has developed with schools around the state.

The Huey Long Assassination Room examines the September 1935 assassination of Louisiana's best-known politician and appeals mainly to people from the state, unlike the "We the People" exhibit. Having said that, survey forms show that its appeal to this group is enormous. Although it is the smallest exhibit room in the museum, it receives the most visitors. Huey Long was to Louisiana what Churchill was to England, de Gaulle to France, and, some detractors argue, what Stalin was to Russia. People loved him or hated him, but no one was indifferent to Long. The Progressive Democrat's political ambitions became the basis for biographies, articles, novels, and movies. Some might argue that the room is simply another example of hagiography dedicated to the "pale males" of political history, but it is much more than that. Voting records, registration polls, editorials, and other assorted political evidence show Huey Long was the first Louisiana politician (many argue the first southern politician) to appeal to voters across racial and economic lines. His carefully constructed political image as a folksy poor boy made good, even though his family was actually quite wealthy, set him apart from other politicians of the era, and his smashing of the Bourbon dynasty ushered in a new era for Louisiana politics. Long's outspoken and carefully orchestrated championing of ethnic minorities and poor whites outraged the former power elites and created as many enemies as friends. His murder, allegedly by the son-in-law of a political opponent, is still controversial and engenders as much debate as his life. Rather than simply reinforcing stereotypes of Huey Long as "Saint Huey" or "the southern Mussolini," the exhibit examines issues of class, extreme power, and corruption in a way impossible in a hagiography.

For the observer, the Huey Long room seems an impartial display, but a visitor versed in museum theory knows that all museum "realities" are staged. The Bourbons created their own vision of their past and then acted to maintain that false reality. Huey Long smashed the power of the Bourbons by using a carefully constructed image which he maintained until his death. Another layer of artificiality is added as modern museum professionals use the events of the past to create their own reality. That the designers of the Huey Long exhibit made every effort to be historically accurate and impartial as well as to place the events in a broad historical context is laudable, but the motivation to showcase (or change) events of the past to suit the needs of the present is as old as the Babylonians and Egyptians who chiseled the names of their predecessors off obelisks and walls. In this respect, the exhibit designers followed a time-honored tradition.

The exhibit's heavy curtains, dark colors, and dim backlighting create a funereal atmosphere, heightened by somber music and ghostly images of Long's life projected onto hanging gauze. The gun allegedly used by Long's assassin rests in a raised central display case, so it is protected from the elements, yet visible from every angle, and an eight-foot statue of Long gazes upon visitors while they are in the room. Yet too much should not be made of the placement of the statue and the gun. The large statue is a copy of the one which stands in Long's hometown of Winnfield, Louisiana, and was put in the display for aesthetic reasons and to give the poorly maintained plaster image a place where it would be conserved. The gun was placed in a raised viewing platform not so it would be seen as a holy object showcased in a shrine, but so it could be seen from all angles. True, some people might argue that a large statue and a raised and showcased object combine to make a martyr's shrine, but neither the exhibit designers, the museum's employees, nor members of the general public have voiced this opinion. Again, it is true that a skillful display might induce a feeling of awe without visitors realizing that they have been manipulated, but this would not really work in the case of Huey Long. He was such a notable and controversial politician that almost all visitors who come to the museum enter either loving him or hating him. An exhibit design is unlikely to change the strong feelings visitors bring with them. It is my opinion that the statue and the gun would neither support a hagiography nor damage one.

Given the pervasive Long mythology, the exhibit designers are to be commended for separating the man from the myth, which many people consider impossible. Placards on the wall state: "Official Version," "Continuing Controversy," and "Recovered Evidence." Explanations accompany each placard. Perhaps as much because many Louisiana citizens hold strong views on Long and his assassination as because it attempts to offer a thorough and balanced history, the exhibit offers no answers, only possible theories. The theme is not only the assassination itself but also the historical detective work needed to draw one's own conclusions.

Another very subtle theme is the cult of personality. How does one person make such a difference and inspire such strong emotion more than seventy years after his death? A thoughtful observer realizes Long manipulated reality as easily as he manipulated people, and the constructed version of his life and death keeps him almost as involved in Louisiana politics now as when he lived. For good or ill, most state politicians since his death have been measured against him. And the museum's effort to confront and bring into question mythologies of the past offers a stark contrast to Wichita's Old Cowtown museum, which will be discussed in the next chapter.

The specter of Huey Long also rises in the Governors of Louisiana exhibit, but he has to share the stage with others. Museum planners turned the former governor's office into an exhibit tracing the role of the office and the histories of individual governors since the founding of *Louisiane.* The paradox of the exhibit is that, although one would consider the governor's position the domain of elites, in many respects the room is most expressive of Louisiana's political and social diversity. The museum's historian and chief archivist in 1994 summed up the focus of the exhibit when he said, "We've had an unfortunate situation in that our more colorful political leaders tend to get a great deal of publicity. But they're not necessarily representative of most of the people of Louisiana. This [display] has a quieter grandeur that to me is representative of our people."[5] Indeed, the Governors of Louisiana exhibit has two themes. The stated theme is, as mentioned, to examine the role of the governor through the histories of individuals who have held the office and through analyses of major issues in their terms as governor. The unstated theme is the way these men's careers reflect the issues and needs of the average citizen. In its mechanics, the exhibit has three main components: an interactive portrait, which is actually a high-resolution computer monitor containing the images of and key facts on each governor from earliest times until the museum's opening; a display case containing smaller images of the governors combined with artifacts and text on key issues in Louisiana politics; and a podium from which one can gaze into a teleprompter and watch video footage of Louisiana politicians from 1932 forward.[6]

Visitors entering the room see the electronic portrait directly in front of them. An image of each governor dominates the screen, while a narrator gives an overview of that governor's career, followed by his "resume," with details about his education, religion, birth and death dates and locations, political affiliation, and other personal information. This is the least-utilized facet of the exhibit. Guided tours and survey forms reflect that the device is generally used only by people curious about how it works or who want information about one particular governor. The average visitor usually watches only for a minute or so and then goes to another facet of the exhibit; many state that they find the detailed information on obscure governors boring, thus showing that technology alone is not enough to hold visitors' attention. Those watching the display are most interested in a family member who was governor, or a governor who shared their ethnicity or home town. For example, Edwin Edwards, the first Cajun governor, is popular among Cajun visitors.[7]

Documents and artifacts in display cases draw much more attention. The objects purportedly offer insight into individual governors but actually illustrate much of the state's diversity. One document outlaws the enslavement of Native Americans and recognizes them as equal trade partners with the French and Spanish. Others reflect the legal status of Africans in the colony, both slave and free. State requirements for pharmacists are detailed, always an important issue in plague-ravaged Louisiana. Two official acts are displayed, one moving the capitol to Baton Rouge in 1846, and the other outlawing African slavery in 1865. Both are recorded in French and English, which in itself says much about the political issues of ordinary people; for over a century, Creoles and Americans fought to determine who would control the state.[8] The largest artifact in the case is a portrait of P. B. S. Pinchback, an African American who served as Louisiana governor for three weeks and was actively involved in Louisiana politics for thirty years. He served as America's first African-American governor and remained the only one until the election of Governor Wilder of Virginia in 1989. As a free person of color before the Civil War, he illustrates an experience not examined much in decades past, but vital to understanding Louisiana's political history.

The exhibit's centerpiece is a raised podium from which visitors watch news footage of various state officials. The Old State Capitol Museum is the largest video and film depository in the state, and one of the museum's major goals is to preserve and showcase these resources for future generations. Clips highlight governors from the last seventy years but also include a civil rights leader and other notable Louisiana politicians. The podium's size and location pique the visitor's attention, but what keeps it is the combination of modern technology with primary documentation. These clips date back to the 1920s and offer the visitor closeness with political figures that could only be matched by actual interaction. To see a leader, hear his dialect, and observe his mannerisms binds the modern viewer to events of the past. Add to that video clips chosen specifically because they reflect the political issues of decades past and present, and the attractions are evident. Selected by the staff when the building reopened as a museum in 1994, the clips are as relevant now as then, and there is no indication they will be changed. Based on visitor responses culled from guided tours, survey forms, and time spent at the podium, the staff readily states that this is the most popular element of the museum. Many repeat visitors say that, of all elements in the building, they remember the video clips the most. Some museum theorists might argue that these clips imply a narrative of progress by being encased in a high-tech device. On the other hand, their opponents might argue—with a great deal of support—that these clips do not bring the speakers into the present so much as draw visitors into the past, and the modern display monitor is simply a servant to the wisdom of the past.

The last exhibit in this chapter is the boxcar which was part of the Merci Train, a present from France to America for aid in World War II. The train was composed of forty-nine boxcars, one for each state and one to be shared between the District of Columbia and Hawaii. To give some background, in 1947 Americans gathered approximately $40 million in supplies for relief of war-torn France and Italy. The seven hundred railroad cars of clothing, food, and fuel were shipped in what was called the American Friendship Train. The French people were so overwhelmed by this generosity that, even with all the hardships of post–World War II Europe, they gathered a series of boxcars filled with French art, wine, food, lace, historical artifacts, children's drawings, and assorted other treasures; as a play on the number of American states, these cars were selected because they were "forty and eight," big enough for forty men or eight horses. These were shipped to the United States, divided by region, and then shipped to individual states. Both because the museum is dedicated to the veterans of Louisiana and America and because of its central location, Louisiana's Old State Capitol was chosen as the site for Louisiana's boxcar. Covered with an open-air roofed structure and painted regularly, the car never deteriorated, and in 2001, it was restored to its original appearance with national French colors and seals of French provinces.[9]

For many people, the exhibit serves one purpose, as a symbol of gratitude between two nations for their combined efforts in the last world war. For many citizens from southern Louisiana, however, the boxcar has an added layer of meaning. World War II records and anecdotal evidence show that many people from southern Louisiana were sent to France to serve as interpreters for other Americans. It is hard to underestimate the effect this had on many Cajuns, because this was the period in which the Louisiana public school system was attempting to eradicate the use of French among schoolchildren, and the word *Cajun* came to be used by many as a synonym for backwards, illiterate swamp dwellers. Yet these southern Louisiana men were sent to France because they were fluent in a language that could keep other soldiers alive and forge bonds with members of another country. Thus, the quality that made them "backwards" in their home state made them ambassadors in the country their ancestors called home. This boxcar reminds them of their efforts and their patriotic service, and it also reminds them of the persistence of their culture.

For many people who stayed in Louisiana during World War II, the boxcar also served as a reminder of their connections to France. I once listened as an elderly woman told me quietly in French how she had received a bridal veil sent from one of France's great lace-making towns on the Merci Train. Too poor to afford such finery as a young bride, the woman said that what she wore on her wedding day was not only the most beautiful veil she had ever seen, but carried the wishes of distant family who had not forgotten grace in the face of war. She smiled into my eyes and said that all women are beautiful on their wedding day, but how can any woman not be beautiful wearing the good wishes of a nation?[10]

The boxcar exhibit is interpreted through tours, the exhibit guide, and a raised marker which gives a history of the "forty and eights." Having said that, the car's central location on the grounds, its condition, and its prominence in the memories of many Louisianans is such that extensive signage is not really necessary. The Old State Capitol's outreach program produced a packet called "The Merci Train: The Friendship Carries On" for educating students, and in 2001, the museum created a program for Louisiana schoolchildren to send gifts to schoolchildren in France, thus strengthening ties between the two countries. This is part of a statewide movement to recover the use of spoken French and reestablish cultural ties to France.

The Old State Capitol Museum is without doubt a specialized entity, but a thoughtful visitor notices themes which present themselves at museums around the world. Who owns the history? How does this museum contribute to national, regional, and local cultures? How does one appeal to a very diverse group, both within the state and without? Lastly, how does one tell a complete story in a state with so many divergent groups? The solution this particular museum takes is to gear exhibits toward as many target audiences as possible. The statehouse itself is a political artifact, and its history tells as much about the state's past as a guidebook. In the exhibits, individual displays address issues of nationalism and internationalism, exclusion versus inclusion, historical detective work, and the power of the individual. The museum ultimately encompasses all of Schawb's commonplaces, demonstrating how telling the story of one individual illustrates the history of many, and how shared experiences establish or reestablish links between social groups. These are not the only themes a curator and museum planner might emphasize, but they affect many history museums. These themes address challenges that are as much a part of the museum as lighting and lettering and are to be welcomed rather than disparaged. These are the challenges which will continue to inspire museum professionals for many years.

NOTES

1. For further examination of the issue of "influence" in the museum setting, see Kenneth Hudson, *Museums of Influence* (Cambridge, England: Cambridge University Press, 1987). Although the issue crops up throughout the work, the most succinct discussion is in the preface; *gombo*, or *gumbo* as many people now pronounce it, is a spicy dish influenced by almost every ethnic group in Louisiana. It is often hot, frequently spicy, very filling, and unique to the state. Many people in the state use this word to describe how they are mainstream Americans, part of a melting pot, yet at the same time very different.

2. Although not examined in this article, there have been a number of displays about the history of the building. The Old State Capitol's staff's belief that the museum itself is an artifact and that by tracing the various statehouses one could trace the history of Louisiana politics is so strong that two of the former curator/historians, Daniel d'Oney and Ray Lukas, researched the locations, architecture, and dates of all the statehouses, collecting images for an exhibit. This research was first on display in a temporary exhibit designed by Dr. John Rodrigue of Louisiana State University and is currently part of a permanent exhibit by Jenny Zehmer of Whirled Peas.

3. Author's interview with Joyce Chaney, Head of Visitor Services, 18 July 2001. Ms. Chaney is in charge of the interpretation staff at the Old State Capitol Museum and compiled a database of thousands of visitor surveys. Data was collected on the visitors' addresses, the amount of time they spent in each exhibit, what they found most interesting, and other factors; author's interview with Mary Louise Prudhomme, Director of the Old State Capitol Museum, 19 July 2001.

4. Old State Capitol visitors' database; survey information from Louisiana teachers.

5. "Capitol Castle," *Historic Preservation* 45, no.3 (May/June 1993): 93.

6. "The Governor's Exhibit," *Capitol Chronicle: The Official Journal of Louisiana's Center for Political and Governmental History* 1, no.2 (October 1993): 3.

7. Author's interview with Joyce Chaney, Head of Visitor Services, 18 July 2001. This statement about the electronic portrait is derived from the thousands of responses in the database.

8. By law, all official documents were printed in both languages until the English speakers managed to pass Act No. 24 of 1914, which outlawed the use of French in state documents.

9. *La Société des Quarante Hommes et Huit Chevaux. Merci Box Car Memorial Book* (n.p., 2 February 1984), 4–5, 16, 40; Louisiana's Old State Capitol in partnership with the Louisiana Department of Veterans' Affairs, "The Merci Train: The Friendship Carries On" (n.p.: Fall 1999), 9–11.

10. Sources for this passage are the Old State Capitol visitors' database and the writer's personal experiences.

III

NOSTALGIA AS EPISTEMOLOGY

For many small historical museums, nostalgia may be considered a kind of epistemology. Nostalgia is a unique way of knowing that valorizes certain positive aspects of the past, endowing them with importance as truths. Events and conditions that do not fit into this worldview may be denied or ignored; they are frequently treated as beliefs for which no evidentiary testimony exists. A good example of the use of nostalgia in museums is the "old-fashioned" Christmas festival at many historic homes. At the Ellwood House in DeKalb, Illinois, Christmas brings a host of activities. The home museum opens during the evening on several weekends before the holiday. These openings include a homey crafts sale, special tours, cookies, and romantic, dimly lit interiors. The emphasis is on Christmas as a communal and family time so that parents and children are encouraged to attend. The tour script about the Ellwoods emphasizes their importance as beneficent individuals and major economic forces in the development of the town.

Competing narratives are minimized. The nostalgic vision of Christmas may in fact have little to do with the way the past inhabitants of the home celebrated the holiday—no doubt they did not host a crafts sale, for example. Similarly, there is no mention that for servants the holidays meant more work. There is little attention to Christmas as a religious ritual and even less critical analysis of

Christmas as a marketing endeavor. Finally, even as the museum attempts to inscribe its holiday celebration as a community and family ritual, it overlooks the fact that many visitors do not belong to traditional "nuclear" families. Thus, the authority of the museum script renders one an idealized vision of Christmas as the genuine one. We might say that the avoidance of implicit political issues itself characterizes the subject matter of the visitors' experience.

Moreover, in such small local museums, nostalgia can privilege the past over the present, and it has a complicated relationship with narratives of success and the American dream. Nostalgia fosters the ideals of the American dream and of the self-made man, even as it gestures at a happier, halcyon time, an age of innocence before the fall into the knowledge of urbanism and industrialism. Thus, nostalgia structures the way knowledge is imparted by museum narratives.

The three chapters in this section discuss museums that rely on nostalgia in just this way. Jay Price's essay, "The Small Town We Never Were: Old Cowtown Museum Faces an Urban Past," traces the shifting relations between Old Cowtown, a living history site commemorating Wichita's earliest days, and Wichita of the twentieth century. In particular, Price demonstrates how Old Cowtown presents a history of the city that is imbued with nostalgia for a fictive West as depicted in Hollywood Westerns. The town consists primarily of single-story buildings of the kind that would have been found in a small city, and it combines original buildings with reconstructions. Price notes that, as one might see in a film, the town contains only one church, one hotel, one fire station, and so forth. Later, a farm and an annual re-creation of the 1800s county fair were added to the site.

Price points out that Cowtown bears little resemblance to the historical Wichita of the 1800s, which was a city incorporating numerous churches, banks, and other businesses, many of them in two-story buildings. The living history site more accurately represents the small town of Delano nearby, and, in a larger way, the history of the county. The nostalgia that pervades the town is for a city that never really existed; the implicit message or curriculum to be taught is that Hollywood versions of the past bear more weight than lived history. It is no wonder, then, that boosters of Wichita business have had ambivalent feelings about the site.

In "'The Dream Then and Now': Democratic Nostalgia and the Living Museum at Arthurdale, West Virginia," Jay Patterson focuses on the New Deal experimental community of Arthurdale. The original town was built on a vision of a cooperative agrarian community and became a pet project of Eleanor Roosevelt. Homes were to be built around a central square with a community center and businesses. The project excluded immigrants, African Americans, and individuals with no savings, guaranteeing that the town would consist primarily of middle-class whites. Even though the project did not succeed in creating a self-sustaining community, in 1984 original residents gathered to create Arthurdale Heritage, Inc., an organization set up to turn the town into a living history version of itself. In the tourist version of the town, inhabitants impersonate townspeople of more than fifty years ago. The emphasis is primarily on the town as a community, and the central hall has been restored as a center for local events. The subsistence household idea is minimized. In this case, then, nostalgia melds with the democratic ideals of the town into a new vision of community, an ideal for those who long for a small-town cohesiveness that, like the agrarian vision of Cowtown, may never have existed. Once again, nostalgia functions as a theory of knowledge for the town's re-creators.

Heather Perry's "History Lessons: Selling the John Dillinger Museum" complicates the notion of nostalgia by emphasizing its embedded ironies. In its original site, the Dillinger Museum was infused with nostalgia for the bank robber as a kind of Depression hero who stole from the rich. When the museum moved and was taken over by the county in 1999, the museum's narrative was perceived as embarrassing by many. Local residents felt that it underscored negative stereotypes of the area as a hub of gang activity; police were angered that the museum celebrated a cop killer, the center of a prison break that scandalized the region.

The reconceptualized museum promoted a different narrative: crime does not pay. Although items from Dillinger's life were still included, the emphasis was on his death. A countermyth, favoring Hoover's FBI, was elevated instead. Police became the museum's heroes, and the exhibits centered on crime fighting. Visitors also had the opportunity to reenact the electrocution of Bruno Hauptmann (who is irrelevant to John Dillinger's history), with themselves pushing the button. The second site replaced nostalgia for an outlaw hero with nostalgia for the golden days of crime fighting when the FBI seemed capable of solving every crime. A subversive community that celebrated the adventures of a robber was transformed into a community that supported an establishment narrative. Here, a revised political interpretation of the role and stature of crime (or at least of celebrated criminals) in a community substantially changed the subject matter of the curriculum offered by the museum.

Perry is quick to note that the site contained certain kinds of irony, too, in its evocation of legal authorities. She suggests that viewers might critically consider the difference between the negative portrayal of Dillinger as an assassin and the state-sanctioned violence of the Hauptmann execution. She also notes that the hubbub that arose when a photo of Dillinger unshackled was circulated indicates that he is still viewed as a threat by the authorities. Significantly, the museum has now closed due to a dispute with Dillinger's family over the rights to his name and reputation.

If the museums discussed in the previous section of this book reveal how tour scripts and museum narratives constantly change to reflect the times, the chapters in this section focus on a more tenacious kind of nostalgia, one that affects the knowledge imparted by the museums. This nostalgia is successful in promoting narratives of community which are critically important to the survival of small museums because they bring in local visitors, volunteers, and funds. While such displays may at times seem oppressively narrow, visitors who approach them with a sense of irony will discover alternative viewpoints.

6

The Small Town We Never Were

Old Cowtown Museum Faces an Urban Past

JAY PRICE

Old Cowtown[1] Museum in Wichita, Kansas, is an outdoor living history museum on the banks of the Big Arkansas River (pronounced *Ar-kan'-sas* in that part of the world). Located about a half-mile west of the original town site, it consists of buildings mostly brought in from downtown Wichita or constructed out of new materials at some point in the museum's fifty-year history. Looking around, the visitor sees what appears to be a small frontier town, a supposedly accurate depiction of what downtown Wichita must have looked like at one time. The log cabin of Darius Munger, one of the founders of the community, recalls the days when the prairie rolled to the horizon. Old Cowtown also features Wichita's oldest frame church and adjoining parsonage. There is the obligatory one-room schoolhouse as well as a general store. A small railway depot stands next to that most iconic of rural Kansas structures, the grain elevator. Just beyond the elevator is an 1880s farm, complete with house, barn, outbuildings, pigpen, and horse pasture. A field separates the farm from the rest of Old Cowtown. Nearby sits the homestead of the Blood family orchard. Throughout, dusty streets with one-story wooden buildings evoke familiar images of other small towns—usually images taken from movies and television. In many ways, Cowtown looks strikingly similar to the sets of *Little House on the Prairie* or *Gunsmoke*. Visitors often assume they are at the original town site instead of at a collection of buildings assembled in the 1950s. They also come away with the sense that Wichita started as a small western town and grew into a modern city, an impression that may be plausible but is incorrect.

Like many boomtowns of the nineteenth-century American West, early Wichita developed into an urban environment almost overnight. In 1870, a handful of settlers started constructing a few wooden frame buildings to replace the sod, stockade, and log structures of the previous years. By 1872, as the cattle era took off and herds of longhorns and rowdy Texas cowboys roamed the streets, Wichita also had two-story brick businesses along its main streets. In the years that followed, the town continued to grow. Churches sprouted up, serving several denominations. Fashionable homes graced wide, tree-lined streets. By the middle of the decade, Wichita boasted commercial establishments such as the three-story, brick Occidental Hotel, whose Italianate details were in keeping with architectural fashion back East.

Wichita was never a "small town" in the Jeffersonian, agrarian sense. It was "born booming," to use one of many monikers the city has received over the years. Wichita's leading citizens wanted their community to be the next Chicago, not a farming hamlet. The following decade was even more striking, and Wichita became a major regional center for agriculture and investment. It was the staging ground for the opening of Indian Territory into what became Oklahoma. By the 1880s, Wichita was the largest city of a region that extended from the southern plains to the Rio Grande and beyond.[2]

Even after the depression of the 1890s burst that initial bubble of enthusiasm, Wichita continued to pride itself as a place of business and entrepreneurship. Broom corn and oil brought new forms of wealth. Since the 1920s, the aviation industry has been at the heart of the city's identity. Wichita is also proud to be the birthplace of companies such as Coleman, Mentholatum, Pizza Hut, and Rent-a-Center. This city reveres its business heritage and generally loathes being thought of as a backward cowtown, a sentiment that has made local history efforts awkward at best.

MUSEUMS AND MEMORY

As Gable and Handler have noted, over the past fifteen years or so, scholars have shown how a community's identity is closely tied to the collective memory embodied in its museums and historic sites. Authors such as Michael Kammen, John Bodnar, Michael Wallace, and David Thelen have shown that this past evolves and changes over time as each new generation selects or suppresses its memories of certain persons and events. In many cases, these memories grow distorted. Uncomfortable controversies, inequalities, and conflicts are ignored, while historic figures become heroes, and earlier times start looking like the "good old days." Not only have Gable and Handler used such studies in constructing their ethnography of Colonial Williamsburg, but other scholars have explored how cities such as Santa Fe, Williamsburg, and Monterey have consciously shaped the past to create palatable images for the present.[3] Others have applied these concepts to museums in the nation's heartland. For example, in her study of outdoor museums in Kansas, Cathy Ambler notes that many outdoor museums in that state portray a past filled with hard-working, religious, and thrifty settlers. With a preponderance of schools, depots, general stores, churches, and barns, these museums present a harmonious whole, tastefully organized and with a minimum of the clutter that would have been part of the real community.[4]

In light of this scholarship on collective memory, an observer might assume that Old Cowtown Museum is simply another shrine to the agrarian myth or to a love of the Old West. Such attitudes are evident at the site, but the dynamics involved are more complicated than mere nostalgia. The notion that Cowtown represents Mayberry-like small town values is understandable but misleading. If anything, Cowtown's rural and cowboy image has been one of the institution's main liabilities. Back in 1956, a visiting reporter mused that although the museum attracted visitors, "Wichita does not love 'Cow Town' because it recalls a time before the virus of bigness bit the community." The commentary was accurate in regard to the 1950s but not the 1870s: the virus of bigness had been part of Wichita's ethos from the very outset.[5]

THE OLD COWTOWN STORY

The story of Old Cowtown Museum goes back to the collective vision of a small group of men and women. The spark came from Victor Murdock, the editor of the *Wichita Eagle* and son of the paper's founder, Marshall Murdock. However, it was Richard "Dick" Long, the manager of the *Wichita Eagle's* morning edition, who began the effort to create an outdoor museum that celebrated early Wichita. In the 1930s and 1940s, Murdock and Long both published vignettes on the community's history in the *Wichita Eagle.* Victor Murdock ran a series of articles about the early days of the city, talking about everything from personalities to prominent homes to the cattle era. Long produced a similar set of illustrated pieces called the "Wichita Historical Panels." Accompanied by line illustrations, Long's panels offered a glimpse into what he felt the history of the community was like. In 1945, Long even published a book of photographs of early Wichita that reiterated the same themes: Wichita traced its heritage to a pantheon of businessmen and entrepreneurs such as Darius Munger, William Mathewson, William Greiffenstein, James R. Mead, and Marshall Murdock. All of these works focused on community-building events such as the platting of the town, the arrival of the railroad, the wooing of the cattle trade, and the construction of the first hotels, stores, stockyards, churches, and utilities. Although the cowboys did bring a measure of rowdiness to this scene, they tended simply to add color rather than to challenge the overall image of enterprising businessmen working tirelessly to boost Wichita into a respectable community.[6]

In the early 1940s, Murdock found out that Wichita's oldest frame church still existed as a dilapidated rooming house. He took an immediate interest in saving the building. Murdock enlisted the help of Dick Long, making Long promise to continue the effort to save the building if he died. Murdock passed away in 1945, and a few years later Long acquired the building and the adjacent parsonage. His initial hope was to have the city take on the restoration of the buildings, but the commissioners turned him down, worried that the project would appear to be an inappropriate use of public funds. Consequently, Long and other local citizens came together to create a nonprofit corporation called Historic Wichita, Inc., to restore the church as a museum.[7] Sensing that there was energy developing around the church restoration, the local chapter of the Daughters of the American Revolution donated the log home of Darius Munger, which they had acquired in the early 1940s. Soon afterwards, Historic Wichita acquired the first jail from the local school district.

Historic Wichita now had to find a site for its new acquisitions. The city's parks director was reluctant to house the buildings in one of his parks but suggested that a site along the Arkansas River owned by the Wichita Water Company would be a good setting. Historic Wichita agreed, and in 1952 subleased the surface rights of twenty-three available acres, moving the church and parsonage, the Munger House, and the jail to the site. In late 1953, the museum opened to visitors.

Very early in the planning process, as Long later recalled, "The idea came for a cowtown village. . . . We decided to go ahead and restore from 20 to 30 buildings which were a part of Wichita during the cowtown period of the community, from 1870 to 1880."[8] Cowtown's founders were generally professionals with good local connections. However, very few of Wichita's richest families and largest businesses embraced the effort. In response, Historic Wichita actively encouraged smaller businesses and clubs to sponsor building replicas. For example, to raise money for one project, Larry Roberts created a mock fire company composed of volunteers and encouraged these volunteers to fund a re-creation of a "typical" firehouse. In many cases, these reconstructions used whatever materials were available, including lots of plywood decorated with strips of wood to simulate board and batten siding, and finished with faux Victorian bric-a-brac. Using techniques such as these, Historic Wichita, Inc., gradually created what it claimed was an authentic recreation of early Wichita.

From about 1955 through 1965, Cowtown boomed, with turn-of-the-century buildings moved on site and remodeled into 1870s-looking structures, while other buildings, like the fire station, were constructed entirely new. The biggest boost came from the celebration of the Kansas centennial in 1961. This was a time when Wichita's city leaders toyed briefly with a Western image for the community, with Cowtown as the chief symbol. The city contributed $15,000 to fund the development of the museum. As part of the arrangement, in September 1959, the city took possession of the twenty-three-acre property and the buildings on it, with Historic Wichita running the facility on behalf of the city.

By this time, nearly twenty years of Western movies had made a Wild West mystique popular, and Wichita's citizens started seeing the image as something positive to embrace. This was the era that inspired dozens of Western-themed attractions, from the Old West amusement park at Knott's Berry Farm in California to the "restoration" of Tombstone, Arizona, to countless establishments of varying quality along Route 66. In 1955, Hollywood produced a movie called *Wichita*, featuring Wyatt Earp as a lawman who brought justice to a lawless region. Even though it was not filmed at Cowtown, the movie helped popularize an image of Wichita as part of the Old West.

For postwar Wichita, Cowtown was the most visible example of a trend that included motels with neon cowboy signs and Western-wear outfitters. As a result, the community began to take an interest in the museum, which had faced the prospect of closing only a few years earlier. By then, the Wichita Chamber of Commerce boasted that "Cow Town authentically depicts the roaring cowboy era of 1869–84."[9] Promotional material touted the museum's accuracy. "'Cow Town' buildings which are not actual relics have been constructed to look as the original buildings in Wichita would have looked," crowed a souvenir newspaper.[10] "Cow Town is an authentic restoration of a frontier day village, looking much like Wichita itself as the town grew from an

Indian trading post in the late 1860s and 1870s," said a piece in the *Wichita Old Cow Town Vidette.*[11] Another article in the same edition began with, "Cow Town in Wichita is believed to be the only authentic restoration of an actual Western cow town village."[12]

Old Cowtown's founders ensured the look of a small town when they decided to go with the Western theme during the construction efforts of the 1950s and 1960s. For many people, the Hollywood Western town has defined what all communities in the nineteenth-century West presumably looked like. In the mythic West, towns existed largely as places for the characters to connect with the necessities of "civilized" life before moving on. Thus a stereotypical Western town could have one or two major streets but no more—and certainly not the streetcars that crossed many larger communities. In the movies, a town could have only one station, one church, and one school—token representations of transportation, religion, and education. By contrast, Wichita, like most real Western towns, actually had several of each. In Cowtown, a jail and sheriff's office were fine, but not an ornate Victorian courthouse.[13]

This Hollywood image, rather than the actual town of Wichita, served as the inspiration for much of Old Cowtown in the 1950s and 1960s. Cowtown had a gunsmith, a saddle shop, and of course, the obligatory jail. There was no bordello—that being just a little too risqué for family-oriented Kansas—but there was a wooden hotel. Other buildings, such as the law office, bank, and fire station, were reconstructions and did not represent specific Wichita buildings. Old Cowtown's main streets featured rows of one-story false-fronted buildings—perfect for the recreated shoot-outs that took place. The world of the cowboy and the Old West became part of the museum's heritage and image, ensuring that the vision of a rugged frontier town persisted, rather than that of an urban center.

NEW DIRECTIONS

Unlike Williamsburg or Greenfield Village, Cowtown has never had a cadre of wealthy patrons who could finance development. Consequently, spurts of support and funding emerged around specific projects. Yet, as the Old West faded in popularity, a Wild West–themed Cowtown seemed increasingly out of place in a Wichita that promoted itself with the slogan "Center City, U.S.A.," and made the futuristic Century II civic center its most iconic structure.

By the late 1970s, as the cost of operating and maintaining the facility went up, the city encouraged Historic Wichita to seek financial assistance from

Sedgwick County. The county agreed to help with the museum's staffing crisis by placing several positions on its payroll. This resulted in a reshaping of the main organization into "Historic Wichita Sedgwick County, Inc." Now the museum also had to tell the story of Sedgwick County, which did have a more rural, agricultural character than "born-booming" Wichita. Ever since, the museum has had to balance the stories of an urban 1870s Wichita and a rural 1870s Sedgwick County within its 1950s vision of the Old West.

This combination of county support and professional staff also helped redefine Cowtown's focus away from the Old West paradigm of earlier generations. The 1984 interpretive plan suggested that the museum do more to depict urban life, industry, and agriculture. Of these areas, it was agriculture that received the most visible support. Much of the energy and inspiration for these projects came from staff who felt that the museum had an obligation to talk about farming, which even during the era of the cattle drives was the primary economic mainstay of the region. In the late 1980s, the staff managed to secure for the museum the grain elevator from Bentley, Kansas. Meanwhile, the museum recreated the 1800s Sedgwick County Fair as a major annual event.

By the 1980s, the facility, renamed "Old Cowtown Museum," also had a broader story to tell to a larger audience. Its commonplaces had changed. As at the House of the Seven Gables, these were years when the museum began to professionalize. The museum hired curatorial and education professionals, who coordinated a crew of devoted volunteers. Old Cowtown Museum in the 1980s and 1990s tried to paint a picture of an entire community, not just the works of great men or mythical gunfights. As a press release from 1981 put it: "More than depicting the cattle era, however, the Old Cowtown Museum . . . depicts a cross section of lifestyles and developments from the time of the earliest settlement to a full-blown Victorian era."[14] The museum marketed itself as a living history site along the lines of Williamsburg and Greenfield Village, where everyday life and activities were the main attractions. As a promotional brochure from 1988 noted, "National and regional media are praising it [the museum] for providing an authentic, quality historical experience rather than an amusement park version of the West." In 1990, a decade of work resulted in the museum being accredited by the American Association of Museums.[15]

In the 1990s, the museum launched a capital campaign to turn a former parking lot into an 1880s farm. As the asphalt gave way to fields, a complex of farm buildings emerged some distance from the main town, creating the impression of a farm located on the plains. When the farm opened in 1998, a fifteen-year effort to tell the story of local agriculture had come to fruition. In an attempt to get away from the mythology of the Western, Old Cowtown Museum looked more agrarian than at any time in its history. Yet the transformation was not total—the story of agriculture was simply grafted onto an already complex image.

Cowtown continues to struggle with reconciling several different, even conflicting, visions of the past. While the museum's basic theme has centered on 1870s Wichita, the history that appears to today's visitor is really an amalgam of several different versions of that past. The museum has fused the trading post era of the 1860s, the Victorian propriety and boosterism of the 1870s, the rowdiness of the cattle era, the agriculture of Sedgwick County, and the mythology of the Western.

Even if Cowtown's founders had wanted to emphasize an urban, booster image, they would have had a hard time making it work. The decision in the 1950s to develop an artificial town on a piece of undeveloped land made the small town look almost inevitable. Urban history, by contrast, lends itself to historic preservation rather than creating "building zoos." Outdoor museums that have a more urban framework, such as the Lowell factory complex, Phoenix's Heritage Square, New York's Lower East Side Tenement Museum, and to a lesser extent, Colonial Williamsburg, are all based in part on existing structures on their original sites. Even in Wichita, the institutions that explain the community's urban past use existing buildings in their original locations. For example, the exhibits of the Wichita-Sedgwick County Historical Museum, located in the late Victorian, Romanesque city hall, feature the development of Wichita as a regional city from very early in the community's history. The visitor is left with no doubt that Wichita was a city early on, far removed from the agrarian myth that still captures the imagery of the Midwest.

These issues have long been apparent to Cowtown's staff. Whether Long and the other founders of Cowtown initially planned on relocating or constructing a brick building is unknown. As early as 1953 they did plan on moving a two-story wooden structure to the site. A wind storm wrecked the upper floor of the building, forcing Historic Wichita to adapt the lower, surviving half into a drugstore. By the 1980s however, the museum's staff recognized a lack of larger buildings. A 1984 story line noted that "with stores, houses, church, and school all in close proximity to one another . . . [Cowtown's buildings] tend also to be miniaturized and small . . . no representation has been given to large stone and brick structures."[16] The 1984 story line envisioned a recreated downtown at the intersection of the museum's two main streets that could contain a brick building and even a stone structure as well as multistoried wooden edifices. Yet moving brick, stone, or multistory buildings would be major undertakings, even assuming appropriate structures could be located nearby, that their owners were willing to part with them, and there was enough money to do the job. Constructing new buildings would also require a great deal of commitment on the part of staff and fundraisers. While a two-story wooden building eventually replaced the earlier drugstore, no further work has been done to acquire or build brick or stone buildings.

Moreover, the scale of Old Cowtown precluded reproducing early Wichita as it originally stood—even in part. The size of the actual buildings alone would have made an accurate reconstruction out of the question on the modest museum site. For example, one major 1870s-era building that survived was the Occidental Hotel. Yet the three-story building's brick construction made moving it to Cowtown far too expensive to be feasible. Even if the Occidental could have been moved to Cowtown, it would have dwarfed every other structure around. Covering the better part of a city block, it would have taken up such a large part of the grounds that there would not have been much room for anything else.

CONCLUSIONS

Old Cowtown Museum looks like a small town for several reasons. It began as an attempt to recreate aspects of Wichita's early history but developed into a place that presented both Wichita's urban past and Sedgwick County's rural origins. The decision to go with the Old West theme in the 1950s and 1960s has, moreover, committed the museum to work with a location that looks like a small town, albeit one defined more by the Old Tucson movie studios than by Jeffersonian agrarian mythology. Attempts to include a more urban story line at the museum have continued to run up against a site that largely features small, wooden structures instead of the variety of buildings that actually existed.

The literature on collective memory often assumes or at least implies that the shaping of memory is largely intentional—whether by elites who want to reinforce their position in society or by a broader public searching for stability in uncertain times. The Cowtown story does reiterate these themes to an extent. The political rationale for preserving the museum's first structures did come from groups such as the local DAR and newspaper editors with ancestral ties to Wichita's founding. They certainly saw in Munger's log cabin and the first church the values of the pioneer founders that they hoped could be perpetuated in the twentieth century. Later on, the decision to go with a movie Western theme for the museum in the 1950s and 1960s resonated with the larger, national obsession with the Old West. This decision in some ways paralleled the emphasis on Hawthorne's characters in certain tour scripts for the House of the Seven Gables, where a famous media image (based on a novel rather than a film) took precedence over the lives of common persons. Even the move toward living history and social history in the 1980s and 1990s embodied a new orthodoxy in historical and museum studies—the influence of an elite of professional training if not wealth. The museum educators were no longer its founders but specially trained individuals.

Most institutions emerge as compromises between the ideals of the founders, visions of later staff and supporters, and the reality of local resources. A major reason why Old Cowtown projects a small town image is because outdoor museums, especially those that are entirely artificial, lend themselves to the depiction of villages, small towns, and rural settings. The buildings are usually small enough to move relatively easily. Buildings that cannot be moved or no longer exist are often small enough to be reproduced on site. Urban settings, by contrast, have buildings whose size and construction make them costly to relocate or reconstruct. Had Darius Munger built a substantial brick Victorian mansion instead of a log home, or if the oldest surviving church in town were out of stone and not wood, Old Cowtown Museum might never have been created at all. The structures would either have been preserved where they stood, or they would have been lost. Cowtown, like many outdoor museums, suffers from space limitations that preclude the addition of all but the most modest of urban structures. A one-story general store can fit into nearly any outdoor museum, while a three-story brick hotel or imposing commercial block would overwhelm most museum sites and look out of place unless accompanied by other structures of a similar scale.

Reading the landscape of a museum can provide valuable insights into the community's vision and values, its ethical and political rationales. However, what exists is as likely to be a product of limited resources as of a conscious, coherent vision of the past. Features that scholars interpret as representing ideological positions might actually be the result of making do with what is available. In some instances, features inherent in a site or its history shape a museum's current operations as much as the intentions of the founders or later staff. At Old Cowtown Museum, a variety of factors including the site chosen, the ideals of 1950s historians, local politics, and availability of resources create a complex memory, the dynamics of which are likely to be typical for many outdoor museums. The story of Cowtown reveals a mixture of historic preservation, careful reconstruction, creative adaptation of later buildings, and complete fabrication based on Hollywood-inspired fantasy, all of which have shaped Wichita's collective memory into the small town it never was.

NOTES

1. When originally founded, the institution was known as Cow Town. The term Cowtown appeared in the early 1980s. For the sake of consistency, *Cowtown* will be used throughout except in direct quotations.

2. Craig Miner, *Wichita: The Magic City* (Wichita: Wichita-Sedgwick County Historical Museum Association, 1988), 9–44; Robert R. Dykstra, *The Cattle Towns* (New York: Alfred A. Knopf, 1968); C. Robert Haywood, *Victorian West: Class and Culture in Kansas Cattle Towns* (Lawrence: University Press of Kansas, 1991); Richard M. Long, *Wichita Century* (Wichita: Wichita Historical Museum Association, Inc., 1969).

3. See John H. Jameson, ed., *The Reconstructed Past: Reconstructions in the Public Interpretation of Archaeology and History* (Walnut Creek, Calif.: AltaMira Press, 2004); John Bodnar, *Remaking America: Public Memory, Commemoration, and Patriotism* (Princeton: Princeton University Press, 1992); Michael Kammen, *The Mystic Chords of Memory: The Transformation of Tradition in American Culture* (New York: Alfred A. Knopf, 1991); David Thelen, "Memory and American History," *Journal of American History* 75 (March 1989): 1117–129; Robert Lumley, ed., *The Museum Time Machine* (London: Routledge, 1988). See also Ivan Karp, Christine Mullen Kreamer, and Steven D. Lavine, eds., *Museums and Communities: The Politics of Public Culture* (Washington: Smithsonian Institution Press, 1992).

4. Cathy Ambler, "Small Historic Sites in Kansas: Merging Artifactual Landscapes and Community Values," *Great Plains Quarterly* 15 (Winter 1995): 33–48.

5. "Visiting Newsman Finds 'Cow Town' Distinctive but Unloved by Wichita," *Wichita Eagle*, morning edition, 7 September 1956. See also, Nucifora Consulting Group, *Wichita . . . It's a Great Place to Visit: A Master Plan for Marketing to the Leisure and Convention Visitor*, presented to Wichita Tourism Council, August, 2000; "Our History's Rich, but Often Neglected," *Wichita Beacon*, 28 May 1965; "Report: Wichita Can Lure Tourists," *Wichita Eagle*, 30 August 2000; "Who Loves Ya, Wichita? Not Wichitans," *Wichita Eagle*, 3 September 2000; "Consultant says Wichita's Vibrant, End of Discussion," *Wichita Eagle*, 3 September 2000. Quotation from "City Dreams Big for Tourism," *Wichita Eagle*, 31 August 2000. Hereafter, *WE* will stand for *Wichita Eagle*; *ME*, for the *Eagle's* morning edition; *EE*, for the *Eagle's* evening edition; *TDC*, for the *Topeka Daily Citizen*; and *WB*, for the *Wichita Beacon*.

6. See Richard Long, *Wichita 1866–1883: Cradle Days of a Midwestern City* (Wichita: McCormick-Armstrong Co., 1945). See also clippings of Long's historical panels in the Richard

M. "Dick" Long Collection, Wichita State University Special Collections, and clippings of Marshall Murdock's historical reflections, Wichita Public Library, local history division.

7. Among his partners were Robert Aitchison, a local artist and textbook publisher; Dr. Jessie Clyde Fisher, a Methodist minister; Tom Fuller, the owner of a uniform company and the grandson of one of Wichita's founders; Larry Roberts from a local mortgage company; former mayors Robert Israel and Phil Manning; and Orville Bell, at the time a semiretired businessman who had served three terms on the county commission.

8. Richard Long, "Wichita Cowtown" [address of the President of the Kansas State Historical Society], *Kansas Historical Quarterly* 26 (Spring 1960): 92–100.

9. "Chamber Asks Recognition of Cow Town," *Wichita Week*, 26 May 1960.

10. "This is Cow Town—," *Wichita Cow Town Vidette*, July 1961.

11. "This is Cow Town—."

12. "An Authentic Pioneer Day Restoration," *Wichita Cow Town Vidette*, July 1961. For more on Cowtown's history see Jay M. Price, "Cowboy Boosterism: Old Cowtown Museum and the Image of Wichita, Kansas," *Kansas History* 24 (Winter 2001–2002): 300–317; *Guide Book of Wichita Cowtown, 1869–1872* (Wichita: n.p., n.d.); "Cowtown Wichita Has Been a 17-Year Project," *TDC*, 25 October 1959; "Cowtown Grows to 71 Structures," *Wichita Eagle*, morning edition, 11 June 1961. See also the following Cowtown publications: "An Illustrated Walking Tour Guide to Historic Wichita Cowtown," c. 1978/9; "Historic Wichita Cow Town: Walk Down the Wooden Sidewalks of the Old West," booklet, c. 1975; and *Wichita Cow Town Vidette*, Centennial Year Souvenir Edition, June 1961, Wichita-Sedgwick County Historical Museum.

13. Michael Coyne, *The Crowded Prairie: American National Identity in the Hollywood Western* (London: I. B. Tauris Publishers, 1997); George N. Fenin and William K. Everson, *The Western: From Silents to the Seventies*, rev. ed. (New York: Grossman Publishers, 1973); Jim Hitt, *The American West from Fiction (1823–1976) into Film (1909–1986)* (Jefferson, N.C.: McFarland & Company,1990); Buck Rainey, *Western Gunslingers in Fact and on Film: Hollywood's Famous Lawmen and Outlaws* (Jefferson, N.C.: McFarland & Company, 1998); Jane Tompkins, *West of Everything: The Inner Life of Westerns* (New York: Oxford University Press, 1992); "The West and the Western" edition of *Journal of the West* 29 (April 1999).

14. Press release, Old Cowtown Museum, 1 March 1981.

15. William E. Unrau, H. Craig Miner, Patricia Christgau, Stan Harder, and Elizabeth Kennedy, *Old Cowtown Museum Story Line and Planning Recommendations* (Wichita: Historic Wichita-Sedgwick County, October, 1984); "Cowtown Polishing Image," *WE*, 29 April 1989; "Reliving the Past," *WE* 12 April 1990; "The Many Faces of Old Cowtown," brochure for Old Cowtown Pioneer Drive, June 1988; Old Cowtown Museum newsletters and editions of *Sagacity* from 1996 through 1997.

16. *Old Cowtown Museum Story Line and Planning Recommendations*, 70.

7

"The Dream Then and Now"

Democratic Nostalgia and the Living Museum at Arthurdale, West Virginia

STUART PATTERSON

Since its founding, the town of Arthurdale, West Virginia, has embodied the mutual accommodation of democracy and nostalgia. Arthurdale's story falls into two parts. The first begins in late 1933 with the town's creation as the pilot project of the "subsistence homesteads idea," an experimental federal resettlement program designed to model plans for "a new pattern of . . . abundant living" during the Depression.[1] In effect, Arthurdale served as the New Deal's city set upon a hill, where a handful of families were, in Eleanor Roosevelt's words, "taught how to live" according to a microcosmic version of FDR's early social and economic agenda for national relief and reform. This model of New Deal charity served ideological and political ends by enacting its residents' presumed cultural history, and Mrs. Roosevelt herself called it the "community spirit" of the "early pioneers."[2] From the first, then, heritage was an integral means of governance at Arthurdale.

The second part of Arthurdale's history reveals how the project of governing through heritage has survived there. In 1984, the town's remaining original residents reunited under a banner reading "The Dream Then and Now" to celebrate the fiftieth anniversary of Arthurdale's opening. Out of this event came Arthurdale Heritage, Inc., a nonprofit set up "to acquire, restore and maintain" original community buildings and to turn them into a "living museum."

According to Arthurdale Heritage's chief visionary, Glenna Williams, who was resettled there as a teen in 1934, "A unique thing about our living museum would be that even as we tell about our community's beginning we would also be serving as a center of community life today."[3]

Both "then and now," Arthurdale has closely approximated what Diane Barthel terms a "staged symbolic community," offering verisimilar enactments of a utopian agrarian past as a kind of moral education for increasingly rootless families. Indeed, the paradigmatic American examples of such "lessons in the 'good community,'" Henry Ford's Greenfield Village and John D. Rockefeller, Jr.'s Colonial Williamsburg, are Arthurdale's contemporaries, all three having been developed during the early 1930s.[4] Wichita's Old Cowtown, too, serves as an example of a living history museum that seeks to teach "lessons" about an agricultural community. With these examples in mind, I will begin by outlining two conditions Michael Kammen has identified within the American public historical sphere of the 1930s: "democratic traditionalism" and "nostalgic modernism."[5] Kammen uses the terms to describe divergent appeals to the past in Americans' negotiations of the changes of the interwar years. The often antagonistic operation of democratic and nostalgic uses of the past can be traced in "the transformation of tradition in American culture" (in Kammen's phrase) throughout the twentieth century, leading me to describe the general American public historical condition as one of "democratic nostalgia."

Resembling in many ways Old Cowtown's growth, Arthurdale's development exemplifies democratic nostalgia. The "community idea" its elite sponsors planned to model there was shaped by a regard for traditional democratic values that took the form of a nostalgic appeal to a heroic American past.[6] Similarly, current residents' nostalgic restaging of their community's origins depends crucially on the democratization of attitudes, practices, and institutions that support and promote nonelite public histories and cultural productions (developments that have important origins in the New Deal). If Arthurdale is indeed unique among staged symbolic communities, it is because its enactments of the past have been integral to its identity as an actual community, rather than the mere semblance of one, though they fulfill this latter aim as well. The lessons in community Arthurdale teaches lie in just how it serves our own simultaneously democratic and nostalgic claims on the past.

DEMOCRATIC NOSTALGIA

Kammen's "nostalgic modernism" was the more pervasive and popular of the two conditions. Nostalgic modernism conceived of past and present as mutually distinct worlds which could be juxtaposed in self-conscious ways to judge the relative merits of tradition and progress. The exemplars of this "oxymoronic condition" were Greenfield Village and Colonial Williamsburg. Both deemed knowledge of history secondary to the experience of history and therefore mounted recreations of the American past. As Ford put it, "The only way to show how our forefathers lived and to bring to mind what kind of people they were is to reconstruct, as nearly as possible, the exact conditions under which they lived."[7]

Of course, as any number of critics of heritage sites have since noted, the fetish for the authenticity of objects and experiences that reigns at these and other staged symbolic communities only masks their function as powerful historical authorizations for present social and political ideals.[8] Michael Wallace offers a succinct account of this point by differentiating between Ford's and Rockefeller's pasts. Wallace argues that Ford "had grappled with history in the course of mystifying it," offering visitors a chance to stroll from slave cabins past Lincoln's courthouse to Edison's Menlo Park laboratory, recalling the simple virtues of the past while celebrating the march of progress—social change devoid of conflict. Rockefeller shared none of Ford's ambivalence about past or present by denying "that history had ever happened," and authorizing a corporate order of harmonious social stratification through tableaux vivants of a slaveless pre-Revolutionary patrician idyll.[9] But whatever their differences, both places sanctified present ideals as recovered actualities and fortified a sentimental devotion to common, imagined pasts offered as object lessons for a contingent and uncertain present.

By contrast, what Kammen calls "democratic traditionalism" represented a more explicit use of history as a medium of power. For the impulse "to accommodate tradition to the democratic ethos," as Kammen puts it, could mean reinventing democratic institutions altogether, lest they became hidebound with custom and lose their vitality. In John Dewey's words, "We can retain and transmit our own heritage only by constant remaking of our own [social] environment."[10] At the same time, it could mean expanding the traditions to which democratic institutions were responsible to include those previously disregarded, disparaged, or simply undocumented histories that Ford and Rockefeller excised from their recreations of the American past. In this regard, Kammen cites the large number of intellectual and cultural elites who embarked on an "emotional discovery of America" during the interwar years by championing regional folkways as materials with which to expand and thereby invigorate public discourse.[11] This trend climaxed with the New Deal's initiatives for collecting, preserving, and disseminating vernacular American culture.[12]

While Kammen's terms represent distinct uses of the past in political discourse, the manifold and negotiated character of the American public historical sphere over the last seventy years provides much evidence of their dialectical operation. For example, populist celebrations of the "folk" during the 1930s served pecuniary as well as political interests, as they commodified sentiment for bygone days as readily as they expanded political and social consciousnesses. Alternatively, while Colonial Williamsburg continues to offer unmediated encounters with the past, the inclusion of slavery within its vision of community, however stylized the presentation, signals the symbolic importance of such living histories to democratic discourse.[13] But perhaps nowhere do we find as concentrated an illustration of this dialectic as at Arthurdale, where nostalgic and democratic impulses were entwined from the beginning.

THE SUBSISTENCE HOMESTEADS IDEA

The town's legislative foundations were in laid in June, 1933, in a terse, undebated amendment to Title II of the National Industrial Recovery Act that called for "the redistribution of the overbalance of population in industrial centers." Congress provided the president with a relatively modest $25 million to begin developing what the bill termed "subsistence homesteads."[14] The task of defining the term and its application to the problem of resettlement fell to Milburn Lincoln Wilson, an idealistic agronomist who was chosen to head the new Division of Subsistence Homesteads within the Department of the Interior. With an ad hoc committee of business leaders, agricultural economists, academics, land planners, and rural sociologists, Wilson outlined what came to be known as the "subsistence homesteads idea."

In its essentials, the idea represented the New Deal's answer to the popular "back to the land" initiatives that flourished during the Depression, which fostered dreams of the simple life away from cities. The New Deal's version proposed to resettle un- and underemployed workers in new homes along with land enough to maintain a subsistence level of household production while they preserved ties to the cash economy in newly decentralized light industries. In the short term, the idea offered a reduction in relief rolls while promising the long-term development of new colonies as families repaid their loans on homes and lands. In fact, as with many of the 1930s back-to-the-land schemes, the initial spirit of relief behind the idea was soon eclipsed by visions of total social and economic reform. In characteristically expansive terms, Wilson stated his agency's agenda as establishing "a balance between urban and rural life—a balance which will offer the crowning advantages of both modes of life in a new structure of civilization."[15]

"Cooperation" was the social and moral complement to economic balance. The term was used to gloss the notion of the business sector's enlightened self-rule under federal oversight, as mandated in the National Recovery Administration's industrial codes. But in a larger sense, New Dealers used it to champion what James Holt has called a "new moral tone" for post-Depression America. FDR himself characterized it as "a spirit of justice, a spirit of teamwork, a spirit of sacrifice, but above all a spirit of neighborliness," in short, "the old principle of the local community."[16] The subsistence homesteads colonies were a miniature emblem of the principle. They were designed to enlist homesteaders in producers' and consumers' cooperatives (based on old Populist models) and other civic associations. Wilson conceived of these colonies as a bulwark for democratic institutions: "Co-operation will be the basis of our future society if we are to maintain our individual freedom and not bow to the force of a dictator. I believe that the subsistence homesteads community can well serve as a cradle for a new growth of the cooperative attitude."[17]

If the subsistence homesteads colonies were designed to stage these progressive New Deal ideals, they did so—like Ford's and Rockefeller's—through idealized versions of a mythic American past. Wilson and his colleagues constructed an elaborate allegorical rendering of Frederick Jackson Turner's frontier thesis, the dominant historical paradigm of the day. Turner's great accomplishment was to lend the legitimacy of professional, "scientific" history to the basic tenets of the agrarian myth (most often associated with Thomas Jefferson) by attributing the rise of democratic institutions to the progress of Western settlement. Turner warned that democratic institutions required reinvention with the closing of the frontier and the transformation of their original social base of pioneer homesteaders and independent small traders.[18] To many, the Depression seemed the terrible fruit of Turner's thesis, the result of American society's lopsided urbanization, industrialization, and incorporation. Restoring and preserving American democracy would be a matter of opening *New Frontiers*, as Secretary of Agriculture Henry Wallace announced in the title of his 1934 volume on regulatory capitalism and the New Deal, which he closed with a tribute to the subsistence homesteading program.[19]

But even as they adopted the historical, political, and social lexicon of Turner's thesis, the homestead planners adapted it to convey the New Deal's transitional ideological spirit. For where Jefferson's yeoman was ruggedly individualistic, self-sufficient, and above all antistatist, as a subsistence homesteader, he reemerged as the wage-earning citizen of a modernized, interdependent social order through the benevolent oversight of a federal welfare state. And among the thirty-some subsistence homesteads colonies eventually developed, nowhere was this redramatization of the frontier myth as fully realized as at Arthurdale.

ARTHURDALE THEN

Arthurdale's origins are typically dated from a visit by Eleanor Roosevelt to the coal mining district of Scott's Run, near Morgantown, West Virginia, in the summer of 1933. She had come at the invitation of the American Friends Service Committee, then operating a small Appalachian crafts cooperative with the Run's families, who had themselves been engaged in an often bloody struggle against repressive conditions of employment for nearly a decade. In part horrified by the Run's squalor, and in part apprehensive that the place might "breed revolution," the First Lady joined an effort to expand the Friends' cooperative into the Division of Subsistence Homesteads' first colony. By the fall of the year, the project was underway near Reedsville in Preston County, twenty miles distant from Scotts Run on fallow farmland purchased from Richard Arthur. The following June, a contingent of fifty families began moving into the new town of Arthurdale.[20] Their effort at creating an agricultural town in an area predominantly dedicated to mining resembles the attempt to replace the urban reality of Wichita's history with a historical and nostalgic reconstruction of an agrarian town.

At Arthurdale, the first task was to transform the colony's setting on the Allegheny Plateau into a set of homesteads, a detailed account of which was left by Bushrod Grimes, a West Virginia University agricultural extension agent who served briefly as Arthurdale's first on-site manager. As Grimes tells it, prominent urban planner John Nolen drew a preliminary design for the town, clustering houses on piney knolls to leave bottomlands open for cultivation. FDR's personal secretary Louis Howe, who had become Mrs. Roosevelt's devoted ally in the project, vetoed Nolen's plan as "too communistic," citing the president's comment that each family should be able to keep its own cow.[21] The final plan called for 165 separate houses on three to five acres each, allowing for the combination of the nostalgic ideal of independent homesteading with the lineaments of middle-class home ownership. At the same time, the homesteads were arranged around a town square where administrative offices sat next to the project's cooperatives, which eventually included a furniture shop, textile crafts shop, forge, filling station, general store, tearoom, barber, and cemetery. The layout conveyed the New Deal ideal of supervised cooperation, though again in appropriately retrograde trappings. The square's most intriguing feature was its Center Hall, a dilapidated Presbyterian meetinghouse moved, restored, and refitted with a pillared portico by architect Eric Gugler (who had come from remodeling FDR's West Wing to replace Nolen).

While the stage was set, the crucial work of selecting homesteaders began. Family Selection Agents (themselves West Virginia University and Friends Service Committee staff) screened hundreds of applicants, looking primarily for families with a few children and some savings, not so much as a surety against payments on new homes and land as a sign of "proper attitudes and ambitions."[22] As M. L. Wilson later observed, rather than being for the most destitute families, subsistence homesteads colonies were ideally "a middle-class movement for selected people, not the top, not the dregs . . . who feel that they are outcasts of the jazz-industrial age, looking for something more secure and satisfying."[23] Wilson's antimodernist nostalgia expressed the middle-class ideal better than most of the candidates for homesteads, though it would have been hard to find people less secure or satisfied than the Run's miners, or more genuine outcasts of industrialization. All the same, the selection committee relied mostly on bosses for applicants' reputations for hard work, sobriety, and a cooperative attitude, which meant abstinence from untoward unionizing as much as a pleasant mien.[24]

The most crucial determinant guiding the selection of families was their "homogeneity," a feature of the subsistence homesteads community idea practiced at Arthurdale. For in first targeting Scotts Run, selection agents had encountered the polyglot reality of many Appalachian mining areas, where new immigrants and African Americans supplied a good deal of the labor. Even though Mrs. Roosevelt had encouraged all of the Run's families to apply for homesteads, very few foreign-born and no black Americans were accepted. Resistance to integrating the project came from a number of directions, but it was the newly formed Homesteaders' Club at Arthurdale that supplied the most comprehensive statement of opposition. In a letter to Mrs. Roosevelt, they argued that the project's neighbors were opposed to integration, which was true; that separate schools would need to be built, which was the position taken publicly by Grimes; and, curiously, that "real Negroes" would themselves "refuse to mix with the white race," which the homesteaders interpreted as evidence of the black applicants' inferiority and lack of dignity.[25]

The episode posed fundamental questions about a federal program proposing to build "community." Assurances that 10 percent of future homesteads would go to blacks did not satisfy protesting African-American leaders. Walter White of the NAACP argued that Arthurdale's segregation put "the stamp of federal government approval upon discrimination." He called for integrated projects, but was countered by W. E. B. Du Bois, who argued that blacks would achieve more with their own projects and avoid becoming second-class citizens in mixed communities.[26] Du Bois's position held sway. While the Division of Subsistence Homesteads did explore prospects for interracial projects, they adopted criteria citing "homogeneity within the group" as a primary consideration for selecting homesteaders.[27] As a result, one project was built "by blacks, for blacks" at Aberdeen Gardens, Virginia, under the sponsorship of the Hampton Institute, though not to the specified quota of 10 percent.[28] Separate projects were also developed by and for immigrant Jews and Native and Hispanic Americans.

The diversity among colonies represented a kind of controlled democratic traditionalism, as it attempted to integrate a plurality of "cultural inheritances, traditions and folkways," as M. L. Wilson put it, within the New Deal's progressive vision of a balanced, cooperative society.[29] But at Arthurdale, the decision to predicate community on "homogeneity within the group" only furthered planners' nostalgic modernism, the oxymoronic nature of which flourished in the project's pedagogic program—homesteaders' lessons in good community.

In this regard, homogeneity represented as much a vision of as a condition for community. Agents took most of their families from areas beyond Scotts Run, where residents had more farming experience. The distribution of skills was only meant to be temporary. All homesteaders were ultimately expected to participate in industrial wage work and their own as well as communal subsistence agriculture. While planners searched for paid employment for homesteaders, they enlisted them in training that revived the Progressive-era Country Life Movement agenda for revitalizing rural life through scientific agriculture, improved health and child care, efficient home management, and tasteful decorating. Indeed, the only lasting divisions of labor envisioned on the project were gendered, insofar as childrearing, most housework, food preparation, and certain crafts were regarded as women's work. Otherwise, homesteaders were expected to develop commitments to common labors to better develop their cooperative "spirit of neighborliness."

Such functional plans for community were subtended by homesteaders' common ethnic and cultural bonds—their "homogeneous Scotch Irish" descent.[30] While agrarianism already supported a certain nostalgic modernist sentiment for a secure farm life, it proved insufficient for reviving what Mrs. Roosevelt termed the "community spirit" of the "early pioneers." To the latter end, Arthurdale's sponsors recruited Elsie Ripley Clapp to serve as Director of Community Affairs and to set up an experimental program of progressive community education (largely with loans from financier Bernard Baruch, a friend of Mrs. Roosevelt).[31] Clapp, a protégée of John Dewey (who was a member of the Sponsoring Committee), developed a program for children and adults, building on her mentor's principle of active learning by making it "function socially," as Dewey wrote.[32] She immersed children in "lifelike problems" rather than "traditional courses of study" by having them mimic their parents: first graders "farmed on the homestead," second graders erected a diminutive Arthurdale, and fourth graders went "pioneering in West Virginia." High school students made glass, spun wool, and practiced other crafts partly to prepare for the project's economic life, but also to appreciate modern conveniences: "After they have tanned a hide, they begin to know more about what goes into making a pair of shoes."[33]

Community education was not limited to the children. Indeed, the isomorphism between children's and adults' activities ran both ways, insofar as life at Arthurdale was in general "lifelike." Clapp's pedagogy and Ford's historical consciousness bear an uncanny resemblance when we consider that homesteaders were intended to "bring to mind what kind of people" their forebears were by steeping themselves in "the exact conditions under which [the pioneers] lived." In this light, the homesteaders were "historical reenactors" long before the term became current. The authenticity of their experience of community was the object in homesteaders' performances. But there were ideologically and politically expedient omissions from Arthurdale's vision of community, just as at Greenfield Village and Colonial Williamsburg.[34]

As Daniel Perlstein observed in an article on the shortcomings of Clapp's community education, even though children "went pioneering" in front of an old slave cabin on the Arthur property, Clapp declined to make it an object lesson in race relations, acceding to the exclusions made by their parents and the project's planners. And in having homesteaders model their forebears in order to expose them to modernity and recuperate their premodern community spirit, Clapp and her associates bypassed the education in modern industrial labor relations at Scotts Run. Thus, while she aimed to improve homesteaders "mired in the existing tradition of minstrel and church plays," Clapp replaced the latter with Scotch-Irish ballads like "Barb'ry Allen," avoiding, as Perlstein observed, "the industrial ballads that animated labor organizing."[35]

In a similar vein, Jane Becker has observed that Arthurdale's Mountaineer Craftsmen's Cooperative Association, the Friends' furniture-making cooperative transplanted from Scotts Run, turned out "traditional" Appalachian furniture and crafts that were produced for wages according to industrial standards and by largely industrial means. For Becker, Arthurdale's crafts trade, including textiles and metalwork, served as another instance of selling tradition in a society demanding mass-produced and marketed goods while yearning for tokens of simpler times.[36] But in Arthurdale's case, what was marketed was not merely a set of goods, but a Janus-headed vision of community joining democracy's New Deal future to its frontier past.

ARTHURDALE NOW

Tourists at the Arthurdale living history museum frequently ask, "Did it work?"[37] But the more apt questions are "How did it work, and for whom," for its specifically utopian features in fact were, and continue to be, a set of signifying practices open to symbolic uses as well as ideological contestation.

For critics of the New Deal, every cost overrun, misconceived plan, and meliorist bit of rhetoric from the "zealots" at Arthurdale was evidence of the sins of statism.[38] The most consequential opposition of this kind came from Congress, and a plan for a Post Office factory in Arthurdale was scrapped after members warned against the "nationalization of industry."[39] This sent planners on a largely fruitless search for private employers, during which years cooperatives like the Craftsmen's Association provided most of the homesteaders' modest incomes. Baruch and other donors to Clapp's school pulled out, and Clapp left as parents sought county accreditation for schools that might provide better prospects for their children.[40] The agricultural program was a success but could not sustain individual families, much less the entire colony. In the end, most homesteaders did not get on a sound financial footing until the war began. By that time, the government was selling off homes and lands at a loss.

By 1946, most of the colony was in private hands. Some former homesteaders pushed to incorporate but were rebuffed by those who valued their independence. A version of the original plan did survive as many families continued to farm their holdings, work in local industries, and ply trades they mastered as homesteaders. More houses appeared as homesteaders' children started their own families, and others returned after years away. A few buildings in the square housed small businesses, but these failed as community life migrated to other places. The old community center buildings were boarded up by the late 1970s, and one burned down. Center Hall fell into disuse and ruin, becoming a symbol of the colony's difficulties and near demise.

In a less visible way, however, Arthurdale's original community spirit seems to have survived. This became evident in June 1984 at the fiftieth anniversary of the project's opening, a "gala event" organized by the Arthurdale's Federated Women's Club.[41] Former homesteaders, their extended families, and notables such as Mrs. Roosevelt's son Elliott and Senator Jennings Randolph (a strong backer of Arthurdale as a freshman congressman in the 1930s) celebrated "The Dream Then and Now." The "dream" had many meanings, the most immediate of which was the Women's Club's hopes of buying back and restoring the Center Complex. To this end, they incorporated as a small nonprofit the next year under the name Arthurdale Heritage.

With help from a West Virginia University public historian and various state and federal preservation offices, Arthurdale Heritage gained National Historic District status for the original eleven-hundred-acre tract in 1987, an effort that gained significant local support when it became known that an oil company had planned exploratory drilling there. Over years of courting donations and grants with volunteer labor, Arthurdale Heritage acquired the structures of the Center Complex from their owners and restored them to something resembling their original functions. The administrative building was converted into Arthurdale Heritage's offices and a museum displaying crafts and objects from old Arthurdale, along with an archive of ephemera and signage about the project prepared by the West Virginia Humanities Council. The forge houses blacksmithing paraphernalia and demonstrations for school groups and special events. The Center Hall's restoration was completed in 1996, its history commemorated with plaques noting its origin as a nineteenth-century Presbyterian meetinghouse. It hosts ice cream socials and square dances reminiscent of those held in the 1930s. Artisans lead crafts and performing arts classes like those once held there and private parties rent it out for celebrations. Finally, the Hall's wings have resumed their purposes; a hairdresser plies her trade near the old barbershop, and Appalachian crafts and mementoes are sold where 1930s homesteaders sold their goods.[42]

Arthurdale Heritage's most recent and ambitious restoration project involves a Wagner homestead at number fifteen E Road, just down from the Center Complex.[43] The house was furnished with objects and furniture from the 1930s donated by former homesteaders and local residents, and, in the summer of 1999, received its new homesteaders, "Jacob and Anna Born." The "Borns" were in fact a local couple who took the house rent-free for a year in order to interpret "homestead living" for visitors on summer weekends. No Borns had ever lived in Arthurdale. Their names and identities were scripted from an amalgam of former homesteaders' stories and characteristics, an interpretive solution hit on, I am told, to avoid either seeming to favor or misinterpret any one family's past. On weekends the Borns could be found tending a garden and a menagerie of animals kept on the property's intact acreage. They gave tours of the house and sometimes introduced their "daughter" Betty, who was borrowed from a neighbor because the couple was unmarried and childless. Mr. Dixon, a young man, took up homestead living after the Borns' departure. On my first visit, he inquired, "Are you with the press," creatively invoking homesteaders' public visibility in the 1930s and involving me in the recapitulation of roles produced by Arthurdale's living museum of itself.[44]

For Glenna Williams, the Women's Club member who led Arthurdale Heritage in its formative years until it began "running itself," the restored Center Complex and Homestead E-15 represent "our own story . . . the way it really was for us." Asked about that story, she describes her arrival at Arthurdale from Scotts Run as a young teen in 1934: "I came from a world of black and white into one of technicolor. . . . It was like a rebirth." Her lifelong friend Annabelle Pervis Mayor, another charter member of Arthurdale Heritage, adds, "I can't imagine who I'd be if I hadn't come to Arthurdale." They offer these insights as illustrations of homesteaders' transformation, the stuff of the "dream" animating Arthurdale "then and now," in the words of the slogan Mrs. Williams coined. She and others differentiate this dream from the subsistence homesteads idea, the failings of which account for the project's reputation as a New Deal experiment gone wrong. She asserts that Arthurdale's chief "success," by contrast, and the dream celebrated there today, is the idea of community.[45]

In this light, Arthurdale Heritage offers, indeed is itself, the community's own answer to the question "Did it work?" Refining the question again into "How did it work, and for whom" reveals how Arthurdale's staged symbolic community thrives on complementary democratic and nostalgic impulses, the inheritance of the attitudes, practices, and institutions that shaped its predecessor.

Arthurdale Heritage has revived the civic voluntarism planners meant to instill in the project's original cooperative enterprises. Indeed, despite its strictly cultural mandate, residents occasionally approach the museum as a kind of proxy town council when they seek to enlist its resources in various matters involving local governance.[46] In fact, Arthurdale Heritage represents one among a growing number of small "community museums" that have developed in this country following the turmoil of the 1960s out of the combination of civic and economic empowerment programs, localized preservation activism, and public social history. But as Michael Wallace and others have shown, these "people's histories" have deeper roots in the New Deal, when the government promoted nonelite historical and cultural activism, notably in such democratic traditionalist efforts as the subsistence homesteads program itself.[47]

At the same time, many such community efforts among strongly identified groups reveal a certain reliance on boosterism, pride, and nostalgic myopia.[48] Arthurdale's celebration of its own democratic traditionalist inheritance proves no exception. Concentrating on mounting performances of homestead living and demonstrations of Appalachian craft production, Arthurdale Heritage has largely foregone reviving the progressive elements of its original communal institutions like health and child care. Indeed, performances of the past are rife at Arthurdale. Eleanor Roosevelt, still regarded by many at Arthurdale with near reverence, is portrayed by a bookseller from Charlottesville, West Virginia, who "interprets" the First Lady on a circuit. As the town's "patron saint" who also serves as the museum's main selling point, Eleanor Roosevelt can thus appear regularly, as she did in the 1930s, at the annual Ice Cream Social fundraiser and New Deal Festival. Dramatic pastiches of homesteaders' lives are also mounted, and Glenna Williams herself has been portrayed by a young 4-H member in local school history competitions.

One clue to the energy dedicated to staging the past at Arthurdale comes in Mrs. Williams's statement that her "Bible" in planning the town's fiftieth anniversary celebration was Elsie Clapp's volume on Arthurdale, *Community Schools in Action.*[49] Mrs. Williams's instincts served her well, insofar as the living aspects of Arthurdale's past—democratic and nostalgic—were then and are now powerfully conveyed through the sort of ritualized authenticity Clapp devised as "pioneer study."[50] Indeed, for Mrs. Williams, Mrs. Mayor, and others of their age in the 1930s at Arthurdale, the transformative experience of staging community was powerful enough to mount a second and just as vital version fifty years later. For children like "Betsy" and Mrs. Williams's young

4-H portrayer, there may be no more powerful means of conveying an authentic experience of "community" than to impart it through performances that invoke the past in their enactment. Nostalgic sentiment thus lends itself powerfully to the ritualized conveyances of the past Paul Connerton has described in *How Societies Remember* and serves to remind us, in Connerton's phrase, of the "difficulty of extracting our past from our present."[51]

The questions facing Arthurdale Heritage today concern the best uses for these inextricable pasts. As the organization's current masthead reads, its mission is "Restoring Yesterday for Tomorrow." Both democratic and nostalgic impulses will continue to shape Arthurdale Heritage. Neither cooperative management nor imaginary performances are dispensable, and together they fully convey the inheritance they represent. But as second-generation homesteaders pass away and the original Arthurdale fades from living memories, its facsimile in Arthurdale Heritage will need to remain vital and to expand its mission beyond ritual reenactments of 1930s homesteads. The prospects are promising and signal a shift from a single commitment to heritage to an embrace of the complementary riches of history. The latest acquisitions are the Arthurdale School buildings, to be developed into a New Deal archive and study center. The plan again demonstrates Arthurdale Heritage's creative adaptation of structures to new but appropriate functions, reinventing the past rather than simply reimagining it.

NOTES

1. Russell Lord and Paul Johnstone, *A Place on Earth: A Critical Appraisal of Subsistence Homesteads* (Washington, D.C.: Bureau of Agricultural Economics, 1942), 4, quoted in M. L. Wilson, "The Place of Subsistence Homesteads in Our National Economy," *Journal of Farm Economics* 16 (1934): 83.

2. Eleanor Roosevelt, quoted in Daniel Perlstein, "Community and Democracy in American Schools: Arthurdale and the Fate of Progressive Education," *Teachers College Record* 97 (Summer 1996): 628.

3. Arthurdale Heritage, Inc., *Arthurdale Heritage, Inc., Mission Statement, 2000*; Glenna Williams, "An Encouraging Word. . . ," *Restoring Yesterday for Tomorrow: The Newsletter of Arthurdale Heritage, Inc.* 2 (Fall 1987): 3.

4. Diane Barthel, *Historic Preservation: Collective Memory and Historical Identity* (New Brunswick: Rutgers University Press, 1996), 36, 50.

5. Michael Kammen, *Mystic Chords of Memory: The Transformation of Tradition in American Culture* (New York: Alfred A. Knopf, 1991), 300. I use the term "public historical sphere" as it is

defined by Tony Bennett in *The Birth of the Museum: History, Theory, Politics*, to designate "those institutions—from museums through national heritage sites to television historical dramas and documentaries—involved in producing and circulating meanings about the past" (New York: Routledge, 1995), 132.

6. Wilson, "The Place of Subsistence Homesteads in Our National Economy," 81.

7. Kammen, *Mystic Chords of Memory*, 300; Henry Ford quoted in Michael Wallace, "Visiting the Past: History Museums in the United States," *Radical History Review* 25 (1981): 70.

8. As Barbara Kirshenblatt-Gimblett puts it in *Destination Culture: Tourism, Museums and Heritage*: "Heritage is a new mode of cultural production in the present that has recourse to the past" (Berkeley: University of California Press, 1998), 149.

9. Wallace, "Visiting the Past," 78.

10. Kammen, *Mystic Chords of Memory*, 301, including quotation from John Dewey.

11. Kammen, *Mystic Chords of Memory*, 302.

12. Wallace, "Visiting the Past," 79.

13. Anders Greenspan, *Creating Colonial Williamsburg* (Washington, D.C.: Smithsonian Institution Press, 2002).

14. United States, *Statutes at Large*, 47, 205–6.

15. Wilson quoted in Mike Smathers, "The Search for the Garden," *Southern Exposure* 8 (Spring 1980), 58. For discussion of the planning for subsistence homesteads, see Lord and Johnstone, *A Place on Earth*, and Paul Conkin, *Tomorrow a New World: The New Deal Community Program* (1959; rpt., New York: Da Capo Press, 1976). On "balance" in New Deal thought, see William Leuchtenberg, *Franklin D. Roosevelt and the New Deal, 1932–1940* (New York: Harper Colophon Books, 1963), 35.

16. Franklin Roosevelt quoted in James Holt, "The New Deal and the American Anti-Statist Tradition," in *The New Deal*, ed. John Braeman, Robert H. Bremner, and David Brody (Columbus: Ohio State University Press, 1975), 35.

17. M. L. Wilson, "The Subsistence Homesteads Program," *Proceedings of the Institute of Public Affairs, 1934*, 7 (1934): 171–72.

18. Frederick Jackson Turner, *The Frontier in American History* (New York: Dover Publications, 1996), passim.

19. Henry A. Wallace, *New Frontiers* (New York: Reynal and Hitchcock, 1934).

20. Eleanor Roosevelt, *This I Remember* (New York: Harper and Brothers, 1949), 126. Secondary published accounts of Arthurdale's origins are not lacking; cf. Arthur M. Schlesinger, Jr., *The Age of Roosevelt*, vol. 2 of *The Coming of the New Deal*, (1959; rpt. New

York: Houghton-Mifflin, 1988); Conkin, *Tomorrow a New World*; Stephen Edward Haid, *Arthurdale: An Experiment in Community Planning, 1933–1947* (Ph.D. diss., West Virginia University, 1975); Blanche Weisen Cook, *Eleanor Roosevelt*, vol. 2 (New York: Viking, 1992); Bryan Ward, ed., *A New Deal for America: Proceedings from a National Conference on New Deal Communities* (Arthurdale, W.Va.: Arthurdale Heritage, Inc., 1995); Perlstein, "Community and Democracy in American Schools"; and Nancy Hoffman, *Eleanor Roosevelt and the Arthurdale Experiment* (North Haven, Connecticut: Linnet Books, 2001).

21. Bushrod Grimes, "Deposition to Public Works Administration. Preston County, West Virginia. September 1, 1934" (Morgantown, W. Va.: West Virginia Collection, A&M 2178 [B. Grimes Papers], 1934), n.p.

22. Haid, *Arthurdale*, 76.

23. M. L. Wilson, quoted in Russell Lord, "The Rebirth of Rural Life, Part II," *Survey Graphic* 30 (December 1941), 691.

24. On one homesteader's difficulty gaining a spot on the project because of involvement in Scotts Run's "National Miners Union," reputedly "a front for the Communist Party," see Hoffman, *Eleanor Roosevelt and the Arthurdale Experiment*, 15.

25. Homesteader Claude Hitchcock to Eleanor Roosevelt, quoted in Haid, *Arthurdale*, 106, and Cook, *Eleanor Roosevelt*, 138.

26. Walter White, "Segregation—A Symposium," *Crisis* (March 1934): 80–81. See Perlstein, "Community and Democracy in America's Schools," 637–41, for a full discussion of this debate in the context of Arthurdale's segregation.

27. Ghirardo, *Building New Communities*, 172.

28. This is the unofficial motto of the Aberdeen Gardens Historic and Civic Association, their contemporary counterpart to Arthurdale Heritage, as they are also developing a community museum of their New Deal origins. The slogan recalls Du Bois's editorial comment that blacks' greatest advances leading up to the Depression were a result of their working "for and by themselves" (W. E. B. Du Bois, "Segregation," *Crisis* [January 1934]: 20.)

29. M. L. Wilson, "How New Deal Agencies Are Affecting Family Life," *Journal of Home Economics* 28 (May 1935): 275.

30. Fletcher Collins, quoted in Elsie Ripley Clapp, *Community Schools in Action* (New York: Viking, 1939), 218.

31. Although the Division of Subsistence Homesteads could not build schools on its own, it encouraged efforts to find state, county, or local governmental funding, and failing that, sought private support for children's education.

32. John Dewey, introduction to *Community Schools in Action*, by Elsie Ripley Clapp, viii.

33. Clapp, *Community Schools in Action*, 73–74, 125, 143, 150.

34. On authenticity as the primary object of living history and historical reenactments, see Richard Handler and William Saxton, "Dyssimulation: Reflexivity, Narrative, and the Quest for Authenticity in 'Living History,'" *Cultural Anthropology* 3 (August 1988): 242–61.

35. Perlstein, "Community and Democracy in American Schools," passim.

36. Jane Becker, *Selling Tradition: Appalachia and the Construction of an American Folk, 1930–1940* (Chapel Hill: University of North Carolina Press, 1998), 93–124.

37. Author's interview with Kenneth Kidd, Arthurdale, West Virginia, August 2000.

38. "Half-Baked Ideas Laid to Roosevelt," *New York Times*, 28 October 1935.

39. *Congressional Record*, 73rd Cong., 2nd session 1934, 1272.

40. Minutes of Arthurdale Homesteaders' Club (January, 1936), in collections of Arthurdale Heritage, Inc., Arthurdale, West Virginia.

41. Glenna Williams, interview with author, Arthurdale, West Virginia, January 2002.

42. Arthurdale Heritage's offices have moved into another wing of Center Hall.

43. The house is named for the architect of many Arthurdale houses, not its former occupants.

44. Information on the Homestead at 15 E Road comes from interviews with Deanna Hornyak Stone, Kenneth Kidd, Jennifer Bonnette (Executive Director of Arthurdale Heritage), and past issues of *Restoring Yesterday for Tomorrow*, Arthurdale Heritage's newsletter.

45. Glenna Williams and Annabelle Purvis Mayor, interview with author, Arthurdale, West Virginia, August 2000.

46. Jennifer Bonnette, interview with author, February 2002.

47. Susan Porter Benson, Stephen Brier, and Roy Rosenzweig, introduction to *The Presence of the Past: Essays on History and the Public*, eds. Susan Porter Benson, Stephen Brier, and Ray Rosenzweig (Philadelphia: Temple University Press, 1986), xv–xxiv. On the forms and functions of community museums and histories, cf. Michael Wallace, "Visiting the Past"; Linda Shopes, "Oral History and Community Involvement: The Baltimore Neighborhood History Project" in Benson et al, *The Presence of the Past*, 249–63; Nancy J. Fuller, "The Museum and Community Empowerment: the Ak-Chin Indian Community Ecomuseum Project," in *Museums and Communities: The Politics of Public Culture*, eds. Ivan Karp, Christine Mullen Kreamer, and Steven D. Lavine, 327–65 (Washington, D.C.: The Smithsonian Institution Press, 1992); John Kuo Wei Tchen, "Creating a Dialogic Museum: The Chinatown History Museum Experiment," in Karp et al, *Museums and Communities*, 288–326; and, on related developments internationally, Dominique Poulot, "Identity as Self-Discovery: The Ecomuseum in France," in *Museum Culture: Histories, Discourses, Spectacles*, eds. Daniel J. Sherman and Irit Rogoff, 66–84 (Minneapolis: University of Minnesota Press, 1994).

48. See, for example, Shopes, "Oral History and Community Involvement."

49. Glenna Williams, interview, Arthurdale, West Virginia, February 2002.

50. Clapp, *Community Schools in Action*, 143.

51. Paul Connerton, *How Societies Remember* (Cambridge, England: Cambridge University Press, 1989), 5.

8

History Lessons

Selling the John Dillinger Museum[1]

HEATHER R. PERRY

Imagine this: You are in an interactive museum and you come to the first station. A plaque hangs on the wall next to a closed door with a semi-opaque glass window. Peering through the window, you can barely discern that you are standing face to face with a man seated in a chair. Seconds later, you notice that a steel helmet covers his head and wires circle down behind his back. His wrists are belted to the wooden chair arms and as your eyes dart downward, you realize his feet are bound as well. The warning sign on the door—"Caution: Electric Current!"—suddenly makes sense.

Once you realize that the man sits in an electric chair, you read the accompanying plaque, eager to know more. A short description relates the crime and the man's conviction, and then a sign asks: "Do you agree with the verdict? If yes, press the button below." How do you react? Do you ponder the verdict? Do you press the button and see what happens? What do you do?

Suppose the sign tells you that the man seated before you was Bruno Hauptmann, notorious kidnapper of the Lindbergh baby. Convicted of the 1932 kidnapping and murder of aviator Charles Lindbergh's two-year-old son, Hauptmann was sentenced to death by electrocution in 1934. The electric chair on display is exactly the kind which executed Hauptmann over seventy years ago. Under those words, you read this quotation: "The electric chair yawns for its fodder of calloused human beasts whose warped minds prompt evil deeds. The wages of sin was [sic] death. Sooner or later it will get John Dillinger. That or the searing death of hot bullets fired from eager guns. Crime never pays."[2] At this point, you are asked whether you agree with the verdict. Do you?

The John Dillinger Museum[3] in Hammond, Indiana, which is currently closed, depicted an aspect of the 1930s that was decidedly different than the version on display at Arthurdale. Not only did the museum expect the visitor to agree with history's verdict, but staff relied on this exhibit and others to teach important lessons about crime. If visitors chose to push the bright and shiny red plastic knob, the first thing they would notice was a flash of light across Hauptmann's face. Nearly simultaneously, a buzzing sound would fill the corridor as the final punishment was audibly carried out. As the buzzing ceased, the lights in the execution chamber dimmed once again, and the visitor moved forward to the next exhibit, unless, of course, a visitor wanted to execute Hauptmann a second time.

Many might have been surprised to find that a mock execution of Bruno Hauptmann was the first exhibit greeting the visitor at the 1990s museum devoted to John Dillinger. Certainly, no one who toured the Dillinger Museum in its previous location in Nashville, Indiana, would recognize this particular display. The original museum, a peculiar—and decidedly most original—cabinet of curiosities to which amateur historian and Dillinger aficionado Joe Pinkston devoted his entire life, closed. It did not have a strongly ideological curriculum or ethical rationale. But in November 1999, a new Dillinger Museum opened, one which no longer resembled the kind of old-fashioned wax museum one might have found on a boardwalk arcade, but instead modeled on new interactive museums. In getting away from what he described as "typically dull and boring historical museums,"[4] the new collection's director, Speros Batistatos, the president and CEO of the Lake County Convention and Visitors Bureau, had this museum designed to be both child-friendly and pedagogical. "It makes learning fun," he proudly declared.[5] This sentiment was neatly expressed over the exhibit's entryway, as well, which proclaimed, "Welcome to the John Dillinger Museum: A Hands-On Historical Adventure." As we shall see, the museum itself has been part of a historical adventure involving not only the (re)presentation of John Dillinger but also dilemmas relating to the ownership of culture and history.

In many ways, the Hammond museum lived up to its name. Through various hands-on exhibits or interactive sites, the visitor was drawn into the world of the Depression-era criminal. The first room focused on Dillinger's early life. There museum patrons could try lifting heavy sacks of grain as they experienced the harsh reality of Indiana farm life during the Dust Bowl years. Nearby, an old-fashioned radio played popular tunes from Dillinger's youth. Among Dillinger family photographs and newspaper clippings recounting his first crime, the museum guest could find a vocabulary wheel and an electronic voting booth. The former was called "Gangster Rap," because visitors were quizzed on their knowledge of 1930s-era gangster slang. A rotating wheel taught guests that a gangster's girlfriend was called a "moll" and police informants were called "stool pigeons." At the next exhibit, "You Be the Judge," participants were invited to pass judgment on Dillinger's early years as a criminal. Specifically, in October 1924, Dillinger and Ed Singleton were easily foiled in a robbery attempt at a grocery in Dillinger's hometown of Mooresville, Indiana. At the time, several townspeople suggested that the twenty-one-year-old Dillinger had been led astray by the older, more delinquent Singleton. After reading a short description of this crime and Dillinger's subsequent trial, museum visitors were asked questions such as whether Dillinger's father exercised enough responsibility over his son or whether Dillinger himself evinced any potential for rehabilitation. After eight such queries, visitors had to decide whether to condemn Dillinger. With only the limited information given, they were asked to form a judgment as to whether Dillinger was truly incorrigible. These opinions were electronically registered and tallied at the station so that museum-goers could compare their votes with history's verdict. Those who wished could then be locked up in Dillinger's reconstructed jail cell, which included a few of his personal belongings. There, museum guests could consider the daily discomforts of prison life, especially while confronted with the minimal amenities offered by the corner bucket. This was certainly a very different kind of simulation from the type found in the Old State Capitol Museum in Baton Rouge, where visitors have the opportunity to pretend they are giving a major political address.

Through these vocabulary games and crime reports, patrons became acquainted with a world which might seem like ancient history to many twenty-first-century visitors. What pedagogical function was really at play in exhibits which asked patrons to condemn a criminal? What exactly did a mock execution teach a child?

In answering these questions, we must look back in more depth at the history and recasting of the John Dillinger Museum. When the Lake County Convention and Visitors Bureau (LCCVB) first announced it had bought the entire collection of Dillinger memorabilia from the estate of an eccentric Dillinger buff in Nashville, Indiana, protests immediately erupted. For years, the original Dillinger museum had enjoyed modest success among America's roadside travelers. Despite its somewhat inconvenient rural location, the unusual museum was a favorite among those seeking an alternative to more traditional Indiana vacation stops. It was always listed in the underground travel classic, *Roadside America*.[6] Joe Pinkston, the original owner and collector of the assorted Dillinger artifacts, died in 1996, and the county seized the opportunity offered when Pinkston's survivors advertised the collection for sale in early 1998.[7] In an effort to boost the tourist economy of northwestern Indiana and take advantage of the traffic around Chicago, they envisioned the museum's popular appeal as the ideal hook to lure interstate drivers into the Lake County Convention and Visitors Bureau. For the LCCVB, the ensuing popular protest against the museum was completely unexpected.[8]

In retrospect, the various public debates surrounding the relocation of the Dillinger Museum might seem predictable. Whereas the original John Dillinger Museum was tucked away in Nashville, a small artists' colony and antique district in southern Indiana some thirty miles removed from the heavy traffic on Interstate 65, the new Dillinger Museum lay at the heart of the Chicago-Indiana freeway tourist and commuter traffic. The new museum was more accessible, more public, and more noticeable than the older one. There were important sociohistorical and geographic differences as well. Nashville is located in rural Indiana's heartland, just south of Mooresville, the site of the Dillinger family farm and the gangster's hometown. The Depression found many victims in this area, and local memories of bank foreclosures both then and now are as strong as those of the bank robberies that resembled appropriate justice to some.[9] Indeed, one Mooresville resident, Dillinger's descendant Jeffery Scalf, suggested that the town hold an annual festival to be called "Dillinger Days" which might capitalize on the exploits of this famous native son.[10] These local memories contrast starkly with those of Crown Point and East Chicago in northwestern Indiana, where Lake County can be found. Indeed, in northwestern Indiana, natives recall a murderer, not a folk hero, and their public debate over the museum reflected this image.

Although uproar could initially be heard across the state, the strongest voices of protest could be distilled into two distinct categories: from law enforcement and area residents. The Indiana State Police and various Lake County law enforcement agencies met the news with righteous indignation.

For them, the idea of a museum that focused on the life of John Dillinger was offensive for two reasons. First, it was simply disrespectful to the memory of William O'Malley, the police officer the gangster had killed.[11] Secondly, in their eyes, the museum also glorified crime by indirectly paying tribute to a man who was a convicted felon and murderer. In short, a museum honoring a "cop killer" posed a direct challenge to their personal and professional mores.

A second wave of protest arose from museum-area residents. Having endured for years the label "murder capital of the United States," Lake County cities such as Gary and East Chicago had spent the 1990s reinventing themselves for the public eye. Renovated downtowns, swanky riverboat casinos, and large tourist-friendly hotel complexes were all part of the rehabilitation project underway in America's rusting steel towns.[12] Outraged letters to the editor, condemnatory op-ed pieces, public protests, and angry phone calls to the visitors bureau were all part of the reaction of the local population to the announcement of the museum's relocation.[13] City planners, economic developers, and area residents could not tolerate the opening of a venture which might destroy the image they had so painstakingly recast. As one editorial pointed out, "Lake County doesn't need a cop-killing bank robber to be the first historical figure visitors to the area see."[14] Whereas community activists were largely responsible for the restoration of Arthurdale, in this case, concerned community activists joined the economy-minded Lake County residents in a move against the museum. Teachers, parents, and police argued that a museum devoted to Dillinger would only exacerbate the increasing problem of inner-city street gangs by providing a negative role model.[15] To them, Dillinger's notoriety threatened to work like a curse over the area's unsuspecting youth. Once immortalized in a museum, Dillinger and his legacy of crime would become an unavoidable and sinister presence in Lake County, one whose strength and power would only grow with ticket sales.

The local memories recalled by the return of John Dillinger to the Lake County area encompassed even more than personal grief, professional solidarity, or public image, however. For the town of Crown Point, not far from the museum, the gangster prompted collective memories of an embarrassing prison scandal that cost the town sheriff her job and brought shame to many of its residents. In early 1933, amidst much publicity, Dillinger was captured in Tucson, Arizona, and delivered to the Lake County police. At the time, the county jail was being heavily promoted in the nationwide media as a veritable escape-proof prison incorporating the latest in penal technology. Yet on

March 3, 1933, against all odds, Dillinger managed to escape from the facility, allegedly bluffing his way out with a carved wooden gun. Rumors quickly spread that Dillinger had received inside help during the escape.[16]

Photos circulated in the local papers which pictured Dillinger chummily clapping the shoulder of Lillian Holley, the local sheriff, in the courtroom at his hearing. The wife of the town's former sheriff, Holley had been appointed to the office upon her husband's death. She had been widely popular and heralded by many as a path-breaker for women in the public sphere. To her critics, however, these photos confirmed her incompetence and inappropriateness for the post. Although she never publicly commented on the events of that spring, in an unofficial conversation made public after her death, Holley suggested that the true organizer of Dillinger's escape was none other than her local political adversary, Lake County Prosecutor Robert Estill. Indeed, Estill did use the scandal to his party's advantage the following year, passing out tiny carved wooden guns to embarrass the Democrats in the 1934 county elections. Neither Holley nor her remaining local supporters initially welcomed the opening of a Dillinger Museum in the area.[17]

Given both the range and volume of protest within Lake County against the Dillinger Museum, one could easily understand that gaining community support was going to require a hard sell on the part of the visitors bureau. At least one important member of the marketing relations community agreed, and on January 25, 2000, the Hospitality, Sales and Marketing Association International (HSMAI)[18] awarded Shawn Platt, vice president of Communications at the LC-CVB, the Bronze Award for his successful efforts in winning public approval for the Dillinger Museum. Indeed, it took over a year of intense image management, careful exhibit design, and a strict pedagogical makeover for the freshly dubbed "Historical Adventure" to open in Hammond, Indiana, with public support. Aware that a museum which in any way glorified the life of the gangster would be met with criticism, the visitors bureau consciously decided to cast Dillinger's story, the museum's curriculum, in such a way that the visitor-patron would leave with the firm understanding that crime did not pay. The visitors bureau then hired ICON Exhibits, an interior design firm specializing in trade fairs and expositions, to design a museum that would tell the fascinating story of Indiana's notorious native son while simultaneously reinforcing the museum's commitment to and respect for law enforcement officers and the surrounding communities.[19] Hauptmann's execution and other exhibits were part of the compromise reached in the selling of the Dillinger Museum.

To win the support of law-and-order advocates and others who condemned the Dillinger enterprise, Batistatos of the visitors bureau agreed to place a police memorial at the entrance of the museum.[20] Indeed, in the entryway next to the Hauptmann execution, a plaque reminded visitors not only of Officer O'Malley's sacrifice but also of each and every Lake County law enforcer slain in the line of duty. Borrowing its text from the National Police Memorial in Washington, D.C., the commemorative inscription upon the plaque read: "It's not how these officers died that makes them heroes. It's how they lived." For city officials and the victims' families, the Dillinger Museum marked a personal site for mourning local heroes. In addition, the death of Lillian Holley in 1999 removed another source of criticism, and it has been suggested that with her passing, the rumors that plagued her (and Crown Point) after Dillinger's escape were finally put to rest.[21] Perhaps to those involved, the nearby relocation of the Dillinger Museum represented a kind of symbolic recapturing of the nation's most famous escapee. Dillinger was incarcerated in Lake County, apparently permanently.

This tribute to public servants and the symbolic recapturing of the criminal did not mean the museum's development was able to proceed without any further objections. Indeed, the LCCVB might have taken a lesson from Holley's own experiences as an early controversy signaled to Platt that photographs long since published elsewhere could suddenly be charged with renewed controversy. Initial publicity shots for the museum used a well-known photo taken during Dillinger's bank-robbing spree in the Midwest. This image of a smiling Dillinger posing rakishly with his Tommy gun proved too much for contemporary critics. Museum protesters argued that the photo presented Dillinger in too positive a light. They contended that his good looks and flirty air lent a boyish charm to the ruthless murderer, detracting from the serious nature of his crimes. Platt immediately pulled advertisements using that photo. Clearly, the gangster's popular legacy as an antiestablishment figure would have to be thoroughly recast. After that, all public images of Dillinger promulgated by the museum offered a much more serious image of the criminal—usually behind bars.[22]

Careful to exclude exhibits that might be construed as glorifying Dillinger, ICON concentrated its efforts on delivering the message that crime does not pay. Despite notoriously popular items from the gangster's life, such as a getaway car riddled with bullet holes and the carved wooden gun he used when bluffing his way out of the supposedly escape-proof Lake County Jail, the museum visitor's journey ended with more somber visions of Dillinger. Having explored the extent of Dillinger's crimes through various exhibits—climaxing with the murder of an innocent police officer—the visitor encountered a diorama toward the end of the "adventure" that recalled the gangster's grisly death. As patrons walked into the room, they stood before the recreated facade of the famous Biograph Theater in downtown Chicago. Motion detectors placed strategically about the exhibit triggered the sound of gunshots as the museum visitor neared the exhibit's descriptive panel. Screams and sirens quickly followed. The panel informed visitors that if they pressed the knob below, they could witness Dillinger's last moments. When the knob was pushed, the lights flashed up and a life-sized wax figure of an already dead Dillinger was revealed face down upon the sidewalk before the theatre. In this way, museum patrons viewed the gangster's death as if they were actually present the night of July 22, 1934, when Dillinger was gunned down by police.

As at the Hauptmann execution display, museum patrons found themselves at the center of the drama, witnesses to history. The nearby plaster death mask cast upon Dillinger's delivery to the morgue along with the bloody "trousers of death" he wore that night completed the exhibit. Next to them, the visitor could find Dillinger's original tombstone, which was donated to the museum in an effort to prevent any further bits from being chipped away by visitor-pilgrims to the gangster's actual gravesite in his hometown of Mooresville. For some patrons, these artifacts lent a macabre authenticity to the exhibit, but for others, they seemed to detract from the seriousness of Dillinger's end. Moreover, the automatic death which was so easily triggered took on a kind of surreal, comic quality, as Dillinger was repeatedly gunned down each time a new visitor entered the room. The boundary between moral lesson and entertainment blurred.

Depicting the gruesome "wages of sin" was certainly the most obvious way this "historical adventure" taught visitors that crime does not pay, but it was not the only one. A second narrative ran parallel to the story of Dillinger's criminal exploits, and it was also possible to read the museum's exhibit as a more general history of law enforcement. Wax figures of J. Edgar Hoover and other champions of justice began to dot the Dillinger narrative halfway through the exhibition after we learned that Dillinger was the FBI's original "Public Enemy Number One." Whereas the folk-hero, antigovernment image of Dillinger and his gang was often downplayed in the museum, the mythology surrounding Hoover's G-men was clearly reinforced. For instance, while figures of outlaws were presented standing at eye level with the visitor, sitting in chairs, or prostrate in death, wax figures of law enforcers were strategically placed high upon pedestals, making them appear larger than life. Copies of board games, novels, movies, action figures, t-shirts, and television shows—all inspired by the real-life adventures of the FBI—were displayed in cases next to the wax statues as part of the popular legacy of crime fighting. Not only was dispensing justice fun in this "historical adventure," but it was also lucrative, as evidenced by the consumer products displayed.

Given the difficulty the new owners faced in gaining police support for the museum, it was hardly surprising that in the Lake County Dillinger Museum the real heroes turned out to be those who fought crime, not those who committed it. Beside each installment of the John Dillinger crime narrative, the museum visitor could learn about a corresponding historical moment in the development of crime-fighting techniques. At one early station, patrons attempted to match written descriptions with unidentified black and white photographs of Dillinger and his gang. After testing their abilities to identify criminals, museum visitors could try on a bulky, cumbersome bulletproof vest from the 1930s, thereby experiencing firsthand how early crime fighters protected themselves from gangsters' bullets. Another somewhat discomfiting exhibit was the station where visitors could fingerprint themselves with real ink using criminal identification filing cards. At the nearby mock FBI crime lab, visitors could compare slides of real blood, thread, and human hair under a microscope. These and many other exhibits constantly reminded the museum patron of the extensive arm and eye of the law.

Walking from exhibit to exhibit, the visitor learned that over the years the state invented and perfected various methods of surveillance and control over its citizens. One of the more convincing stations illustrated the important contributions of technology in this area. Halfway through the adventure, the museum patron entered the foyer of a bank, unwittingly interrupting a robbery in progress. Wax figures in a variety of poses—one teller behind the counter and several bandits in action—combined with an automated recording of threats, gunshots, and screams. As they left the crime scene, visitors had the opportunity to check their memories by answering a series of questions about the robbery at the nearby witness station. The objectives of this exhibit extended beyond testing the audience's ability to recall important crime scene details. Rather, once museum visitors had the opportunity to be witnesses, they were invited to compare their recollections with evidence from a surveillance camera and video monitor. On the small exhibit screen, they could review the crime and note how the technological memory of the videotape was much more reliable than a human witness. The conclusion was inescapable—human memory is fleeting, selective, and fallible.

This parade of techniques and advances made over the past seventy years played an important role in ensuring a healthy respect for the law. ICON's decision to include a history of criminal detection in a museum about John Dillinger suggested that depicting Dillinger's gruesome demise was more effective in deterring crime when coupled with a reminder of the state's increasingly pervasive surveillance. If the example made of Dillinger was not enough to deter all visitors from crime, the seeming inevitability of capture and prosecution was supposed to convince the rest. By the end of the museum tour, the patron had to realize that crime does not pay.

But how did the Hauptmann execution fit into all of this? If reminding the visitor of the power and authority of the state was crucial to conveying the message that crime does not pay, why not simply show a film or photograph of Hauptmann's execution? Or, to repeat my original question, what were we supposed to learn from a mock execution?

Hauptmann's execution served a more complicated pedagogical function than the explicitly didactic sites such as the "Gangster Rap"[23] vocabulary wheel. As with "You Be the Judge," the station where patrons reevaluated Dillinger's first nine-year jail sentence, museum visitors had to decide for themselves whether the verdict—the death penalty in Hauptmann's case—was justified. A patron who agreed with the verdict would push the execution button and reenact this historical moment. But what if the visitor hesitated or wanted to reconsider the case? Nowhere was there space for the patron to hear both sides of the story, review the evidence, and come to an individual conclusion. Nowhere could the visitor actually register dissent or reject the verdict; nor could history be rewritten to reflect the individual visitor's choice. Hauptmann was executed on April 3, 1936. This is historical fact and could neither be pre-empted nor debated within the "historical adventure" of the museum. In order to participate in this module of the exhibit, the visitor was forced to choose to execute the criminal. In fact, the exhibit seemed expressly to play upon our instinctive reflexes to press red buttons and not upon our evaluative skills. No real choice was offered.

Indeed, if Arthurdale brought into question some of the government's New Deal policies, perhaps what was being offered at the Dillinger Museum was the opportunity to confirm or reject the historical legitimacy of the state's monopoly on violence and punishment. Death, bloodshed, and surveillance played an unavoidable role within the Dillinger "adventure"; the museum's message was not antiviolence. Rather it seemed to be vaguely distinguishing between those who use violence with permission and those who do not. In his own extensive work on the historical emergence of the state's authority, Michel Foucault argued that it was through the spectacle of the public execution that the state displayed its monopoly on violence, power, and control over the individual.[24] As the exercise of punishment gradually receded to the less prominent sphere of the prison, the residual threat of the public execution displaced the spectacle thereof in deterring crime. That is, the potentiality of the state's power—its permission to use it—became tantamount to its actual display. Fear of the state's punishment became enough to keep the citizenry in line. Clearly, by witnessing Hauptmann's execution, the museum visitor was confronted with the "wages of sin" or the consequences of crime.

The Hauptmann execution exhibit also employed another, more complicated pedagogical function, however. Within the Foucauldian paradigm briefly sketched above, an internalized fear of the state works to prevent crime. We could argue, however, that instead of relying on an *already internalized* support for the state's authority, the Hauptmann exhibit actually *created* it. By choosing affirmatively, the museum patron simultaneously confirmed the state's decision and legitimated its authority. It was an unconscious act of validation. Beyond this, however, executing Hauptmann offered the museum visitor a kind of temporary—or imagined—role within the state's apparatus of power. Unlike the spectacle of eighteenth-century executions at which crowds fundamentally excluded from the execution and the performance of authority gathered round the scaffold to mock the event, pray for the condemned, or sell souvenirs, this execution drew in the crowd—that is, the museum's audience or students. It created an "imagined community"[25] by offering every museum visitor the opportunity to take part in a larger chain of events: the dispensation of justice, the exercise of power, and the legitimate use of violence. Each visitor who arrived at the museum knew that he or she would simply be following those who went before. Paradoxically, each and every patron had the chance to be the one who executed Hauptmann. At that point, visitors were not simply observing the power of the state; they were becoming aware of their own positions and potentiality within it. The Hauptmann execution reinforced in children and adults that they were citizens in an imagined community dedicated to supporting—not undermining—the state. Indeed, the display seemed to outline the public space within the community—or all communities for that matter—for "acceptable" violence.

Hauptmann's execution was placed at the entrance of the museum; it was the first episode in the John Dillinger "historical adventure." By the end of the visitor's tour, the museum's ethical rationale seemed abundantly clear. Exhibits such as "Where Are They Now?" depicted for the visitor the grisly end which met each of Dillinger's gang members, replete with black and white photographs. For those who failed to be impressed by the museum's elaborate productions and games, one more reminder appealed to them as they left. The text, printed on an $8\frac{1}{2}$" x 11" sheet of paper taped to the exit door, read simply: "Crime Never Pays!" What seemed perhaps less apparent, however, was the museum's position on the legitimate use of violence in society. The distinction in authority, legitimacy, and moral responsibility between a police officer shooting an unsuspecting Dillinger behind a movie theater and a visitor simply carrying out orders on an already tried and convicted Hauptmann was never actually made clear. A vague idea that justice was served hung in the air, but no clear discussion of justice, crime, and punishment existed. Exhibits which automatically trigger death or place it on the other side of a shiny, plastic knob seem to detract from the seriousness of both crime and punishment. Decision-making appears flippant and all too neat. In the "John Dillinger Hands-On Historical Adventure," crime—and the grave consequences thereof—was clearly not being depicted as *fun*; however, within the "historical adventure" of the museum itself, killing disturbingly *was*.

The museum's power to control and instruct its visitors is well known; the role of museums in instruction has been delineated in the chapter by Elizabeth Vallance. Likewise, discussions of museums as producers of national or cultural identity are nothing new. As Tony Bennett points out, governments have been deploying the museum as a civilizing agent within the public sphere since the middle of the nineteenth century.[26] What makes the selling of the Dillinger Museum such a fascinating story is not simply that its ultimate pedagogical message is conservative or even mundane. We have come to expect our public institutions to promote, even demand, the display of citizenship. Rather, what makes the story so interesting was that for years the Dillinger Museum—and any message it may have suggested—sat relatively tranquil and unnoticed in a small town in Indiana. It was only with the announcement of its sale and proposed relocation that many disparate social groups began competing for control over both the collection and its message. The story of the Dillinger Museum highlights the fact that although museums are powerful institutions, they are not necessarily autonomous ones. A museum's local setting, that is, the geographical and social space in which it is positioned, can exert significant influence on the institution's orientation.

Clearly, the selling of the Dillinger Museum was far more complicated than simply moving the collection from one end of Indiana to another. In this case, public opinion heavily influenced the museum's pedagogical orientation. In seeking compromise with its critics, the museum lost the story that Joe Pinkston originally told. Gone was the quirky story of a local farm boy turned folk hero whose bank-robbing escapades represented a kind of antiestablishment, vigilante justice against government and bank farm foreclosures during the Great Depression.[27] The ethical rationale for displaying the story of Dillinger was recast, grafted onto a larger project devoted to teaching civic duty and responsibility. Danger, intrigue, and the thrill of hot pursuit were still being used to draw in the visitor, but the glory belonged to the supporters and wielders of the state's power, not its challengers. In the twenty-first century, the John Dillinger Museum became a force of order, not subversion.

Yet the story of the selling of the Dillinger Museum in Lake County took another unexpected turn when Dillinger's grand-nephew Jeffery Scalf sued the museum, forcing it to close in early 2006. Scalf claimed the museum was in violation of Indiana's 1994 Personality Rights law, which states that individuals have a right to control publicity using their names or images and to derive profits from the same. The law was intended to protect famous persons from having others make money from exactly the kind of toys, t-shirts, and figurines on display at the museum, but Scalf and his attorney are attempting to broaden its interpretation and to protect Dillinger's reputation. According to a May 2006 National Public Radio story by Harriet Baskas, the irony of the case is that Scalf ultimately hopes to open his own museum, sell the collection, or allow others to display it. The pending case seems to suggest that whereas crime does not exactly *pay*, it just may *profit* a gangster's heirs. Further, the treatment of the case in the media might well confirm the police's worst fears: Dillinger memorabilia promotes the glorification of robbers. Indeed, the very title of Baskas's piece—"Museum *Honoring* Dillinger Faces Roadblock" [emphasis added]—celebrates the criminal.[28]

On another level, the lawsuit raises critical issues pertinent to all museums devoted to chronicling historic personages and vital to any discussion of the ownership of culture. If the court finds that museums are bound by the publicity rights laws existent in many states, then these institutions may be unable to exhibit displays about famous personages without full permission from the heirs (not all of Dillinger's kin are participating in the case).

In the end, the selling of the Dillinger Museum tells us nearly as much about the conflicting ethical rationales behind museums as it tells us about the gangster himself. In reaching compromises with various segments of the local public, the Convention and Visitors Bureau created a museum that told multiple stories while simultaneously offering a memorial to the slain and the restoration of city pride. More recent legal conflicts involving the museum remind us that the selling of any aspect of culture must inevitably invoke questions about whether culture can be owned, and if so, by whom. One nagging question remains: Why was it that an area so intent on erasing its violent image could not condone the circulation of a photograph of an unshackled Dillinger, but found it appropriate to have visitors execute strangers immediately upon their arrival? Does crime pay?

NOTES

1. An earlier version of this essay was presented at the Fourth Annual Museum Studies Symposium at Indiana University, 29 April 2000. I would like to thank Dror Wahrman, Jeff Wasserstrom, Amy Levin, and Jude Richter for their suggestions and comments.

2. The museum attributes this quotation to "an unnamed 1934 documentary film about John Dillinger."

3. Beginning in the late 1990s, the John Dillinger Museum was located inside the Lake County Convention and Visitors Bureau (LCCVB) in Hammond, Ind.

4. Speros Batistatos, interview with author, 7 January 2000.

5. Batistatos, interview with author.

6. Doug Kirby, Ken Smith, and Mike Wilkins, *The Roadside America Homepage*, www.roadsideamerica.com/tour/94day6.html (accessed 26 June 2006).

7. According to Batistatos, the Pinkston family wanted to dissolve and sell the collection immediately.

8. Batistatos, interview with author.

9. John Toland, *The Dillinger Days* (Cambridge, Mass.: Da Capo Press, 1995), quoted in Bob Hammel, "68 Years Later Dillinger Still an Era's Symbol," *Hoosier Times*, 21 July 2002.

10. "'Dillinger Days' Fest Rejected by Town," *[Louisville] Courier-Journal*, 12 January 2002 www.courier-journal.com/localnews/2002/01/12/ke011202s136837.
htm (accessed 28 August 2003).

11. In 1933, Dillinger shot and killed East Chicago Officer William O'Malley during his robbery of the local First National Bank branch. For more on law enforcement protests, see "Police Object to Dillinger Museum," *Chicago Sun-Times*, 8 May 1998.

12. For more information, see for instance, the GARY 2000 economic development and urban renewal initiative on the Gary, Indiana, municipal website, www.gary.in.us/gary2000.asp (accessed 28 August 2003). This initiative was part of President Bill Clinton's nationwide Millennium Communities project designed to encourage cities to preserve their municipal histories and their arts and humanities programs. For additional information, see *America's Millennium: Communities, Programs, Partners* (Washington, D.C.: White House Millennium Council, 1999).

13. Shawn Platt, interview with author, 7 January 2000.

14. "Dillinger Should Be Escorted All the Way Out of Visitor Center," *[Gary] Post-Tribune*, 10 July 1998.

15. "Dillinger Should Be Escorted All the Way Out of Visitor Center."

16. Rich Bird, "Crown Point, IN, March 3, 1933," *[Munster] Times*, 7 February 2002, www.thetimesonline.com/dillinger/crownpoint.html (accessed 28 August 2003).

17. Rich Bird, "Sheriff Holley: Politics Fueled Dillinger Breakout," *[Munster] Times*, 11 October 1998.

18. The Hospitality, Sales and Marketing Association International (HSMAI) is an international association of marketing and sales professionals.

19. Lake County Convention and Visitors Bureau, "Dillinger Museum Opens in Lake County, Indiana: Illustrates Crime Does Not Pay" (Undated LCCVB Press Release given to the author by Shawn Platt, 7 January 2000).

20. Platt, interview with author.

21. Bird, "Sheriff Holley."

22. Platt, interview with author.

23. A discussion of the semiotic shift that occurs when the gangster slang of rural, predominantly white 1930s America is inserted into the urban diversity of twenty-first-century Gary lies outside the scope of this essay. However, the "gangster rap" with which many of the museum's contemporary visitors were familiar was decidedly different and merits further discussion elsewhere.

24. Michel Foucault, "Torture," in *Discipline and Punish: The Birth of the Prison*, trans. Alan Sheridan (New York: Vintage Books, 1979), 3–72.

25. Benedict Anderson, *Imagined Communities: Reflections on the Origin and Spread of Nationalism* (London: Verso, 1983).

26. Tony Bennett, *The Birth of the Museum* (New York: Routledge, 1995), 28; Anderson, *Imagined Communities.*

27. For more on this see, for instance, the narratives offered in G. Russell Girandin, *Dillinger: the Untold Story* (Bloomington: Indiana University Press, 1994), and Toland, *The Dillinger Days.*

28. Harriet Baskas, "Museum Honoring Dillinger Faces Roadblock," *All Things Considered,* National Public Radio, 30 May 2006. For earlier coverage of the controversy, see "Dillinger Relative Wins Suit over Rights," *[Bloomington] Herald-Times*, 9 November 2002. Scalf was thwarted in his own attempts to profit from his famous relative when the Mooresville Town Council rejected his proposal that the city initiate an annual festival called "Dillinger Days" to celebrate its infamous son ("'Dillinger Days' Fest Rejected by Town").

IV

MUSEUMS AT RISK

Changing Publics

Every so often, those attuned to museums hear of an institution being closed. Occasionally, these closures are due to legal disputes involving legacies or heirs, as with the John Dillinger Museum in Indiana or the Terra Museum in Chicago. There is also a long history of museums going bankrupt, such as the famous Peale family museum of the nineteenth century. Still other institutions appear simply to be too esoteric, for instance, the National Coin-Op and Video Game Museum in St. Louis, or they become too dependent on the labor of a single person, such as the former Museum of Menstruation. The defunct Continental Sculpture Hall in Portis, Kansas, described in Elizabeth Vallance's chapter of this book, is one example of a museum that fell under both of these categories. More recently, museums have had to decide whether to continue after losing major parts of their collections as a result of Native American Graves Protection and Repatriation Act (NAGPRA) policies. In Huebner's terms, these museums "technically" failed—they did not work as intended, and from their closing we may "scientifically" learn something of how museums work, as well as about how they teach.

In comparison to the number of museums that close, however, an even larger number of small, specialized, or local institutions struggle for long periods of time for a combination of reasons, including not only financial hardship but also changing audiences. Some museums, like the one at Dickson Mounds in the next chapter, are able to reconstitute themselves; others, like the Fick collection in the same chapter, retain a certain fascination, but for limited audiences. The museums discussed in this section of the book are evidence that we can learn as much about America from museums whose scope is reduced as from those that thrive, from those whose methodology is somewhat out of date as from those that use cutting-edge technology. Moreover, such museums pose a variety of interesting questions focusing on the third element in Schwab's commonplaces—the students or audience. For example, why do these particular kinds of museums lose some of their audience appeal? Why do other museums maintain their appeal? What does the fate of such museums reveal about Americans' appreciation for the past?

The previous three chapters of this volume focused on museums whose narratives for visitors were structured by a particular kind of nostalgia. The institutions examined in this section of the text also evoke feelings for the past, not only for the history of their subjects, but also for previous incarnations of the museums being discussed. In "The Politics of Prehistory: Conflict and Resolution at Dickson Mounds Museum," Donna Langford discusses the history of a collection consisting largely of human remains that was amassed by a chiropractor in Illinois. Langford illustrates how prehistory can be used to forward more contemporary political agendas, tracing the story of conflicting claims to ownership of the Dickson Mound remains. Initially, the Dickson family claimed ownership of the site and gained a certain cultural capital from the private museum. When the site shifted to state control, it continued to be a source of local pride, even though the objects were displayed and maintained poorly. In the 1980s, Native Americans contested the ownership of the remains, and a struggle erupted when the governor attempted to close the site to placate Native Americans, only to be met with protests from regional residents. With the passage of the Native American Graves Protection and Repatriation Act (NAGPRA) in 1990, a compromise was reached, allowing scientists to study the remains before they were reburied. The current museum displays objects that do not fall under NAGPRA restrictions and shows more cultural sensitivity to Native Americans, including them in exhibition planning and special events. Native Americans are no longer exoticized as primitives, but are brought into contemporaneousness. According to Langford, another effective museum strategy has been "diminishing the interpretative authority of the museum staff and expanding that of community members and other contributors," thus keeping the museum as a center for all local constituencies.

Langford briefly discusses the Fick Fossil and History Museum in Oakley, Kansas, as a contrast to the site in Illinois. The Fick has not had to transform itself with the passage of NAGPRA because its antiquities are primarily animal fossils. Yet the Oakley museum faces some of the same issues relating to professionalism faced by Dickson Mounds. The museum has been a source of local pride, its founders claiming that the institution maintains its popular appeal by deliberately not embracing more current museum theories or scientific techniques. The museum remains almost stubbornly quirky, a large part of its collection consisting of art works created out of shells and fossils by one of its founders. In the end, this institution remains at risk not because of larger national policies and changes, but because it is defined so thoroughly in terms of its founders and their collections.

The museums in the following two chapters have other features in common with the Fick Fossil and History Museum; their collections are tremendously varied but of limited interest to the general public, the curators have made little formal effort to interpret objects in labels or other signage, and their displays are partly composed of fragments or pieces of items. Members of the public accustomed to multimedia might find such institutions charming but somewhat outdated; in fact, these miscellanies take on certain qualities of modernism and postmodernism with their alternate emphases on an encyclopedic scope and collections of fragments, on the importance of objects themselves and their dislocation from a more coherent past. In these chapters, readers will learn about two very different institutions of this kind—the museums of the Daughters of the Utah Pioneers (DUP) and the National Museum of Health and Medicine (formerly the Army Medical Museum) in Washington, D.C. Thus, this section of the book will focus on museums that are or have been at risk because they have been caught in the public's changing expectations of museums.

The DUP museums in Utah are also seemingly without accession policies, accepting almost any donation from members. A DUP museum might therefore display a hundred quilts rather than ten of its best fabric works. Each work is accompanied by a simple note describing its date and provenance, but no information about quilting techniques. A donor may be pleased to see her grandmother's work on display, and a quilt expert might enjoy the variety, but someone seeking to learn to appreciate the various kinds and qualities of coverlets might be daunted. DUP museums retain their fascinating mélanges of materials to please donors; at the same time, their display techniques reflect their reliance on volunteers rather than professionals and their limited funds. Once prominent across the state of Utah, DUP museums are facing difficulties as older generations of volunteers retire and younger people show less interest in volunteering for or visiting the collections. In terms of curriculum theory, the DUP museums' collections may be aesthetically chaotic, resulting in inconsistent lessons. While Langford offers the Fick Museum as a contrast to Dickson Mounds, Embry and Nelson set the DUP museums in contradistinction to the larger Mormon church museum in Salt Lake City, which has adopted multimedia and other current technologies to maintain its appeal.

In contrast, Michael Rhode and James Connor illustrate how the National Museum of Health and Medicine was intended for national prominence in the nineteenth century, when it grew from a small research collection into an institution on the National Mall in Washington. However, curators' growing interests in pathological specimens rendered the museum increasingly specialized, and even though the institution was visible at the great Columbian Exposition, its public appeal diminished until it was moved from the Mall to Walter Reed Army Base, where the public can gain only limited access to portions of the collection. Like the DUP exhibitions and the Fick collection, the medical museum has come to represent a kind of modernism with its emphasis on fragments largely without interpretation, which contrast with the broader collecting scope of the institution. Contemporary medical technology is rapidly superseding the collections of pathological specimens as well, so that the medical museum is disconnected in some ways from its former mission.

To some extent, the Fick, the DUP museums and the National Museum of Health and Medicine have chosen to retain the apparently antiquated nature of their displays. Yet ironically, one could argue that in doing so, these institutions counter the narratives offered by other museums in a way that emphasizes modern and postmodern orthodoxies. In particular, the emphasis on fragmentation found also at Dickson Mounds, with scraps of materials as well as complete objects, reflects a kind of modernism. The labels convey a partial and subjective knowledge of objects. That these seemingly "unhip" sites reflect more contemporary concerns will be especially evident when we move to the discussion of the New York Freakatorium and City Museum, St. Louis, in the next section. Significantly, the latter two collections and other new sites are choosing to return to tactics used by early American museums, ones that might contradict more hegemonic discourses created by traditional museum elites.

9

The Politics of Prehistory

Conflict and Resolution at Dickson Mounds Museum

DONNA LANGFORD

Readers who have stopped at roadside museums and ventured into the historic society collections in small towns will no doubt have encountered a variety of ancient objects—Boy Scouts' arrowhead displays; eminent citizens' fossil collections; prehistoric Native American pot shards and occasional human remains; and dusty dinosaur bones. A quick web search yields listings for dozens of museums dedicated to fossils or Native American prehistoric objects. Like many other small museums, these collections exist primarily to serve tourists, and are not intended as centers for scholarly research. For example, a statement of facts about the Dakota Dinosaur Museum begins, "The mission of the Dakota Dinosaur Museum is to promote tourism by providing a facility for preservation and display of geological and paleontological specimens for public review and education."[1] The Langenrich Museum of Paleontology in New York State sells fossils and meteorites, combining commerce with exhibition. Still others combine historical and archeological instruction and research.

The recent repatriation of many such museums' holdings in human remains and associated funerary objects to Native American tribes has become controversial due to divergent ethical or moral principles among the various cultural groups involved. Conflicts between Native Americans and non-Native archaeologists revolve around resource definition as well as object ownership, significance, and use. According to J. C. Winter, "Cultural resource laws and policies contribute to this conflict with their failure to address Indian values."[2] The objections of Native Americans to professional archaeology are based on "spiritual, legal, moral, historical, political, and ethnic beliefs."[3] The objections include "1) The disrespectful treatment of burials; 2) The implied attitude that Indians are laboratory specimens; 3) The failure of anthropologists to consult Indians concerning the design and execution of research; 4) The 'looting' of Indian heritage properties by archaeologists."[4] The "disrespectful" attitude of archaeologists towards burials is often due to misunderstandings of Native American practices and spiritual beliefs. These "beliefs range from disregard of the mortal remains to a belief that the spirit or soul is tied to these remains as long as there is any physical integrity."[5] Some Native Americans also believe that disinterring human remains interrupts the spiritual journey of the deceased and affects the living descendants. The Navajo, Apache, and Pawnee "believe that anyone who disrupts a grave . . . plans to use the dead as a means of harming the living."[6]

The opinions of archaeologists and museum officials regarding repatriation conflict with many of these Native American views. Their opinions range from the view that all collections should be preserved in museums to avoiding excavation whenever possible and thereby preventing conflicts.[7] An inclusive perspective is derived from consulting with appropriate groups before conducting the research.

The controversies surrounding the Dickson Mounds Museum in Fulton County, Illinois, between 1980 and 1992 serve as an excellent example of the problems generated by repatriation and the possible solutions that may ensue. These disagreements also ultimately forced the museum to redefine its audience (or students) in a more inclusive manner. Conflict at Dickson Mounds focused on the skeletal remains of 248 individuals on public display, with archeologists and Native Americans representing the various views described above. Resolution came in the form of compromise, with the museum being transformed from a display of curiosities to an institution providing scholarly exhibits that respect the native cultures they interpret.

Originally, the Dickson family farm included a grouping of two Native American cemeteries and ten mounds surrounding a low mound that may have been the base for a building used for ceremonies. These mounds were used by the Late Woodland and Mississippian cultures. The terms *Late Woodland* and *Mississippian* refer to archaeological chronology based on adaptive shifts towards more efficiently using woodland environments.[8] The Mississippian tradition grew out of the Late Woodland with the people occupying Illinois about 1500 years ago.

Scientific excavation of Dickson Mounds began in 1927 when Dr. Don Dickson uncovered burials adjacent to his home. Dr. Dickson and his wife continued partial excavations of the skeletons until 1929, when 248 skeletons were exposed and left in their original positions for public viewing. Their intent was simply to display an archaeological excavation. The Dicksons were curating the remains to preserve and learn about past cultures and refute stereotypes about Native Americans that existed at that time. The unintentional use of irony appeared at this point during the history of the museum.

The general public viewed native cultures as primitive curiosities to be examined. Thus, the display drew many European Americans wanting to see different, exotic cultures. During the early twentieth century, European Americans thought of native people as interesting and nearing extinction. They flocked to see something out of the ordinary in Native exhibits. Native American groups were not consulted about the display, as it was not common practice in the late 1920s for museums to confer with native groups.

The Dicksons first covered the excavation area with a tent, then replaced it with a temporary wooden building, and finally constructed a permanent private museum directly over the burial mound. The Dicksons considered the structure their private museum because the family funded the excavation. Yet the word *private* also conveys the impression that the Dickson family owned the skeletal remains and had the authority to decide how the skeletons would be treated and displayed. Indeed, as J. C. Winter has indicated, European Americans have traditionally viewed cultural items as commodities "which can be bought, sold, demolished, used as visitor displays, or otherwise manipulated by our market economy."[9] This holds true for their own European heritage (for example, the trade in antiques) as well as for Native American items. Antiquities are also attractive to European Americans because they may be possessed and cannot be duplicated.

The act of constructing a building over the burial ground changed the site from a cemetery to a museum exhibit. The act of creating an exhibit involved the Dicksons as museum "professionals" deciding what was to be exhibited and how it was to be interpreted. In general, museums are seen as the "keepers of culture" and therefore as the voice of authority. Museum settings isolate objects, separating them from their natural habitat, enhancing their inherent qualities, and turning them into objects with increased visual interest.[10] And, as Elizabeth Vallance has shown, visitors consciously decide to visit museums with the expectation of learning. Thus the creation of an exhibit from the burial mound acted to separate the remains from their culture. The skeletal remains became "objects" to be seen and interpreted. This interpretational focus on the object gave the visitor a false sense of the culture the object came from in that only a part of the culture was being explained. The Dickson Mounds excavation also drew attention to the rich cultural history of west central Illinois, and interest in the excavations during the 1930s served as a catalyst to the archaeological community. The museum soon became a leader in the development of Illinois archaeology by establishing many field techniques and methodologies that became standards in modern archaeology. This established national and international ties to the academic community. Over the years, the museum became a part of the culture of west central Illinois. County residents had lived with the museum as part of the community, and it was a source of pride.

In 1945, the state of Illinois purchased the site, with Don Dickson and his family operating the museum as employees of the Illinois Department of Conservation. After Don Dickson's death in 1964, control of the site was transferred to the Illinois State Museum. The museum opened a new facility in 1972 and welcomed 161,000 visitors in the first year. The new three-story brick building also added to the irony taking place. The large imposing structure resembles a ziggurat, a native symbol. The building itself gave a silent message of being an authority on native cultures, even though Native Americans were not consulted in the process of developing exhibits.

By 1989, a visit to the museum let the visitor view a display of partially excavated human skeletons. The ceiling over the burials was covered with plastic, and buckets were placed among the skeletons to catch dripping water. The display was supported by a state institution, yet the attitude conveyed to visitors through the use of makeshift buckets was one of apathy. Directly below the banister on the walkway were museum flyers and candy wrappers that previous visitors had dropped. The wrappers suggested a shortage of resources to keep the exhibit clean. The few labels to interpret the display were located on the opposite wall, behind the viewer. This label placement did not encourage visitors to read the information, but rather to focus on the display itself, presenting a partial view of the culture with the visitor interpreting the objects on display. Other exhibits within the museum included a timeline of projectile points and stone artifacts in an attempt to describe the prehistoric cultures found at the site. Exhibits were arranged in rows of artifacts in chronological order with identifier labels using the technical jargon of archaeologists. The exhibits left visitors passive and included little interpretation of Native American life ways or interaction with viewers, making it difficult for viewers to obtain and retain information. Tours were self-guided, with little orientation at the entrance to the museum. This tour method gave the impression of a focus on the science of archaeology and the museum's role as a repository rather than on the learning needs of the visitor.

During the 1980s, the traditional European-American concept of ownership began to change. There are three basic alternatives to the concept of owning prehistory. The first is that cultural heritage belongs to everyone; it is "humanity's past."[11] A second alternative is that a certain group such as "indigenous peoples, scholars, collectors, museums, or nations" is the legal owner or repository for archeological data.[12] The third alternative is that the past cannot be possessed; as Sockbeson states, "one cannot own a human body but one can provide for the final disposition of human remains."[13]

Simultaneously, Native Americans were gaining a louder voice in the national political arena and were protesting the treatment of their mortuary complexes. Specifically, the large number of burials on display served to place the Dickson Mounds Museum at the forefront of the controversy regarding ownership. The exhibit became an example and means of gaining media attention for Native American groups. By 1989, museum officials had also become sensitive to Native American issues, and the Illinois State Museum management suggested to Governor Thompson that the burial display be closed. The governor agreed with this suggestion, but reversed his position in 1990 due to public pressure.

Native American groups from outside Fulton County began to hold protests at the museum building during 1989 and 1990. While the Native Americans were voicing their opinion that the excavation be closed to public viewing, many others wanted the excavation to remain open. When the media announced that the exhibit would be closed, local residents, who were mainly uninformed about repatriation issues, did not understand the reasons for this loss to their community. The exhibit had drawn large numbers of tourists to the area, boosting the local economy. Protesters and police officers began to replace visitors at the museum, and the museum staff began to have difficulty implementing their educational programs.

The Native American Graves Protection and Repatriation Act (NAGPRA) passed on November 16, 1990, which served to give further support to the Native American claims. This act regards the past as something that can be owned and gives the first priority of ownership of human and cultural remains to lineal descendants. After many debates, then-Governor Edgar, through his special assistant Allen Grobell, met with Native Americans, residents of Fulton County, and the Dickson Mounds Museum staff to work out a compromise. The compromise entailed the entombment of the remains after physical studies were conducted. Measurement, photographic, age, and gender data collected from skeletal remains during these physical studies could reveal a wealth of information regarding disease, diet, workloads, and life expectancy among the early Native Americans. Archaeology could also provide clues about belief systems, housing, and movement patterns. Native American groups agreed to this collection of archaeological data prior to entombment in order to learn more about their cultural past. The Illinois State Museum and Dickson Mounds staff invited Native Americans to the discussions, giving them a voice in the decisions. They gained power and the chance to determine how Native Americans would be portrayed within the museum context.

In 1991, Governor Edgar announced that the burial display would be closed and that new exhibits would be developed to replace it. During the week prior to the April 1992 closing, 15,000 people visited the display; 3,500 visited on the last day alone. The museum received $4 million from the state of Illinois to develop new exhibits and programs before it closed for renovations in 1993. Alan D. Harn summarized, "Museum renovation began in September . . . after final mapping and photographic records of the burial site were completed and detailed measurements and physical studies were made of the skeletal remains."[14] The process of data collection transformed the skeletal remains from objects to be viewed to individuals belonging to an ancient culture. The remains gained a voice through the data. This ancient voice revealed information that was used to develop diorama exhibits, contributing to a sense of realism within the new displays.

The museum reopened on September 14, 1994, with new exhibits that addressed many sensitive Native American issues and expanded educational programming. The ethical rationale for educational programming changed to include sensitivity to the variety of ways people learn, resulting in a shift in focus from an archaeological repository to an educational methodology emphasizing visitor needs. Large visual graphics and repetition were added to exhibits and educational programs to enhance learning. According to Julie Barr, education coordinator, "Today, almost all of the programs include some type of audiovisual and verbal interpretation, things to touch, things to create and take home, occasionally, things to plant or read. Our programs are often themed festivals that feature performances, living history reenactments, craft demonstrations, food, guest experts, and private workshop instruction."[15] Another new focus of the museum is to illustrate how information is gained through archaeology as well as ethnology and oral history. Information on how knowledge about Native American cultures was obtained was also added to the exhibits, diminishing the interpretative authority of the museum staff and expanding that of community members and other contributors.

The museum's reopening marked the end of the transformation from a small display of curiosities to a professional museum. The viewpoints of the museum staff were also transformed and now continue to reflect a middle ground. As at the Heye Center for the American Indian discussed in the penultimate chapter of this book, staff work to consult Native American groups and to be sensitive to their beliefs. Native Americans are invited to be part of the exhibit planning process. A Native American voice in the exhibits adds to the voice of authority and serves to make a connection with visitors by humanizing the exhibits. Scholars with expertise in prehistory and Native American cultural traditions are also asked to contribute to exhibits and program development.

Since 1998, the burial area has been covered and is no longer accessible to the public. The first floor now contains a desk where visitors are welcomed and oriented to the layout of the exhibits; the Discovery Center with interactive activities for all ages; a resource center to give visitors the opportunity for research; the museum gift shop; and an exhibit gallery. Increased orientation projects professionalism and reflects the shift to respecting visitor needs for education to take place.

The newly added Discovery Center includes a play landscape that allows individuals of all ages to build towns and decide how to use the environment. Discussion is sparked as the environment is developed. Reproductions of ancient toys and symbols as well as animal pelts and tracks are available to be handled for sensory learning. A photographic exhibit, "Dickson Mounds Museum Exhibit," describes how the museum developed and changed through its seventy years of existence. Brochures from the early years of the museum show how people were encouraged to visit the museum, with skeletons as the main attraction. Including these early forms of publicity in the exhibit illustrates how opinions of the exhibitors have changed over time. Today's visitors are able to see the voice of authority in the context of the 1920s and contrast that with today's voice that can be seen throughout the rest of the museum.

The second floor contains an extensive exhibit that illustrates the sequence of Native American cultures from the earliest known to today. Life-size dioramas and interactive displays communicate the information and explore how it was obtained. A sense of greater realism is now present in the exhibits due to the use of data collected from the remains as well as consultation with Native Americans. One exhibit explaining the science of archaeology follows the progression from excavation through interpretation and research to a final display, demystifying the exhibit process and adding support to the museum as the voice of authority. The museum focus has expanded to explore more fully the rich archaeology of the region and include other cultural traditions that exist nearby. The exhibits now provide a wider context for the Mississippian mounds at the museum site. An impressive light and sound show titled "Reflections on Three Worlds" is also located on the second floor. This presentation explores the three worlds of Mississippian belief "and illustrates how artifacts, ethnographies, and historic accounts of rituals can be used to interpret the lives of people of the past."[16] Native American symbols, music, voices, and carved images blend to interpret the Mississippians' worldview with no hint of temporal separation, merging the past with the present. The program stresses that ancient cultures were made up of people living in their cultures as all people have done throughout time. This is an attempt to transcend time and indicate that ancient people were really not that different from people today. The use of oral histories and ethnographies also serves to illustrate that knowledge can be obtained from a variety of sources.

This display uses modern technology to interpret the past and illustrates that methods other than science may be used to learn about the Native American worldview. The blending of time periods within the exhibit also serves to illustrate a goal of the museum—to help visitors remember the past in a way that transcends time. The way this exhibit collapses the past into individual memory resembles visitors' experiences at Williamsburg, which were discussed in the chapter by Gable and Handler.

The third floor exhibit includes a photo gallery of human interaction with nature in the Illinois River Valley, a video titled "Legacy," which describes the various cultures in the area throughout time, and an observation deck. The Illinois River Valley can be seen from the observation deck, and information panels point out various mounds in the area. Today all of the exhibitors are given a voice as well as a face and visitors are able to recognize the source of particular opinions about different periods in the museum's history. Another important change in the museum is a photographic display of contemporary Native American groups. This provides a link between the past and present, which in turn makes the prehistoric cultures seem less remote.

The museum also hosts special temporary exhibits on various Native American topics. Dickson Mounds provides space for artifacts from the Illinois State Museum, such as the "Pueblo Pottery of the American Southwest" exhibit. The opening for the Pueblo pottery exhibit was a weekend event that included a special guest, potter Barbara Gonzales, who talked about her family and craft. She conducted two workshops, one specifically for children and the other for adults, and she also provided a slide presentation on her pottery-making career. The use of speakers helped make the event a richer experience for visitors and showed the museum's efforts to enhance learning. The speaker was also a visual expert, adding support to the information that was being disseminated to the visitors. This display and the "Pole to Pole: The Arctic and Antarctic" exhibit broadened the scope of the museum by presenting information on Native American cultures outside of Illinois.

Each season at the museum offers a round of special activities. The events use demonstrations, performance art, and hands-on activities to provide entertainment along with education for visitors of all ages. A Choctaw Celebration presented by an extended family of the Choctaw Indian tribe took place on July 22, 2001, on the grounds of the museum. Visitors were able to participate in traditional dances, play stickball, and use a blow gun. Craft demonstrations and the serving of fry bread during the event allowed participants to use all of their senses. The use of Native American presenters offered yet another opportunity for the museum to authorize and give voice to the cultural source of its information. The site also sponsors bus tours to other museums, such as Chicago's Field Museum of Natural History, to view exhibits not available in west central Illinois and to promote lifelong learning. Temporary exhibits and other special activities promote repeat visits, which reinforce learning through multiple exposures to similar ideas presented in different ways.

The compromise at the museum quieted the controversy, changing the display from contested terrain to a forum, a place for reflection and learning. The floor plan of the reopened museum emphasizes this shift. The Resource Center near the entrance provides a quiet place for visitors to read and further learn about native cultures. A library of related sources and computer access to a variety of programs encourages visitors to ask questions and seek answers. The museum also encourages groups to use a 135-seat auditorium and a large meeting room to discuss a variety of topics. Learning is no longer static but dynamic and ongoing. The Museum Store reinforces the ideas presented within the museum's exhibits by providing another source for learning materials. Thus, by altering the setting, the museum was able to significantly improve its curriculum as well.

In contrast to the Dickson Mounds Museum, the staff of the Fick Fossil and History Museum in Oakley, Kansas, seems less preoccupied about visitor learning or Schwab's commonplaces than about pleasing its owners and entertaining tourists. The collection mingles fossils with miscellaneous nineteenth- and twentieth-century local history items, such as a replica of a sod house, photographs of pioneers, cattlemen's brands, a player piano, and art created by one of its owners out of shells and other items. Like Old Cowtown, the Fick seeks to inscribe itself in Western myth and history by touting its connections to Buffalo Bill and Wild Bill Hickock, and it retells the story of an Indian attack on a family of nine.[17] With its collection of miscellany, the museum tries in some ways to appeal to all tastes, but risks not satisfying anyone. Moreover, as much as the display seems to hark back to the antiquities collections of earlier eras, its composition of fragments and varied items yields an odd kind of modernism.

This miscellany gives visitors the flavor of local life in a way that no major national museum could. Its claim to uniqueness is also based on a folk art collection which "includes pieces created with fossils, rocks, and paper mache [sic] by Vi Fick."[18] Some pictures were made from fish vertebrae and shells. In a 1980 *Oakley Graphic* article reprinted on the Web, Mrs. Fick's creations are described in greater detail: "The fossils have a background of acrylic. Some others were painted with hot colored crayons. She used a sewing machine to make the rider and the sunset. The roosters in another work are flints used by the Indians. 'Earnie [her husband] posed for the head of a caveman,' she said pointing to the work on the wall, 'because cavemen had half a brain!'"[19] As evident from the quotation, the Fick, together with many museums like it, continues to conflate the prehistoric with the primitive, and the primitive with the Native American, presenting a dated and prejudicial portrait of minorities.

The folksy nature of this account is countered by reference to the contributions to the museum and local history of George Sternberg, whose discoveries are exhibited in a museum at Fort Hays State University, in Hays, Kansas. In this way, the interview and article on the Fick collection reveal the tension between the populist appeal of the exhibit and a desire to give it some scholarly authority. Mrs. Fick, for instance, describes how she and her husband studied "from a learner's book on fossils. As old as I am, I'm not going to learn Latin!" The town's involvement in providing a building for the museum bears neither the hallmarks of the development campaigns of major city museums nor the involvement and archeological expertise contributed by the state at Dickson Mounds. Yet, says Vi Fick, "Oakley came at the right time. . . . We had 2,000 people go through our home in the last four months we had the collection there."[20]

The Fick shows a central feature of such local museums: the desire to cater to popular tastes ("I'm not going to learn Latin!") but also to provide professional credibility. The Fick also demonstrates how a museum may play a critical role in establishing a distinguishing character for a locality, drawing tourists and other economic benefits to the area. It shows the intermingling of personal success and wealth with local governmental initiatives, and it reflects debates about the history and status of Native Americans. All of these features make the museum's approach to the prehistoric and what early collectors considered the "primitive" Native American cultures political in a way that might disturb many more than the politically inspired changes at Dickson Mounds. Even such quirky, small American museums are inextricably linked to politics and inevitably call into play Huebner's political rationale, in addition to an ethical rationale.

The Kansas museum's collection of fossils and private status does not appear to have drawn it into controversy regarding NAGPRA, even though its approach to displaying the past is idiosyncratic. The lack of conflict surrounding this institution did not force it to change or substantially reconsider its educational strategies. Dickson Mounds Museum, on the other hand, was able to resolve the conflict surrounding the burial display through a compromise with Native American groups which rendered the museum more inclusive. The compromise included allowing museum officials to study the skeletons and record as much as information as possible. In return, the museum entombed the skeletons in their original positions, changing the site back into a burial mound. Public access to the burials was denied out of respect for native cultures and beliefs. New exhibits were developed in collaboration with Native Americans to provide more accurate descriptions of ancient life ways, giving a richer, fuller picture of the cultures.

The Dickson Mounds Museum, therefore, shifted from a display of curiosities like the Fick to an archaeological collection whose purpose is to discover, preserve, and interpret the Native American cultures of Illinois. Even the role of archaeology was expanded to include other sources of information such as ethnology and oral history. As a whole, the Dickson Mounds museum fosters discussion, contemplation, education, and understanding. Through this successful resolution, the Dickson Mounds Museum has become an example of how museums created by European Americans can collaborate with Native Americans to satisfy their own needs and acknowledge the beliefs of different cultural groups. The museum continues to evolve in response to the changing community and offers an alternative to the less informative roadside museums of the past.

NOTES

1. "General Info" www.dakotadino.com/General_Info.htm (accessed 27 June 2006).

2. J. C. Winter, "Indian Heritage Preservation and Archaeologists," *American Antiquity* 45, no. 1 (1980): 124.

3. J. Riding In, "Without Ethics and Morality: A Historical Overview of Imperial Archaeology and American Indians," *Arizona State Law Journal* 24 (1992): 25.

4. A. L. Cheek and B. L. Keel, "Value Conflicts in Oste-Archaeology," in *Ethics and Values In Archaeology*, ed. E. Green (New York: Free Press MAC, 1984), 195.

5. Cheek and Keel, "Value Conflicts in Oste-Archaeology," 195.

6. J. Riding In, "Without Ethics and Morality," 13.

7. C. W. Meighan, "Archaeology: Science or Sacrilege?" in *Ethics and Values in Archaeology*, ed. E. Green (New York: Free Press MAC, 1984), 212.

8. Brian M. Fagan, *Ancient North America: The Archaeology of a Continent* (New York: Thames & Hudson, 1995).

9. J. C. Winter, "Indian Heritage Preservation and Archaeologists," 124.

10. Svetlana Alpers, "The Museum as a Way of Seeing," in *Exhibiting Cultures: The Poetics and Politics of Museum Display*, ed. Ivan Karp and Steven Lavine (Washington, D.C.: Smithsonian Institution Press, 1991), 25.

11. Karen Warren, "Introduction: A Philosophical Perspective on the Ethics and Resolution of Cultural Property Issues," in *The Ethics of Collecting Property: Whose Culture? Whose Property?* ed. Phyllis Messenger (Albuquerque: University of New Mexico Press, 1999), 2nd ed., 3.

12. Warren, "Introduction," 3.

13. H. J. Sockbeson, "The Larsen Bay Repatriation Case and Common Errors of Anthropologists," in *Reckoning with the Dead: The Larsen Bay Repatriation Case and the Smithsonian Institution*, ed. T. L. Bray and T. W. Killion (Washington: Smithsonian Institution Press, 1994), 158.

14. Alan D. Harn, "Two Centuries of Development at Dickson Mounds," in *A New View of the Past* (Springfield, Ill.: Illinois State Museum, 1995), 14, adapted from *The Living Museum* 57, no. 1 (Spring 1995).

15. Julie Barr, "New Directions in Educational Programming at DMM," in *A New View of the Past* (Springfield, Ill.: Illinois State Museum, 1995), 6, adapted from *The Living Museum* 57, no. 1 (Spring 1995).

16. Barr, "New Directions in Educational Programming at DMM," 6.

17. "Fick Fossil and History Museum," www.artcom.com/Museums/nv/af/67748-12.htm (accessed 27 June 2006).

18. "About Fick Fossil Museum," http://discoveroakley.com/Document.aspx?id=1353 (accessed 27 June 2006).

19. Willie Mannebach, "How It All Started . . . In a Pasture," *The Oakley Graphic* 9 Sept. 1980, rpt. http://discoveroakley.com/Document.aspx?id=1353 (accessed 27 June 2006).

20. Mannebach, "How It All Started . . . In a Pasture."

10

"Such is Our Heritage"[1]

Daughters of Utah Pioneers Museums

JESSIE L. EMBRY AND MAURI LILJENQUIST NELSON[2]

Found throughout Utah and southeastern Idaho, local or county chapters of the Daughters of Utah Pioneers (DUP) sponsor museums to tell the story of the Mormons who came to Utah in the nineteenth century. The museums range from the one-room gallery in Castle Dale to the Pioneer Memorial Building in Salt Lake City, with three floors and an attached carriage house. Regardless of the size, though, most Daughters of Utah Pioneers museums' collections look much the same. The museums "preserve . . . relics of their [the Daughters of Utah Pioneers'] parents and their grandparents [so they can be] enjoyed by others."[3] They are filled with cases upon cases of pioneer treasures. It seems as if it would be impossible for them to have too many of the same artifacts, and their selection of items seems never to have included any consideration of aesthetic or other rationales. In this way, the museums are a far cry from the hands-on adventures of the Dillinger museum or the representative buildings at Old Cowtown. Instead, they resemble the earliest museums, the "curiosity cabinets" established during the Renaissance, where collectors displayed everything they had with little explanation.

In many other kinds of museums, this pattern of indiscriminate collecting continued throughout the nineteenth century but changed after World War II, when museum work became more professional. Those involved encouraged interpretation based on research and designed installations that included carefully selected objects with thematic text. Moreover, after World War II, long-entrenched ideas began to fall prey to a reordered worldview. Over the second half of the twentieth century, this questioning of norms grew into full-fledged relativism and skepticism. As historian Keith Jenkins explained, "The old meta-narratives no longer resonate with actuality and promise, coming to look incredible from late twentieth century skeptical perspectives."[4] Many of the other institutions discussed in this book, such as the House of the Seven Gables, are examples of museums that revised their structuring narratives.

In the latter half of the twentieth century, this postmodern trend of challenging authoritative positions and ideas led to an extreme situation where little or no authoritative foundation managed to survive. With regard to museums, these trends created a situation in which no one central focus was sufficient. Indeed, museums are now expected to present various perspectives, highlight unexplored topics, and do this in unique and innovative ways.[5]

The DUP museums have not followed more recent curatorial trends that led to the restructuring of many exhibits to highlight their educational goals or commonplaces by presenting carefully selected items with a well-ordered narrative. Yet by doing what they have always done, that is, exhibiting everything and leaving interpretation largely to the public, the DUP museums follow one postmodern theory—the idea that people visiting a museum, reading a journal or novel, or studying the past should be allowed to understand the experience within their own context and adapt the learning experience (limited by what is presented) to fit their own needs, regardless of others' interpretations. In this way, DUP relic halls follow current museum theories even more than the Daughters are aware. Some other museums have even returned to exhibiting everything they own, putting the DUP back in step with the times without ever changing.[6]

To show how Daughters of Utah Pioneers exhibits fit into the larger picture of local museums, this article will explain the history of the DUP and the religious pioneers that the DUP commemorate. After laying this groundwork, I will turn to the DUP's establishment of relic halls and examine their exhibits. Finally, the DUP relic halls will briefly be compared to the Church of Jesus Christ of Latter-day Saints (LDS or Mormon) Museum of Church History and Art in Salt Lake City. The latter museum tells the same stories as the DUP relic halls but offers more interpretation of exhibits through the use of recent museum technologies.

ORGANIZATION OF THE DAUGHTERS OF UTAH PIONEERS[7]

The Daughters of Utah Pioneers grew out of a celebration. In 1897 Utahans and the Mormon Church, following an Old Testament tradition, observed a jubilee, the fiftieth anniversary of the arrival of the Latter-day Saints in the Salt Lake Valley. The events impressed Annie Taylor Hyde, daughter of the third LDS church president, John Taylor, and Jane Ballantyne Taylor, so much that she wanted to do more. On April 11, 1901, she invited to her home a group of Mormon women whose names read like a who's who of Mormon history. Hyde told the forty-six women, "Ever since the pioneer jubilee I have felt deeply impressed with the importance and desirability of the children of the pioneers becoming associated together in some kind of an organization" for friendship and remembrance.[8]

Hyde's idea for an organization followed a pattern started at the end of the nineteenth century to honor forbears. As Americans entered the industrial age in the late 1800s, they started moving to cities and adopting new lifestyles. Searching for identity, they formed associations, many of which looked to the seemingly simpler days of the past.[9] These motivations, together with concerns unique to Utah, led to the establishment of Mormon hereditary societies.

There were also other issues besides preserving the memories of ancestors. Mormons' lifestyles changed dramatically near the end of the nineteenth century. The LDS church eliminated institutions and practices that had set them apart from other Americans. In 1890, for example, the LDS church discontinued the practice of polygamy. In 1896, Utah became a state, and Mormons became part of national political parties, no longer solidly voting along religious lines. Mining and other industries attracted non-Mormons to Utah. Mormons were no longer isolated, and they faced a future of closer interaction with the non-LDS world. They looked back to a time when the Mormon identity had been easily defined in an attempt to solidify their differences from others.

These Mormons shared the religious motivation that brought them to Utah, away from the persecution that they had experienced in the Midwest. The first pioneers who came with Brigham Young in 1847 were the ones Annie Taylor Hyde honored. So initially, potential members had to prove that they were related to those pioneers. Members voted on admitting them.[10] Over the years, there were organizational modifications. Early on, the DUP expanded its membership to descendants of those who came in before the railroad arrived in 1869.[11] According to the DUP Constitution and Bylaws, the organization's mission is "to perpetuate the names and achievements of the men, women, and children [who] were the pioneers" and to "teach . . . their descendants and the citizens of our country lessons of faith, courage, fortitude, and patriotism."[12] Local camps, county companies, and a central committee work together to meet the organization's objectives.

DUP camps hold monthly meetings directed by a captain. At these meetings, a member presents a history of one of her pioneer ancestors, and then another member gives a lesson on aspects of pioneer life. Since 1939, the DUP central committee has published a yearly volume containing the required lessons. A group of camps form a company. The first members, now known as the central committee, organized companies in Cache and Salt Lake counties, Utah, in 1907. According to a 1949 history, there were eighty-four companies throughout the United States and over seven hundred camps. As the DUP expanded, the organization changed its name from the Daughters of Utah Pioneers to the National Society of Daughters of Utah Pioneers and then to the International Society of Daughters of Utah Pioneers in 1994, as camps were established outside of the United States.

ROLE OF DUP RELICS, RELIC HALLS, AND MUSEUMS

The DUP camps and companies carry out their own programs and also support the central committee's plans. An important goal for all three groups is preserving and exhibiting relics. The early Utahans recognized the importance of saving the treasured pieces of pioneer life; in 1883, Phil Robinson, an English tourist, went to the southern Utah commune of Orderville and found that there was already a "rudimentary museum."[13] The DUP values such pioneer objects because, according to the national leaders, "These often-primitive belongings tell of the sacrifice and poverty, struggle and self-denial of these humble followers of the pioneer band." They continue, "The history of things is so inseparably interwoven with the history of men."[14] This is the philosophy of the eighty-six DUP museums, mostly in Utah, with a few in Idaho and Nevada by 2001.[15]

The first relic halls were often cabins that the DUP saved from demolition and restored. Sometimes they were moved from private property to public parks or LDS church grounds for use as DUP museums. The LDS church donated or leased for a minimal charge buildings that it no longer needed. These included buildings used to store donations in-kind (called tithing offices), granaries, or small meeting halls used by the women's organization, the Relief Society. Sometimes the DUP used abandoned schools, courthouses, and city halls that local governments donated. When no building was available, the

DUP occasionally built a log cabin similar to those used by the pioneers. Regardless of the building type, the relic hall frequently served as a place for the monthly meetings as well as a home for artifacts.

Because the surplus buildings were on valuable property, the LDS church or a government agency often asked the DUP to move relic halls, and the buildings were demolished. In the interim, relics were sometimes stored in a member's home, or the government or LDS church provided temporary storage. At other times, the artifacts continued to be on display, but in a public building. The arrangement varied in every community.

The central committee's relic hall in Salt Lake City followed the transient pattern of many other museums. The DUP central committee started collecting and exhibiting relics in 1903. During her three years as DUP president, Susa Young Gates, Brigham Young's daughter, started a relic department and placed the first pioneer artifacts in a yellow bookcase that Brigham Young used. The display was in the LDS church tithing office. When the Daughters outgrew that space, they moved their relics to the Lion House, Brigham Young's former home.

By 1911, the DUP shared exhibit space with the Deseret Museum in the Vermont Building in Salt Lake City. The latter museum was formed as a private institution in 1869, but the LDS church assumed control of it in 1878. In 1915 the DUP and the Deseret Museum moved to the LDS church's Temple Square. But the DUP did not consider itself a part of the Mormon church and wanted state support. It asked for assistance, and in 1919 the state provided space to the DUP in the two-year-old state capitol building for an office, exhibits, and a small gift counter.[16]

The DUP central committee's dream was to have a museum building of its own. Flora H. Horne, who was custodian of the relics when they were in the Vermont Building, explained, "We pictured a magnificent building that . . . feature[d] our Utah history." Horne expressed this concern at a party in 1911 and requested donations, which began to flow in. In 1921, the state legislature authorized the governor to appoint a committee "to investigate and report regarding the provisions of a suitable place for the preservation and housing of relics, documents, etc." about Utah which would also house the DUP relics. Two years later, the committee recommended that the legislature select a site on Capitol Hill for such a building.[17]

In 1936, the DUP formed its own committee, appointing Cornelia S. Lund, then president, the lifetime chair of the memorial building committee. The

DUP women decided that they wanted a triangular piece of property at the top of Main Street in Salt Lake City, directly across from the capitol building. The committee expressed that desire to Utah Governor Henry H. Blood.[18] In 1941, the DUP's lobbying paid off—the legislature agreed to lease the property to the DUP for a nominal charge.[19] The Daughters worked with architects and designed a Grecian-style building complete with columns, modeled after the demolished pioneer Salt Lake Theater.

The DUP hoped to have the building completed for the Pioneer Centennial in 1947. However, that goal was impossible to meet. World War II stopped all construction. Then neighborhood residents sued, claiming that the state was supporting a religious organization. The case went to the Utah Supreme Court and the U.S. Supreme Court before the DUP won, after proving that the women's organization was not part of the LDS church. With the passage of time, costs increased, and the DUP had to raise additional funds. After all these setbacks, the building was finally completed in October 1949, in time for a DUP national convention.[20]

Although the new building had three stories, DUP President Kate B. Carter worried that there was no place for the large pioneer transportation items. Carter talked with DUP member Saramarie Jensen Van Dyke of Tucson, Arizona, who told Carter that she would give her estate to the Daughters. Her money along with other donations from DUP members paid for a carriage house named in Van Dyke's honor, which was dedicated on October 6, 1973.[21]

New buildings for the central committee in 1950 and 1973 did not change the DUP's mission for its relic halls. Now the governing organization had room to display all its artifacts, just as smaller museums throughout Utah had always done. But the central committee needed more money, so the DUP asked businesses, local camps and companies, as well as individual families to fund exhibits. The businesses created replicas of their nineteenth-century counterparts. With this additional community funding and assistance, the central committee created more elaborate displays than the smaller museums that depended on donated space and volunteer time.

DUP MUSEUM POLICIES

DUP museum policies have changed little since they were first determined nearly one hundred years ago. In many ways, they reflect little or no attention to modern museum theory, updated conservation methods, or new exhibition techniques. As discussed earlier, the DUP does follow some new ideas such as exhibiting artifacts in an open storage format, but this is the case only because the DUP never changed the old format, not because they are attempting something new. While it may be tempting at first glance to condemn the DUP museums for falling behind the times in regard to museum theory, it is important to examine the reasons behind the DUP's choices in these matters. In the end, it may be that the DUP's decisions are those that best fit its goals, resources, and abilities.

The most significant policy of the DUP is that its museums are staffed by its members, who work as volunteers. This circumstance influences many other administrative decisions in the DUP museums. Staff members devote limited time to the museum. Their training is rarely formal. Most volunteers are older, and age restricts their activities. Their devotion and dedication are high; in Provo, some families have served for two generations. Consequently, rather than presenting a single narrative of the pioneer experience, the DUP wants to tell every pioneer story possible, and especially the stories of members' ancestors.

To meet that goal, DUP exhibits rarely change. An early flier for the Pioneer Memorial Museum reads almost identically to the one distributed by the museum today.[22] Both fliers describe the type of objects displayed on each floor, and except for objects added to the collection over time, there is no change in the type or placement of objects within the museum.[23] For example, when the Pioneer Memorial Museum opened, Union Pacific furnished a room that showed the coming of the railroad. Among other things, it housed a replica of the golden spike used to unite the railroad in 1869; this room remains unchanged today. ZCMI (Zion's Cooperative Mercantile Institution), a local store and the first department store in the United States, also furnished a room showing what a pioneer business looked like in the nineteenth century.[24] It, too, remains the same. In 1950, these rooms and similar ones showing a pioneer kitchen and bedroom were "modern cases."[25] Today these fifty-year-old exhibits appear dull and lifeless in comparison to recent displays that incorporate multimedia components, interactive elements, and innovative design concepts.

Most DUP galleries are filled with cases arranged by object type. For example, quilts and other bedding might fill one room, while rifles and pistols fill another. When I visited the Pioneer Memorial Museum, I was overwhelmed by the variety of artifacts on display and the number of examples of each type. It was almost impossible to look at them all. There was not just one quilt to look at; there were several cases and hundreds of examples of them.

The museum exhibits repetitive displays for several reasons. First, the DUP considers its own members its main audience and expects that members who have carefully done their genealogy and are familiar with their ancestors will appreciate seeing their particular family donations on display. The only labels included in the exhibits are the short, explanatory notes from the donors that accompanied the artifacts into the museum. Generally, these notes give the names of the original owners of the objects and sometimes brief explanations about the articles. These notes are helpful in locating family donations and provide some information to the general visitor but fail to create a larger understanding of the period, contemporary events, or the relevance of a given object to its surroundings.

While the exhibits described above seem to have little place among modern museum practices, they fit perfectly within the scope of a volunteer organization such as the DUP. For volunteers with little time or training, it is more feasible to make room for new objects than to design a new thematic presentation of the pioneer period, complete with interpretative text, specially designed cases, and carefully selected objects. As it is, the DUP museums do not even have to pay attention to a consistent label format over time, as volunteers simply place the handwritten note from the donor on top of the object in the case.

DUP museums are also affected by the organization's collecting policy. The DUP collects artifacts belonging to and related to pioneers who arrived in Utah between 1847, the year the first Mormons arrived in Salt Lake, and 1869, the year the railroad arrived in Utah. Accordingly, artifacts in these museums illustrate only the Mormon experience in Utah, ignoring Native Americans, other religious groups, and military personnel who were also part of Utah's early history, even though these are state galleries.

No one seems to question the museum's focus on Mormons. While Utahans attempt to be inclusive, inviting other religious groups and ethnic organizations to participate in the Pioneer Day parade on July 24, Mormons remain the central focus because they were the ones who came to the valley on that date. During the 2002 Winter Olympics in Salt Lake City, the organizers tried very hard to avoid perceptions that the event was the Mormon Olympics. Native Americans, for example, were involved in the Olympic planning and sponsored events. But there was also a pervasive feeling that Mormonism was an important part of Utah culture, and history should not be ignored. Similarly, Mormons continue to be honored in the DUP museums.

Few Utahans today are aware of the connection between the state and the DUP. Many not directly involved with the DUP perceive the organization as Mormon, and indeed, most members are Latter-day Saints.

Nearly all DUP artifacts are Mormon related. Especially honored are objects associated with Mormon pioneer leaders such as Brigham Young. Just as Americans in general want to feel a connection to early leaders like George Washington, Mormons want to feel a bond with Young. The Pioneer Memorial Museum exhibits the wagon that Young rode in when he entered the Salt Lake Valley, his bathtub, and several display cases with his personal belongings. Artifacts of daily pioneer life, particularly those items that crossed the plains, are also an important part of the DUP's collecting effort and are more easily available than "big name" objects. As a result, all DUP museums own and display similar guns, dishes, clocks, and other household items, such as butter churns.

A final significant DUP policy pertains to conservation. For some time, the DUP has been aware of conservation problems within the collections. In 1950, when artifacts were transferred from the state capitol to the Pioneer Memorial Museum, some samplers were already so damaged by mice that they were not moved. As an adjunct to preservation activities, the DUP documents its collections carefully, often through lesson manuals, where artifacts are introduced through photographs, descriptions, and histories of donors and object provenance. The 1979 lesson manual, for example, included a discussion of samplers; black and white photographs of samplers at the museum; a description of what was on the samplers, such as the alphabet and sayings; and finally, a history of the women who made them.[26] Even though formal conservation training is limited among DUP members, the organization is taking steps to improve their abilities in this area; in the 1990s, the organization received a grant to train DUP members to care for artifacts. Thus, while the DUP's staffing, exhibition, collecting, and conservation policies stand out among museum policies at the beginning of the twenty-first century, they do provide a way for small museums to meet their goals while operating with limited resources and staff.

THE DUP AND NATIONAL MUSEUMS

The limited size and scope of DUP relic halls allow them to function in ways that larger, more mainstream museums cannot and enable them to avoid certain issues faced by modern museums. One such issue is interpretation. As we have seen in many of the previous chapters, history can be told from myriad perspectives; there are thousands of details and anecdotes that can be shared, and various segments of society will consider different aspects most important. The curator must sift through these numerous views and stories to select a few cohesive exhibition themes. This can be a difficult and controversial task. A classic example of this is the "Enola Gay" exhibition at the Smithsonian National Air and Space Museum in the 1990s. The exhibition was intended to provide a searching look at this important moment in U.S. history, but many Americans—particularly veterans' groups—protested against such a broad perspective. They believed that their deeds as members of the U.S. military should be honored by the government-sponsored institution and not called into question. In the end, the political power of such groups forced the museum to reduce the exhibition to a simple display of the "Enola Gay" to commemorate the anniversary. The display was offered without interpretative text or a contextual exhibition—a format reminiscent of DUP exhibits.

While it is questionable who was best served by this public outcry against and retreat from self-examination, it is true that the interpretative efforts of the Smithsonian curatorial staff created expensive and time-consuming problems for the museum and its public. By simply displaying artifacts, the DUP avoids the potential difficulties of overinterpretation and limits the possibilities of visitors misunderstanding the intent. It provides its public with the artifactual basis for learning and discussion but leaves the actual process up to others.

The LDS Museum of Church History and Art in Salt Lake City also focuses on early Mormon pioneers, but it addresses the topic in another manner. In the latter part of the twentieth century, the LDS church has placed emphasis on educating members and nonmembers about its history. These efforts have included a reformatted historical department, movies about early pioneers, and a modern museum to tell its history. The museum's permanent exhibition, "A Covenant Restored," was designed to teach members of the church about their history and also to be informative to non-Mormons.

Artifacts were chosen for the exhibition based on their ability to support the theme of a people who make covenants with the Lord. While the DUP museums group objects by category, the LDS church's exhibition hinges on an interpretative text created to tell its story or present its curriculum. The DUP wants people to leave knowing more about their particular ancestors or having a general appreciation for early pioneers. The LDS church wants people to leave with an understanding of why people become Latter-day Saints. According to Don L.

Enders, senior curator at the LDS museum, "We hope visitors discover that a combination of conversion, covenant, and community is the answer."[27]

These two museums have similar subjects but distinct missions. While the DUP has remained faithful to the "curiosity cabinet" method of exhibition, the LDS museum follows more modern, innovative trends. One example is the idea of putting "artifacts in an environmental setting" so visitors can "imagine the event."[28] At the LDS museum, the curatorial staff carefully selects a few suggestive objects from storage to illustrate a particular topic, organizing their displays so that objects may be "identified and set within categories of meaning . . . positioned and understood within their social . . . contexts."[29] The DUP museum, however, values artifact appreciation over historical comprehension and displays every example of each type of artifact. A visitor interested in historical chronology and development may need only a few items to help him or her understand the story of the Mormon pioneers. However, a visitor studying variations in nineteenth-century quilts will need to see every one available to conduct his or her research thoroughly. Thus the pedagogical strategies and curricula of the museums diverge.

In each museum, for example, visitors may see a wooden leg belonging to an early pioneer. In both institutions, the wooden leg represents disabled people. The DUP museum is content to let the leg's teaching value go at this level. Certain individuals will visit the museum and know from other sources that the leg belonged to John R. Moyle, superintendent of construction on the Salt Lake Temple, who made the leg for himself in 1876,[30] but the DUP does not accept responsibility for presenting this information alongside the artifact. Celebration of the artifact itself is sufficient. At the LDS museum, a wooden leg is accompanied by written text and a docent script that tell the story of Thomas David Evans, a pioneer who used this leg to walk across the plains while experiencing great pain so that his pregnant wife Priscilla could ride in the handcart.[31] The presentation of this artifact and the related story contribute to the LDS museum's stated goal of helping visitors to understand the story of a covenant people. The leg is a physical reminder of Evans's sacrifice to fulfill his promises to God and his wife.

In another example, both museums display items made in Utah that reflect the experiences of the pioneers after they arrived at their destination. Once in Utah, Brigham Young's goal was for the Mormons to become self-sufficient and independent of the outside world. For the early Latter-day Saints, planting gardens and fruit trees, tending irrigation ditches, and producing their own textiles and clothing were all part of their commitment to God. These tasks were as important, and sometimes more so, than attending services. The church museum displays examples from the cotton mission and the local silk industry to show how members took up the task of making these items as part of their covenant. There are examples of the silk cocoons and thread along with a silk quilt made by Anna Musser. In another area of the exhibition emphasizing covenants church members make at marriage, a silk wedding dress made in Payson, Utah, is on display.

The DUP museums also exhibit Utah silk, but the focus is on the objects themselves. There is no religious or historic context. In the Salt Lake Pioneer Memorial Museum, for example, there is a silk display with bottles of cocoons and materials used in making silk. There are small examples of finished products. Other DUP museums also show the silk industry in much the same way as the one in Salt Lake City. The silk items are separated from the cotton objects, and there is no attempt to tell the larger story about Brigham Young, textiles, and self-sufficiency.

In DUP museums, the value of visitors' experiences depends almost completely on the effort they devote to the visit. According to Gaynor Kavanagh, this setup allows visitors to "encounter and use museums on many different levels and access the meanings that best fit their own agenda."[32] It also becomes a more personal experience. Susan A. Crane, author of *Museums and Memory*, explains that "we go to museums to learn more about ourselves."[33]

Modern institutions like the LDS museum contend that personal identification with individual artifacts is still possible within the interpretative framework of their exhibitions, and that modern museums allow for both consistent educational and unique personal experiences. Built on the postmodern constructs of challenging norms and promoting new thought, modern museums are in essence educational institutions that present new ideas to the public in ways often more palatable than monographs and scholarly lectures. Historian Richard H. Kohn, a professor at the University of North Carolina at Chapel Hill and former chief of Air Force history, explains that the role of contemporary museums is to "stimulate viewer interest and evoke controversy; to educate as well as to commemorate."[34] While not necessarily controversial, the LDS museum follows this pattern in designing its exhibitions. It uses objects to tell the story of the Mormon pioneers and includes interpretative text that makes objects come alive. The wooden leg becomes a symbol of a man's love for his wife and the sacrifices he made to reach Utah. The silk exhibits honor the industry of the early pioneers while also educating the public about silk making and the economic plan Brigham Young used to govern his people. The LDS museum also hosts an exhibit of artifacts created by Native American members of the LDS church. This wide range of exhibits illustrates the broad context of the Mormon experience, while the exhibits are all expressions of the principal theme of the museum.

The LDS museum can do this because it has the support of a large financial organization. However, smaller institutions like the DUP museums that have to rely on donated space and time or limited financial resources have found it more and more difficult to adopt new technologies or even to stay afloat. In the 1980s, the DUP museum in American Fork, Utah, attempted to use contemporary museum methods, and the central committee cited it as a model for preserving and displaying relics in 1984.[35] A DUP lesson manual explained how other DUP museums could incorporate interpretative material into their exhibitions. It illustrated how the American Fork museum placed "a silk spinning reel, silkworm cocoons, raw silk fibers, processed silk fibers and a silk blouse" together with images of a mulberry tree, a woman using a silk reel, and a chart showing the life cycle of the silkworm to tell the story of the Utah silk industry. The manual explained that "labels can be added to give historical information such as reasons the industry was begun, who participated and other pertinent facts." With these additions, "the story of the silk industry in American Fork is told dramatically and effectively."[36] But this pattern did not expand or even continue in American Fork. When Gloria Scovil,[37] the museum's volunteer director, took a job with the LDS Museum of Church History and Art, the volunteers who replaced her returned to the typical DUP method of exhibiting everything.

Why did the American Fork museum return to its original exhibition methods, and why didn't other museums follow the pattern? One reason is membership. The DUP, like many other organizations formed in the late nineteenth and twentieth centuries, has a hard time attracting younger members. Younger people find it difficult to fit a monthly meeting into their busy schedules. It is even harder to donate time to the museums. The older members do their best to keep the museums open, but their energy is limited. Often, visitors are few, and many that do come want to see their ancestors' artifacts, and not general pioneer history. They are not so much interested in a structured curriculum or educational experience as in an opportunity to connect with aspects of their families' pasts. Labels are seen as parts of the donations, so they are not replaced by more professional signs. Many Daughters see no need to change. They feel the mission of the DUP is sufficiently fulfilled by their current work. As DUP members continue to age, it will become harder to staff the museums. Like other small and even larger historical museums, the DUP relic halls may eventually die out.

CONCLUSION

My great aunt Mary Ann Brown, a Utah pioneer, made a pair of stockings for my mother, Anna Elizabeth Coulson Embry. My mother and I donated the stockings to the DUP museum in Castle Dale, along with a 5″ x 8″ card telling my mother's story. The museum exhibits the card with the stockings, where they remain to be seen by relatives and other visitors.

Through similar personal donations, the DUP museums continue as they are, contributing much within their small sphere of intention and influence. Within today's museum community, there is more emphasis on improvements and contemporary technologies, but there should also be room for those local museums that choose to stay outside the mainstream. A variety of missions and ways of fulfilling those missions enhances the diversity of the contemporary museum world. And, according to postmodern theory, such diversity should be welcomed and appreciated for its contribution to the presentation of our past.

NOTES

1. Daughters of Utah Pioneers pamphlet, Cache Museum, Logan, Utah.

2. The "I" in this paper refers to Jessie Embry.

3. Daughters of Utah Pioneers, *An Introduction to the International Society Daughters of Utah Pioneers* [pamphlet] (Salt Lake City: The Pioneer Memorial Museum, n.d.).

4. Keith Jenkins, *Rethinking History* (London: Routledge, 1991), 63.

5. Gaynor Kavanagh, "Preface," in *Making Histories in Museums*, ed. Gaynor Kavanagh (London and New York: Leicester University Press, 1996), xi.

6. In about 1970, the National Museum of Popular Arts and Traditions in Paris returned to exhibiting everything in open storage. While the main exhibits focus on a theme, the basement is a study gallery where visitors can look at artifacts arranged by type. Other museums are moving toward open storage by providing access to the entire collection on computers.

7. The Daughters of Utah Pioneers organization has published a volume annually since 1939 with lessons for its members. The DUP uses the manuals and lessons to record its accomplishments and local history. The volumes were edited and largely written by Kate B.

Carter until 1976, when she passed away (when citing the early manuals, Carter's name has been listed as author if no other author was listed). The volumes were collected into sets published later: *Heart Throbs of the West, Treasures of Pioneer History, Our Pioneer Heritage, An Enduring Legacy*, and *Chronicles of Courage.*

8. Kate B. Carter, "Presidents of the Daughters of Utah Pioneers," *An Enduring Legacy* 1 (1978): 220.

9. Peggy Anderson, *The Daughters* (New York: St Martin's Press, 1974), 56.

10. Norma B. Winn and Emma R. Olsen, "Daughters of the Utah Pioneers Through the Years," *An Enduring Legacy* 12 (1989): 94.

11. Winn and Olsen, "Daughters of the Utah Pioneers Through the Years," 95–96. There is no record of why the DUP expanded membership eligibility to 1869. Perhaps it was to attract more members and because the DUP central committee judged train travel too modern a means of transportation for genuine pioneer immigrants.

12. Kate B. Carter, "Markers Placed by Daughters of Utah Pioneers," *An Enduring Legacy* 10 (1987): 293–94.

13. Phil Robinson, *Saints and Sinners* (New York: AMS Press, 1971), 231–32.

14. Kate B. Carter, "Museum Artifacts," *An Enduring Legacy* 3 (1980): 329.

15. Carma Wadley, "100 Years of Protecting the Past," *Deseret News*, 5 April 2001. In 1984, the DUP collected museum histories from many relic halls, but admitted that the list of museums was incomplete. After a careful examination of other DUP manuals and some personal knowledge, I identified seventy-five relic halls—sixty-nine in Utah, ten in Idaho, and one in Arizona. Not all of these museums have been in operation at the same time; some have been combined or eliminated.

16. Carter, "Presidents of the Daughters of Utah Pioneers," 227; Winn and Olsen, "Daughters of the Utah Pioneers Through the Years," 103. The decision to be a state organization was made in 1908. Susa Young Gates, then president of the organization, wanted the organization to be more closely connected with the Mormon church. According to historian James B. Allen, "[She] saw increasing secularization as a threat to [her] plans for [Mormon] temple work" (Quoted in James B. Allen and Jessie L. Embry, "'Provoking the Brethren to Good Works': Susa Young Gates, the Relief Society, and Genealogy," *BYU Studies* 31 [July 1991]:122–23). When the DUP refused to go along with Gates's suggestions, she resigned and continued her genealogy work within the Mormon Church's organization.

17. Carter, "The Daughters of Utah Pioneers," *Heart Throbs of the West* 10 (1949): 426.

18. Winn and Olsen, "Daughters of the Utah Pioneers Through the Years," 104.

19. Carter, "The Daughters of Utah Pioneers," 426–27.

20. Carter, "The Daughters of Utah Pioneers," 427–28; Winn and Olsen, "Daughters of the Utah Pioneers Through the Years," 107. While the DUP was not officially connected to the

Mormon Church, the membership was often the same as the church's Women's Relief Society. As a result, some Salt Lake City residents objected to the state helping with the DUP museum. Currently, women whose ancestors came to Utah prior to 1869 can become DUP members, and non-Mormons serve on the central committee (Wadley, "100 Years of Protecting the Past").

21. Carter, "The Pioneer Memorial Museum and Saramarie J. Van Dyke Carriage House," *An Enduring Legacy* 1 (1978): 341.

22. Advertising leaflet for the Pioneer Memorial Museum touting it as the "finest Relic Display in the West" is available at the L. Tom Perry Special Collections, Harold B. Lee Library, Brigham Young University, Provo, Utah.

23. In 1987, the Pioneer Memorial Museum had 200,000 artifacts and was still accepting contributions. Winn and Olsen, "Daughters of the Utah Pioneers Through the Years," 135.

24. Kate B. Carter, "Story of Pioneer Memorial Building and Museum," *Treasures of Pioneer History* 3 (1954): 478, 480.

25. Kavanagh, "Preface," xii. According to Kavanagh, "It was once believed that the juxtaposition of a few objects to make a 'Victorian bedroom' . . . would be sufficient," but in modern times, exhibits are "dazzling in the range of material and oral evidence presented."

26. Carter, "Old Samplers," *An Enduring Legacy* 2 (1979): 89–122.

27. Carter, "Old Samplers."

28. Carter, "Old Samplers."

29. Gaynor Kavanagh, "Making Histories, Making Memories," in *Making Histories in Museums*, 2, 6.

30. Wadley, "100 Years of Protecting the Past."

31. Mauri Liljenquist [Nelson], "Postmodern Philosophy and Its Influence on Modern Museum Theory and Development," *The Thetean: A Student Journal for Scholarly Historical Writing* 28 (1999): 89.

32. Kavanagh, "Preface," xi.

33. Susan Crane, *Museums and Memory* (Palo Alto: Stanford University Press, 2000), 12.

34. Richard H. Kohn, "History and the Culture Wars: The Case of the Smithsonian Institution's Enola Gay Exhibition," *Journal of American History* 82 (1995): 1047–48.

35. Kate B. Carter, "Preserving Pioneer Relics," *An Enduring Legacy* 7 (1984), 373–411.

36. Carter, "Preserving Pioneer Relics," 405.

37. Gloria Scovil Oral History, conducted by Mauri Liljenquist Nelson, 2001, Charles Redd Center for Western Studies, Brigham Young University, Provo, Utah.

11

"A Repository for Bottled Monsters and Medical Curiosities"

The Evolution of the Army Medical Museum

MICHAEL G. RHODE AND JAMES T. H. CONNOR[1]

Founded in 1862 as a Civil War research institute, the Army Medical Museum fast became an unparalleled repository of fluid-preserved and dry specimens, photographs, and case histories from ill and injured soldiers. From its inception, the museum's staff conducted research on surgical and medical problems facing the U.S. Army by collecting bones with gunshot injuries as well as diseased organs. In contrast to traditional medical or anatomical museums, which were usually formed by medical societies, schools, or private collectors and often maintained a local focus, the Army Medical Museum was designed to be a national institution, run by the federal government from the beginning. In particular, the museum's fourth curator, John Shaw Billings, is best remembered as the physician-librarian who, during his Washington period from 1865 to 1893, turned the library of the Surgeon General's Office into what would become the National Library of Medicine. In turn, the library has moved beyond collecting books to sponsoring digital human dissections with their Visible Human Project. From 1883 to 1893, Billings also headed the Army Medical Museum and continued to turn the limited military medical museum into a national one. In spite of his efforts, the Army Medical Museum was overshadowed by its library counterpart and outdated by medical developments; thus, it never truly became the national museum that Billings envisioned. Due to advances in medical knowledge such as Koch's germ theory and Roentgen's discovery of X-rays, parts of the collection became obsolete. The pace of medical knowledge began to grow more rapidly by the second half of the nineteenth century, and the museum was buffeted by this change. In the twentieth century, the concept of what the medical museum should be shifted, and it became a national pathology institute with a museum that occasionally was seen as a burden by the pathologists overseeing it. The museum's broad range of collecting narrowed as early as World War I when the study of microscopic tissue samples became the focus of the collection and the museum's rationales shifted again. Currently, the National Museum of Health and Medicine is a small division of the Armed Forces Institute of Pathology, which holds over two million pathological specimens. The museum is situated in Walter Reed Army Medical Center, far from the Smithsonian's museum complex.

The museum began out of practical medical necessities. In 1861, civil war broke out, and in May 1862, reformer Surgeon General William Hammond established the Army Medical Museum as the first federal medical research facility.[2] When it became obvious that the Union Army Medical Department would have to grow to cope with new demands, Hammond seized the opportunity to create the museum and staff it with like-minded Philadelphians.[3] The museum was quickly established as a research institution with open storage for displays. Filling it with collections and drawing conclusions from them came more slowly. Groups of gunshot-damaged bones, arranged by body part, filled shelves of exhibit cases like an array of books on a theme. Specimen labeling was minimal, though printed catalogues were provided for consultation. Labels were written in appropriate language for an audience of doctors; the exhibits were not driven by a narrative as they are in modern museums.

Although it was displayed to the public, the material collected by the museum during the Civil War was primarily used to produce the *Medical and Surgical History of the War of the Rebellion*.[4] This project defined the museum's public and professional outreach for almost two decades. The six-thousand-page, fifty-six pound *History* took twenty-three years to finish and was a systematic, statistical compilation of the types of injuries and diseases a military doctor could expect to treat. The project was assigned to museum curators Dr. John Hill Brinton,[5] Dr. J. J. Woodward, and George Otis. The specimens collected for the preparation of the history, whether shattered bones or diseased organs, were catalogued, studied, and publicly displayed. The books purchased in support of this research formed the foundation for the Surgeon General's Library.[6]

By 1866, less than a year after the war's conclusion, the museum had expanded its scope of collecting to "embrace the whole field of pathology."[7] Studies of the medicine and surgery of the Civil War continued, while research into other areas such as physical anthropology and photomicrography was undertaken. After President Lincoln's assassination, the government purchased and renovated Ford's Theatre as a home for the museum. The building also housed the Surgeon General's Library and the Records and Pension division of the Surgeon General's Office. The move to Ford's Theatre in December 1866 permitted the museum to expand its range of interests and open its larger new exhibit space more widely to the general public. Otis wrote to Dr. William Forwood, the surgeon at Fort Riley, Kansas, explaining the new situation, "We have . . . now an abundance of room and are anxious that the Medical Officers at distant posts should send us contributions of Indian weapons, and of specimens of comparative anatomy."[8] The museum would broaden its audience and become a public landmark.

At Ford's Theatre, the medical specimens, which included many anomalies and curiosities, fascinated both lay and professional visitors alike. No doubt part of the fascination lay in the innate morbid curiosity of seeing human remains, but the Civil War had just ended, and the displays of specimens from maimed soldiers from both sides led the museum to function as an unintentional national memorial. Soon after its move, the museum was described in *Appleton's Journal* in terms calculated to bring in thrill-seeking visitors:

> It is, indeed, not such a collection as the timid would care to visit at midnight, and alone. Fancy the pale moonlight lighting up with a bluish tinge, the blanched skeletons and grinning skulls—the same moon that saw, in many a case, the death-blow given, or the bullet pierce. . . . But in broad daylight, with the sun shining outside, and brightening up, with its tinge of life and activity, the tessellated floor, with the noise and traffic of the street outside, and the hum and murmur of numerous clerks and attendants inside, even those of timid proclivities do not then hesitate to inspect closely and with curiosity the objects which, twelve hours later, when the building is dark and deserted, they would scarce care to approach.[9]

Opened to the public on April 16, 1867, the museum drew around 6000 visitors by the end of the year. Mary Ames, writing a guidebook in 1874, felt, "It cannot fail to be one of the most absorbing spots on earth to the student of surgery or medicine; but to the unscientific mind, especially to one still aching with the memories of war, it must remain a museum of horrors. . . . The museum is a very interesting, but can never be a popular, place to visit."[10] The museum certainly appealed to morbid curiosity, but the wounds of the war were too recent for visitors to divorce the specimens on view from the maimed soldiers visible on the city's streets. In spite—or because of—Ames's concerns, by 1874, the number of monthly visitors sometimes reached more than 2600 people,[11] even though standard hours on weekdays were 10 a.m. to 3 p.m. and from 10 a.m. to 2 p.m. on Saturdays. The museum was well-known enough to be mentioned in Dr. S. Weir Mitchell's fictional story, "The Case of George Dedlow." Mitchell's Dedlow, who had lost both his legs during the war, was contacted by spirits during a séance. The spirits proved to be his amputated limbs, preserved in the Medical Museum: "A strange sense of wonder filled me, and, to the amazement of every one, I arose, and, staggering a little, walked across the room on limbs invisible to them or me. It was no wonder I staggered, for, as I briefly reflected, my legs had been nine months in the strongest alcohol."[12] Undoubtedly, readers of the story would have wished to visit the museum to look for Dedlow's (fictional) limbs. Like Hawthorne's House of the Seven Gables, the site became invested with meanings derived from contemporary popular literature that may have obscured some of the historical actuality of the displays.

With the surge in the museum's popularity, John Shaw Billings was the man most determined to make the Army Medical Museum into a *National* Medical Museum. In 1860, Billings graduated from the Medical College of Ohio in Cincinnati; when the Civil War began, he enlisted as a contract surgeon and eventually served at the front. In 1865, he was transferred to the Surgeon General's Office, where he would work for the next thirty years. Billings took over purchasing for the Surgeon General's Library from the Medical Museum staff in 1865 and was in charge of the library by 1867. The museum and library worked closely together, complementing each other, sharing staff and locations. As he would do at the museum, Billings rapidly increased the library's holdings. The library held about 2,200 books in 1865; by 1870, it had grown to 10,000 volumes.[13] He arranged, upgraded, and expanded the library's catalogue. These activities undoubtedly influenced his view of how the museum's collections should be built and arranged.

Recognizing Billings's abilities, in 1883 the Surgeon General placed him in charge of the newly merged Army Medical Museum and Library. Billings inherited an institution that had already enlarged its focus from collecting specimens of military medicine and surgery. Three initial collections (medical, surgical and microscopical) had been reorganized and increased with sections for pathological (replacing and subsuming medical and surgical), anatomical, and comparative anatomy specimens, as well as miscellaneous objects, such as instruments and equipment. Two provisional sections were devoted to pathology and anatomy and contained specimens contributed for diagnosis or donations that the museum did not intend to keep. Billings began increasing the museum's collections with the energy he had brought to building the library's holdings. In addition to collecting, Billings had the responsibility for running the museum, including exhibiting the collections and compiling a catalogue. By this time, Civil War research was winding down, with only one remaining volume of the *Surgical History* scheduled to appear, but other research, especially in anthropology, was undertaken at the museum.

Not only did Billings's systematic collecting practices develop the museum's comparative and human anatomy collections along with its anthropological ones, but these practices also demonstrate how Billings moved the museum into a more historical direction by collecting and exhibiting the material culture of medicine. Under Billings, the museum's collection policy was informed by American and European scientific and scholarly trends, yet linked to the research strengths (microscopy and photomicrography) of the Surgeon General's Office. Billings focused on human anatomy and embryology, pathology, numismatics, ethnography and physical anthropology, comparative anatomy, specimen preparation, and the development of the microscope. Towards the end of his tenure, he collected medical instruments and military artifacts, including equipment and supplies, especially those of foreign armies. These new collections were an attempt to build a national medical museum with an encyclopedic reach. Billings's conception of the museum collection was stated in *Medical News* in 1886:

1. To illustrate the effects, both immediate and remote, of wounds and of the diseases that prevailed in the Army.
2. To illustrate the work of the Army Medical Department; models of transportation of sick and wounded, and of hospitals; medical supplies; instruments; etc.
3. To illustrate human anatomy and pathology of both sexes and of all ages.
4. To illustrate the morphological basis of ethnological classification, more especially of the native races of America; including anthropometry and craniology.

5. To illustrate the latest methods and apparatus for biological investigations and the various methods of preparing and mounting specimens.[14]

Research continued to be conducted on these diverse museum collections.[15] Museum staff, especially Dr. William Gray, provided pathological diagnoses for army physicians, setting the stage for the eventual transformation of the Army Medical Museum into the Army Institute of Pathology and later, the Armed Forces Institute of Pathology.[16]

Billings approached collecting for the museum in the same aggressive and systematic way that he had expanded the library, making the collection current and independent of the increasingly irrelevant experiences of the Civil War. He asked for a large new exhibit space which would provide for expanded public appeal and showcase the growing changes and advances in medicine. He used his preexisting network of book dealers to acquire items from Europe. In the United States, he had a nationwide network of army posts staffed by medical colleagues who gathered material for the museum over two decades. Material from army posts, usually dealing with injuries and deaths to soldiers, but also items of anthropological, archaeological, or bacteriological interest, arrived at the museum daily. A typical donation in 1885 was of "a leg amputated for dry gangrene following ligation of the superficial femoral artery."[17] Material from Washington doctors also arrived regularly.[18] Often museum and library donations came in together, as when Dr. Samuel Francis donated a "model of a surgical table, an old fashioned syringe and a manuscript of Medical Notes of the year 1763."[19] The two institutions were growing together, but the library would far outstrip the museum.

Although most medical museums have a large collection of instruments, Billings did not collect these aggressively until late in his term. He occasionally bought pieces earlier,[20] especially if they were of foreign origin. He preferred to purchase historical pieces but acquired modern equipment through donations from their manufacturers or government agencies. He gladly accepted free objects from the World's Industrial and Cotton Centennial Exposition in New Orleans in 1885, including bone drainage tubes and Lister's catgut.[21] By 1894, Billings had begun actively buying new surgical instruments from companies like Tiemann or Kny.

Microscopy had been a key focus of the museum under Woodward, and Billings, too, continued supporting it. Dr. William Gray was the staff microscopist whose work was displayed in the museum, as Woodward's had been earlier.[22] In consultation with English microscopist John Mayall, Jr., Billings began to collect antique and contemporary microscopes in the 1880s. Mayall initially offered Billings eleven antique microscopes, which the latter purchased while noting that it would "exhaust the funds which are at my disposal in this direction. . . . It must be something very rare and extraordinary that will induce me to purchase any more microscopes [this fiscal year]."[23] Nevertheless, by 1888, 141 historic microscopes and 11,000 microscope slides were in the collection.[24]

Billings's initiative resulted in today's museum owning the most comprehensive microscope collection anywhere. While the microscope was the most important instrument for biomedical research, its history remains the province of amateur collectors and not professional historians of medicine or technology. Yet the specialized collection has allowed the museum to develop a niche, though it is not one that will necessarily draw large public audiences. Many of the collections inaugurated by Billings labor under this difficulty. Changes in medicine, especially medical research and education, as well as the popularization of museums as "edu-tainment" have lessened the importance of these types of collections.

In addition to microscopes, anatomical preparations of preserved human tissue, especially pertaining to surgery or pathology, were important to Billings, who eventually devoted a large amount of exhibit space to them. In 1885, he spent $500, one-tenth of his annual appropriation for the whole museum, on purchasing "a series of preparations to illustrate the surgical anatomy of the principal regions of the human body" by Dr. D. J. Cunningham of Trinity College, Dublin.[25] Foreshadowing the National Library of Medicine's Visible Human Project, Billings purchased a band saw in 1887, "to cut skulls and very fine sections of bones and frozen flesh for our museum." Billings began purposefully purchasing embryos in 1885, committing $250 to buying from Harvard biologists Alexander Agassiz and later, Charles Minot, "foetuses well advanced in development."[26] He also bought many new anatomical models, made either of wax or papier mache, complaining that those in the existing collection were "made 30 or 40 years ago and are cheap exaggerated specimens prepared to illustrate lectures."[27] Suppliers included European firms such as Baretta, Talrich, and the famed Auzoux, all of Paris.[28]

Comparative anatomy was a growing late-nineteenth-century field, driven by studies in evolutionary biology. In 1885, Billings came to an agreement to necropsy "carcasses of wild animals" received at the Smithsonian Institution across the street from the museum. Billings wrote to Smithsonian Secretary

Baird of his "desire to obtain specimens illustrating the embryology and development of these organs, regions, etc., in man himself, and their morphology in certain of the lower animals."[29] While Billings continued to collect comparative anatomy throughout his ten years, he became more discriminating in the acquisition of specimens. Eventually, he was seeking live specimens and specific organ systems from dead ones. A letter to biological supplier Henry Ward reads, "I want more than the skeletons; I want the entire animal . . . I want him alive. . . . I want a full series of hearts . . . I want embryos and foetuses . . . I want a series of joints."[30] Being conscious of avoiding any popular misconceptions of the museum's role in collecting either human or animal monstrosities or examples of abnormal development, he repeatedly rejected dead or improperly prepared specimens. In reply to an offer of a stuffed two-headed calf, Billings wrote, "It is the internal structure of such a monstrosity which makes it of interest to this institution; the stuffed specimen is of no special value, unless it is for a Dime Museum."[31] Such specimens with little scientific interest were collected by other museums. In fact, just such a creature resurfaced in this century's response to the Dime Museum, the New York Freakatorium discussed in the following section of this book.

The museum staff's long-standing interest in collecting anatomical specimens meant that it could easily embrace a broader interest in anatomy. Ethnography and anthropology were growing scientific fields, also relating to evolutionary biology, and the museum had a preexisting core of army officers in the West to draw on for donations. The museum reached an agreement with the Smithsonian Institution over its collection of American Indian material as early as 1869. The Smithsonian—at the time just one of the government's three major museums (namely Natural History, Agriculture, and Medical)—had proposed "an exchange of specimens which are now in possession of the Army Medical Museum, relative to Indian Archaeology and Anthropology, for specimens relative to human and comparative Anatomy in the Smithsonian Institution."[32] Billings renewed this exchange when he took over the museum.[33] The museum thus returned to being the main government collector of human remains, with a corresponding plan for anthropological research. In response to an offer of crania, Billings noted, "All the crania from the Smithsonian Institution are now being deposited in the Medical Museum, and it is intended to have them all carefully measured and to publish a catalogue."[34]

By 1887, the museum had purchased so many skeletal remains that they had set prices—$3 to $5 for skulls and $10 to $20 for skeletons.[35] Billings's interest in, and support of, anthropology research culminated in the museum's assumption of the failing Hemenway archeological expedition in Tempe, Arizona. In 1887, Washington Matthews and museum anatomist Dr. J. L. Wortman took over the excavation and preservation of the human remains. Billings had a second motive in attempting to secure these remains. He wrote to Wortman that he was "having urgent requests from European museums for Indian crania and skeletons for which interesting and valuable exchanges are offered, and it would be very advantageous to the Museum if we could accept some of the proposals."[36] These specimens were transferred to the Smithsonian, as were most of the nonpathological anthropology collections in the early twentieth century. The few remaining specimens that fall under NAGPRA are being returned.

Despite Billings's avid interest in collecting, he showed little desire to purchase military medical and surgical artifacts early in his tenure, which was ironic given the theme of the museum. A typical purchase was a set of stretchers and ambulance equipment from St. John Ambulance Association Stores Department of London in September 1884,[37] but such purchases were rare until the late 1880s. At that time, he began actively seeking equipment from foreign militaries. By the end of his tenure, he was collecting weapons, which had not been a focus of the museum. Billings wrote to the Assistant Surgeon General, "it seems to me that it would be well to obtain, if possible, specimens of the arms now in use."[38]

Billings also rarely collected dental material, probably because it was considered outside of medicine. However, shortly before retiring, he worked with the American Dental Association to have the museum become a repository for dental materials, thus beginning yet another new collection focus.[39] Billings did let some earlier collecting agendas fade, and he was never very interested in portrait or photographic collections. The museum's photographs of medical and surgical sections were allowed to fade, although he began a "New Series" of pathological pictures. Gray made photomicrographs to be exhibited in the museum, rather than for publication as Woodward had. Billings did not attempt to buy photograph collections although donations were accepted and placed in the "Contributed Photograph" collection. Portraits were found in both the library and museum, especially oil paintings, which were probably donated, because he generally preferred to use money for books.[40] *Materia medica* (botanical compounds and pharmaceuticals) was also out of the scope of his interests since the Smithsonian covered it, although pharmaceuticals used by the American and foreign armies were collected.[41] Memorialization, whether of medical men or the common soldier, remained an understated role of the museum. While Surgeon General Joseph Barnes stated explicitly in his introduction that the *Medical and Surgical History* was a memorial to wounded soldiers, the exhibits themselves did not entirely exemplify this viewpoint as they were arranged by body part and not by battle. One physical example of memorialization, however, is Billings's acceptance of the hat, dress coat, and sword of Assistant Surgeon George Lord, who was killed at the Battle of Little Big Horn in 1876, the Army's most infamous loss in the Indian Wars.[42]

For a time, the museum did in fact have a national scope. Congress provided land and money for a building in 1885. In 1887, the museum and library moved to their new home on the National Mall near the Smithsonian Castle, which enabled the two organizations to work even more closely together. The building was four stories tall and roughly H-shaped. In the two wings were large halls: one for the museum and one for the library.[43] Billings supervised the move of the museum and library to their new building.[44] When planning for the move, Billings expected the library to occupy 160 wagonloads, and the museum 150, to be moved at a rate of 8 loads per day.[45] Billings used the larger space to expand the collection and looked specifically to obtain "specimens to illustrate the methods of work of the best anatomists, physiologists and pathologists of Europe."[46] He had the Surgeon General issue to army doctors an extensive wish list with twenty-four categories including "abnormities" [sic] and "deformities."[47]

During this phase, the museum reworked its organizational system to be consistent with its goal of being a major national collection. With Washington Matthews, Billings designed a classification and exhibition system for the museum based largely on Billings's system for the library.[48] He had planned to have a new catalogue[49] issued for the museum, replacing the obsolete set of three from the 1860s. "This Museum contains 26,800 specimens including the results of all forms of disease and injury, and what is probably the largest and most valuable collection of Indian crania in existence," he wrote to the Surgeon General in 1887. Billings, probably drawing on his experience with the *Index Catalogue*, continued confidently, "Such a catalogue will much increase the value of the collection, and will be the means of bringing great accessions to it; it will be of great interest to scientific men and physicians, and will, it is hoped, be a useful contribution to the science and practice of medicine in all parts of the world." The projected cost for illustrations alone for the three-volume set was $40,000.[50] Congress never funded this project, but it continued to fund the library's *Index Catalogue,* demonstrating that the value of the library was easily understood, while the museum's value was less so. The published scientific article was now seen to possess greater medical significance than the scientific artifact on which the publication may have been based.[51]

In 1888, Billings gave an address in which he outlined his vision of the "National Medical Museum," building on the preceding quarter-century's experience. Excluding microscope slides, the collection held over 15,000 specimens. Billings noted that the museum was not devoted to the narrow study of anatomy but to the broader study of medical practice of which anatomy is a necessary part.[52] Billings detailed his ideas of what a national medical museum should be, in contrast to a typical local anatomical collection devoted to teaching. Borrowing the Smithsonian's motto, he stated,

> The objects of a medical museum are to preserve, to diffuse and to increase knowledge. Its conservative function is to form a permanent record of what has been demonstrated and to fix the meanings of terms. . . . A large proportion of the pathological specimens in this museum illustrate conditions which now rarely occur, forming a group which it is safe to say will never be duplicated. It is not only that they were gathered during a great war, but that they illustrate the results obtained when antiseptic surgery, as now understood and practiced, was unknown. Never again, I hope, will there be brought together such a collection of the effects of pyogenic microorganisms [i.e. bacteria] on gunshot wounds, especially of bone, as may be seen in its cases.[53]

Billings was correct in this assumption, and the bones from the Civil War are still used for research. Billings also foresaw the fall of independent medical museums: "A medical museum is really used, for purposes of study, by very few persons; but through the teaching of those few its lessons are made known to the whole profession. American physicians in investigating a subject do not, as a rule, think of inquiring as to what museums can show with regard to it, simply because they have not had convenient access to large collections and are not accustomed to make use of them."[54] Billings expected other medical collections to be formed to fill this void, as had happened with medical libraries. He was correct, but the others became very specialized collections, usually associated with universities, such as McGill in Montreal.

In regard to the relationship of the museum and the library, Billings stated, "We must have both."[55] However, Billings's budgets reflected the reality of the situation. In 1889, he requested $5,000 for the museum, but $10,000 for the library, $12,000 for its catalogue, and $10,000 for bookbinding.[56] This suggests that Billings saw the research function of the library as most important and reflected the continuing tension regarding the purpose of the museum, which for the army, was largely to conduct medical research.

In spite of the library's better funding, the museum was supported in exhibiting at world's fairs and expositions, increasing its popular audience. Woodward was responsible for the Army Medical Department's exhibit at the Centennial Exposition. In 1876, this included a newly built hospital filled with displays and several catalogues of collections. Billings oversaw the museum's exhibits for the World Columbian Exposition of 1892 and wrote two small new catalogues, one on the history of the microscope and one on selected specimens, continuing the museum's tradition of exhibiting at World's Fairs.[57] Including microscope slides, there were 29,486 pieces in the collection, with one-third of those being pathological specimens, reflecting the origins of the collection and its eventual growth into a pathology institute.

Between Billings's 1888 address and 1893, over 2000 items were added to the collection. Billings succeeded in growing a major museum, but in spite of the diversity within the collection, only the pathological microscopic specimens never lost their importance to medicine. The fate of the Medical Museum in the twentieth century could be seen as either a repudiation or an extreme refinement of Billings's theories. In the twentieth century, the turn towards pathology meant that museum acquisitions consisted of large amounts of human biopsy material—small, select specimens of no interest to a general audience. The Institute of Pathology now holds millions of specimens, in much the same way the museum did earlier, but there is no potential for these to be understood by the public, whose expectations of museums have changed.

In 1895, Billings retired and Walter Reed took charge. Reed pursued the new science of bacteriology, which, along with pathology, made the traditional concept of a medical museum increasingly obsolete (though his approach yielded a typhoid vaccine). The museum's space and collections were also used by the Army Medical School, further limiting public exhibit space. The lack of major American wars as well as the development of the X-ray and aseptic surgery meant that the study of damaged bones was less necessary. Gunshot bone specimens were rarely needed, although projects like Louis LaGarde's *Gunshot Injuries*[58] did use them. LaGarde's book has been reprinted and remains in use, while his specimens languish in storage.

Although it was a popular attraction, the museum became even more research focused. Colonel W. D. McCaw wrote to the Surgeon General,

> While the Army Medical School occupied a large part of the present building, the energies of the Museum staff in practically all the laboratory work were expended in teaching the class and in making original investigations, principally bacteriological, into questions of great importance for the Army at large and the Medical Corps in particular. The results have been so brilliant . . . that no excuse is needed for having temporarily ceased to develop the Museum feature proper. . . . Many new specimens have indeed been accumulated; the Museum has been added to in some new directions and much obsolete material has been taken from exhibition to give place to more valuable and up-to-date specimens. The only room in the building especially adapted to exhibition and built for that purpose is now much overcrowded and yet it contains only the pick of the collections.[59]

Soon after McCaw's report, World War I led the museum staff to further concentrate on pathology; in fact, a formal order was issued in June 1918 for pathological specimens to be sent to the museum.[60] World War I also reinvigorated the museum with new divisions for motion pictures and photography and a push for a new building on the campus of Walter Reed General Hospital. Thousands of pathological specimens arrived. The museum contributed to the diagnosis of diseases during the war and the publication of *The Medical Department of the United States Army in the World War*[61] afterwards. A new numbering system for specimens was adopted, and new displays of wartime concerns such as trench foot were developed. World War I set the museum firmly on the road to becoming a pathological institute. As part of a "modern" medical research institution, the museum staff saw little value in some of the earlier collections and began discarding material, especially from the Civil War. As a result of the reforms of the Flexner report on improving medical education, the rise of laboratory medicine and especially the growth of specialization in medicine, the museum's traditional wide-ranging roles and relevance diminished. Nevertheless, the importance of pathology continued to grow in the institution. The historical component of the museum's collection became more of an antiquarian collection, rather than a documentary or reference one. This antiquarian function was elucidated in 1934 by College of Physicians of Philadelphia's librarian W. B. McDaniel. Ignoring his own institution's Mutter Museum, McDaniel wrote of a museum being an adjunct to a medical library—a "shrine" essentially devoted to the hagiographic worship of the saints of medicine.[62]

World War II confirmed the Army Medical Museum's primary role in pathology consultation. James Ash, the curator during the war and a pathologist, noted, "Shortly after the last war, more concerted efforts were instituted to concentrate in the Army Medical Museum the significant pathologic material occurring in Army installations."[63] He closed with the complaint, "We still suffer under the connotation museum, an institution still thought of by many as a repository for bottled monsters and medical curiosities. To be sure, we have such specimens. As is required by law, we maintain an exhibit open to the public, but in war time, at least, the museum *per se* is the least of our functions, and we like to be thought of as the Army Institute of Pathology, a designation recently authorized by the Surgeon General."[64] The museum became functionally a division of the Army Institute of Pathology in 1944, and officially in 1946, and the triservice Armed Forces Institute of Pathology was created in 1949.[65] Ash's idea of the museum's mission can be seen in the American Registry of Pathology, which was established in the 1920s. The registry was intended to be a collection of specific anatomical specimens, usually tumors, which could be made available for specialized research.[66] In some ways, this concept was not very different from Billings's desires for aspects of a National Medical Museum collection, but it was more limited by being restricted to pathological specimens. Additional registries were added throughout the 1930s, and with the backing of Ash, these became a foundation for the Institute of Pathology. "Through close cooperation with various national societies of medical specialists, records and material in these several fields are brought together at the Army Medical Museum for systematic study. . . . The number of specimens received is considerable; thus, during 1942 over 1,500 enucleated human eyes and nearly 300 tumors of the bladder were investigated," Ash wrote in 1944.[67] That consultation service now provides the vast majority of specimens retained in the Institute's repository.

As the institute grew, the museum's exhibits were frequently shunted into temporary buildings. The museum often featured specialized medical exhibits in the 1950s, such as "Distinctive Tumors of the World," "Round Worm Infections" and "Urologic Antiquities." Despite these graphic titles, the museum remained popular with the general public. Yet a division began in 1947: "This reorganization prescribes that the Museum shall consist of a curator, assistant curator and two departments—the *Medical Science Museum* which is the principal scientific museum maintained for study and research for government and civilian physicians . . . and the *Lay Public Museum* department which maintains that portion of the museum which is open to tourists and others of the lay public who seek information on the general functions and activities of the Medical Department."[68] By 1954, this division entailed displays and collections in two locations because a new building for the pathological institute opened at Walter Reed Army Medical Center. A survey in 1954 revealed atypical visiting patterns for a Washington museum: "42.9 percent were teachers and students and 30.5 percent were doctors, dentists, nurses and others with a scientific background. The remaining 26.6 percent were of diversified occupations."[69] Acting Curator Samuel Kime noted the museum's enduring appeal two years later,

> The AFIP Medical Museum has the only collection of actual pathological specimens accessible to the general public in the U.S. That's an interesting fact when you consider that in 1956 the American public is generally the best informed people that has ever existed. . . . TV demonstrates surgery to them; the *Reader's Digest* discloses wonder drugs to them; increasing numbers of "Marches," "Crusades" and Campaigns request money from them. What they hear about, hear so much about but have never actually seen, they can see . . . at your Medical Museum.

Kime's observations remain true of the museum's current visitors.[70]

Continuing moves and storage of parts of collections added to the difficulties of the museum. The museum returned to its traditional building on the Mall in 1962. In 1966, it had 765,157 visitors, but the relocation of the Hirshhorn collection of modern art on the Mall led to the demolition of the building. The museum closed in 1968 and moved to Walter Reed Army Medical Center, a secure military post about six miles from the museum core of Washington, in 1971. The museum closed again from 1974–1978 while its space was used for establishing a new military medical school.[71] Attendance never recovered, and while the Smithsonian has grown immensely, the museum did not benefit as it would have on the Mall.[72]

In 1988, it was finally named the National Museum of Health and Medicine, after having been called the Medical Museum of the Armed Forces Institute of Pathology and then the Armed Forces Medical Museum. Its location on a military base, which had seemed a good idea as early as World War I, has limited public awareness of its existence and the number of visitors, even though the collections have grown at a breathtaking rate in the past decade. It remains difficult to gauge the impact that the museum has had and will have on its visitors. As there is no master narrative or curriculum, and much of the content of a medical museum remains contested knowledge, visitors viewing the many exhibits no doubt do create "order and understanding for themselves." But is this necessarily bad? As a recent review noted, the museum is not for the "squeamish, [and] it is definitely a great destination for those tired of squeaky-clean political correctness." This reviewer continued, "I won't soon forget my pilgrimage to the National Museum of Health and Medicine. In fact, I'm fairly certain it will linger with me in perpetuity whether I want it to or not."[73] Having metamorphosed over 140 years, the future of the museum remains impossible to predict. Perhaps with continuing changes in popular taste, such museums may regain their audiences. Gunter Von Hagen's exhibits of plastinated humans are proving extremely popular. Given the resources devoted to health care in the twenty-first century, one could easily see the need for a popular educational institution like a medical museum.

NOTES

1. The opinions or assertions in this article are the private views of the authors and are not to be construed as official or as reflecting the views of the U.S. Department of Defense. Nevertheless, this piece is a U.S. government work, and, as such, is in the public domain of the USA. An earlier version of this paper was presented as "Curating America's Premier Medical Museum: The Legacy of John S. Billings to the Professional and Public Understanding of Medicine" for a conference titled, "Anglo-American Medical Relations: Historical Insights," 19–21 June 2003, organized by the American Association for the History of Medicine and the Wellcome Trust Centre for the History of Medicine at University College of London.

2. A more traditional history of the museum can be found in Robert S. Henry, *The Armed Forces Institute of Pathology: Its First Century, 1862–1962* (Washington, D.C.: Office of the Surgeon General, 1964).

3. Bonnie Ellen Blustein, "The Philadelphia Biological Society, 1857–61: A Failed Experiment?" *Journal of the History of Medicine and Allied Sciences* 35 (1980): 188–202.

4. An important secondary use was in providing evidence for pensions for injured soldiers. See Robert Goler and M. Rhode, "From Individual Trauma to National Policy: Tracking the Uses of Civil War Veteran Medical Records," in *Disabled Veterans in History*, ed. David Gerber (Ann Arbor: University of Michigan Press, 2000): 163–84.

5. Brinton was curator from 1862–1864, and was apparently relieved of this duty for political reasons. Woodward was curator of the medical and microscopical section. Otis succeeded Brinton as curator of the surgical section and ran the museum as a whole. See John Hill Brinton, *Personal Memoirs of John H. Brinton, Civil War Surgeon, 1861–1865* (Carbondale: Southern Illinois University Press, 1996).

6. John Shaw Billings, "Who Founded the National Medical Library?" *Medical Record* 17 (1880): 298–99; reprinted in Frank Bradway Rogers, *Selected Papers of John Shaw Billings*, (Chicago: Medical Library Association, 1965), 115.

7. Otis to Cook, 24 March 1866, OHA 15 Curatorial Records: Letter Books of the Curators, 1863–1910, Otis Historical Archives, National Museum of Health and Medicine, Armed Forces Institute of Pathology, Washington, D.C. Hereafter just the correspondents and date will be cited.

8. Otis to Forwood, 4 January 1867.

9. Louis Bagger, "The Army Medical Museum in Washington," *Appleton's Journal* 9, no. 206 (1 March 1873): 294–97.

10. Mary Clemmer Ames, *Ten Years in Washington: Life and Scenes in the National Capital as a Woman Sees Them* (Hartford: A. D. Worthington & Co, 1874), 477.

11. Daniel S. Lamb, *A History of the United States Army Medical Museum, 1862 to 1917, Compiled from the Official Records*, unpublished typescript, 43–44; Parker to Otis, 30 April 1874.

12. S. Weir Mitchell (as Anonymous), "The Case of George Dedlow," *Atlantic Monthly* 18, no. 105 (July 1866): 1–11.

13. Wyndham Davis Miles, *A History of the National Library of Medicine: The Nation's Treasury of Medical Knowledge* (Bethesda: U.S. Department of Health and Human Services, 1982): 32, 34.

14. *Medical News* 18 September 1886, quoted in Lamb, *History of the U.S. Army Medical Museum*, 88–89.

15. For example, forty-two histories of aneurysms were provided to the Surgeon General's Office, along with a request for the return of another forty-four histories. John Shaw Billings (hereafter JSB) to Pope, 4 April 1884.

16. JSB to LaGarde, 21 May 1885. A letter from 1891 describes how the AFIP works today: "When a physician presents to the museum a pathological specimen which requires microscopical examination a section of it is sent him if he requests it." JSB to Seymour, 21 August 1891.

17. JSB to Ainsworth, 7 January 1885.

18. Many unsolicited specimens were placed in either the provisional anatomical or pathological sections and then discarded or transferred as desired.

19. JSB to Francis, 18 February 1886.

20. JSB to Tiemann, 27 August 1885.

21. JSB to McElderry, 28 August 1885.

22. See letter from Billings to Surgeon General's Office, U.S. Army (hereafter SGO), 27 May 1893, about buying special equipment to exhibit "microscopic specimens."

23. JSB to Mayall, 1 November 1884.

24. JSB to Mayall, 7 April 1886; John Shaw Billings, "On Medical Museums, with special reference to the Army Medical Museum at Washington," *Medical News* 53, no. 12 (22 September 1888): 309–16.

25. JSB to SGO, 19 December 1885. Billings had contacted him while traveling in Europe and indicated his interest in having a set made for the museum.

26. JSB to Agassiz, 11 April 1885; JSB to Agassiz, 15 April 1885; JSB to Minot, 28 October 1887.

27. JSB to Hough, 15 August 1887.

28. JSB to Gaulon, 14 March 1887; JSB to SGO, 21 October 1887.

29. Billings, writing to Smithsonian Secretary Spencer Baird, noted that "to form such a collection as [would have a bearing on points in human biology] would certainly be within the province of the Army Medical Museum," 18 April 1885.

30. JSB to Ward, 25 February 1887.

31. JSB to McDonald, 21 July 1888.

32. Joseph Henry, the Smithsonian's first Secretary, proposed the following:

> I address you at present in regard to an exchange of specimens which are now in possession of the Army Medical Museum, relative to Indian Archaeology and Anthropology, for specimens relative to human and comparative Anatomy in the Smithsonian Institution. The specimens referred to as now in our possession consist of a series of skulls which I am informed will be required for the preparation of a monograph, under your direction, of the crania of North America. Those for which we propose to make an exchange and which are in the Medical Museum, consist of a collection of objects illustrative of the manners, customs and arts of the Indians of this continent.

Henry to Barnes, 14 January 1869, quoted in Lamb, *History of the United States Army Medical Museum*, 2–3.

33. JSB to Spencer Baird, 6 February 1884; JSB to Spencer Baird, 7 February 1884.

34. JSB to Pocock, 31 October 1884.

35. JSB to Ashbaugh, 12 April 1887.

36. JSB to Wortman, 16 February 1888. For further information on the expedition, see Charles F. Merbs, "Washington Matthews and the Hemenway Expedition of 1887–88," *Journal of the Southwest* 44, no.3 (Autumn 2002): 303–35.

37. JSB to Trubner, 30 September 1884.

38. JSB to Alden, 16 February 1894.

39. Lamb, *History of the United States Army Medical Museum*, 109.

40. The fifth volume of the *Index Catalogue* indexed over 4000 portraits in the library, although many of these were illustrations in books or journals. Miles, *A History of the National Library of Medicine*, 82.

41. Billings, "Who Founded the National Medical Library?"

42. JSB to Lord, March 10, 1888. For more on memorialization, see J. T. H. Connor and M. Rhode, "Shooting Soldiers: Civil War Medical Images, Memory, and Identity in America," *Invisible Culture: Visual Culture and National Identity* 5 (Winter 2003): www.rochester.edu/in_visible_culture/Issue_5/ConnorRhode/ConnorRhode.html (accessed 26 June 2006).

43. Henry, *The Armed Forces Institute of Pathology*, 81–83.

44. JSB to Paget, 17 September 1885.

45. JSB to SGO, 16 June 1887.

46. JSB to Carter, 19 November 1886.

47. Lamb, *History of the United States Army Medical Museum*, 96–101.

48. Lamb, *History of the United States Army Medical Museum*, 90–91.

49. JSB to W. G. Johnston of McGill College's Pathological Laboratory, 21 May 1887.

50. JSB to SGO, 17 December 1887.

51. Billings suggested scaling back the project to one catalogue of pathological specimens at a cost of $16,600, but this was not successful either. JSB to SGO, 17 January 1890.

52. Billings, "On Medical Museums," 311.

53. Billings, "On Medical Museums," 314.

54. Billings, "On Medical Museums," 314.

55. JSB to SGO, 17 January 1890, 315.

56. JSB to SGO, 10 August 1889.

57. See Julie K. Brown, *Making Culture Visible: Photography and Its Display at Industrial Fairs, International Exhibitions and Institutional Exhibitions in the United States, 1847–1900* (Amsterdam: Harwood Academic Press, 2001). See also Brown's paper, "Making a Public Image for Health: Government Exhibits of Health and Medicine at International Expositions in the United States, 1876–1904," Annual Conference of American Association for the History of Medicine, Madison, WI, May 2004.

58. Louis A LaGarde, *Gunshot Injuries: How They Are Inflicted, Their Complications and Treatment* (New York: William Wood, 1914).

59. McCaw to SGO, 21 November 1913, quoted in Henry, *The Armed Forces Institute of Pathology*, 150–51.

60. Beginning at the end of the twentieth century, eighty-year-old influenza-infected lungs were used to study the virus of the 1918 pandemic; see Henry, *The Armed Forces Institute of Pathology*, 165, for collecting specimens during World War I.

61. Surgeon General's Office of the U.S. Army, *The Medical Department of the United States Army in the World War*, 15 vols. (Washington, D.C.: Government Printing Office, n.d.).

62. W. B. McDaniel, II, "Medical Museum as an Adjunct to Medical Library," *Bulletin of the Medical Library Association* 23, no. 2 (October 1934): 87–92.

63. J. E. Ash, "The Army Medical Museum in This War," *Southern Medical Journal* 37, no. 5 (May 1944): 261–66, quotation from page 1 of offprint that is repaginated.

64. Ash, "The Army Medical Museum in This War," 7.

65. Following along, the museum changed its name to the Medical Museum of the Armed Forces Institute of Pathology, and then to the Armed Forces Medical Museum.

66. Henry, *The Armed Forces Institute of Pathology*, 207–25.

67. Ash, "The Army Medical Museum in This War," 5–6.

68. Armed Forces Institute of Pathology, *Annual Report 1947* (Washington, D.C.: Department of the Army, 1947), 22

69. Armed Forces Institute of Pathology, *Annual Report 1954* (Washington, D.C.: Department of the Army, 1954), 24.

70. Samuel Kime, "John Q Public, Glass, Plastic, and Our Specimens," *AFIP Letter* 12, no. 31, (31 July 1956). For further information on visitors and attendance, see Randi Korn & Associates, *National Museum of Health and Medicine Visitor Survey*, April 2000.

71. See Armed Forces Institute of Pathology *Annual Reports* for the appropriate years.

72. The Smithsonian Institution has held some displays on medicine, but no space has been devoted specifically to the topic recently. Curator Judy Chelnick notes, "Medical artifacts have been incorporated into larger exhibitions throughout the museum which I really like. The new exhibit on the American military has a surgical kit and a cupping kit from the American Revolution, and these put medicine in a larger context." Personal communication, 2 December 2004.

73. Megan Edwards, "Road Trip Washington, D.C.—On Beyond the Smithsonian: The National Museum of Health and Medicine," www.roadtripamerica.com/places/National-Museum-of-Health-andMedicine.htm (accessed 14 November 2004).

CHALLENGING THE MAJOR MUSEUM

Major museums tend to be structured into departments and galleries, first, because they have space, and second, because they have the staff. Their organizational plans reflect the privileging of certain kinds of information as set out by Foucault in *The Archaeology of Knowledge*,[1] which may limit viewers' perspectives even more than the types of narratives found at, say, the Dillinger exhibit. For instance, an institution that separates human evolution from the evolution of animals may reinforce the distinctions between *Homo sapiens* and other species, thus palliating creationists and others who object to the notion of humans being descended from animals.

As evident with the Daughters of Utah Pioneers collections, smaller museums that offer visitors accumulations of apparently miscellaneous items present much less cohesive—and coherent—narratives, but they do allow visitors to create a kind of order and understanding for themselves. There is no "master" plot. The advantage of such collections is that they are less directive than more structured ones; the disadvantage is that uncritical visitors may never find an organizing principle to help them remember the site. In many ways, these places challenge or ignore the most basic tenets of contemporary museology—and their doing so may be as much a choice as the result of limited financial resources.

In fact, certain smaller museums seem to exist primarily to challenge or parody the authority and organizational structures of other institutions as well as their definitions of art, history, or science. Their chief appeal may well be that they make a statement about the kinds of collections they reflect and perhaps can best be understood in terms of Huebner's political rather than scientific rationale. The politics of questioning concepts such as *art* or *museum* may be central to the content of their curricula. On the other hand, one could almost say that these museums lack ordering principles, so varied are their collections. The museums are glorious examples of the conglomerations visible at local sites, but visitors seeking a highly didactic experience may be disappointed. The Museum of Jurassic Technology in Culver City, California, with its odd objects and histories, might be considered an example of such an institution. One more openly devoted to questioning the authority of other museums, however, is the Museum of Bad Art (or MOBA—an abbreviation deliberately reminiscent of the Museum of Modern Art's acronym, MoMA) in a Boston suburb. Some of the works in the museum's collection stand alone; others are deliberate parodies of famous artworks. "Sunday on the Pot with George" is a satire on "Sunday in the Park with George" by Seurat. The description of the painting mocks the vocabulary of high art criticism, "This pointillist piece is curious for meticulous attention to fine detail, such as the stitching around the edge of the towel, in contrast to the almost careless disregard for the subject's feet."[2]

The Museum of Bad Art challenges traditional museums in two ways: first, it raises questions about what constitutes art, and second, it confronts the apparatus by which museums constitute themselves as important authorities by offering its own newsletter, events, mission statement, and the like, all of which parody those of formal institutions. The latter quality of the Museum of Bad Art is particularly important to our discussion of small museums, since most of the institutions in this book devote themselves to history rather than art. The museums discussed in this section, City Museum of St. Louis, the National Architectural Arts Center (also in St. Louis), and New York's Freakatorium, are examples of similar institutions which attract audiences by displaying the spectacular, incredible, and mundane side by side.

The City Museum of St. Louis includes everything from the world's largest pair of underpants to industrial salvage. As Eric Sandweiss, author of the chapter on this site, indicates, the museum is indebted to P. T. Barnum's American Museum and the histories of certain museums as theaters for public amusement rather than sites for scholarly discourse. It is a place where one is more likely to find children petting stingrays in an aquarium than researchers studying urban history in shadowy archives. Labels are often typed sheets hung on the wall with none of the attention to design found in larger museums. Sandweiss offers a contrast between City Museum and the National Architectural Arts Center, a collection not yet open to the public, which offers a different, more serious view of urban St. Louis.

Like City Museum, New York's Freakatorium is a direct descendant of the American Museum with its exhibits of two-headed animals and other oddities. As Lucian Gomoll indicates, the institution challenges the careful categories and structures of knowledge inherent in the organizational plans of traditional museums. In doing so, the museum questions what qualifies as science and forces visitors to confront their notions of normality. Whereas nineteenth-century museums often had a not-so-hidden mission of acculturating immigrants and the lower classes by setting standards for "civilization,"[3] the Freakatorium embraces disorder and diversity.

Although tourists with a limited amount of time would be likeliest to visit the major museums in their vicinities, the Museum of Bad Art, the Freakatorium, and City Museum are all popular attractions. They exemplify particular qualities of Americans— irreverence combined with humor and irony. Such institutions can be enjoyed on their own, but visitors may appreciate them most when they know and understand the kinds of sites that are being challenged. Thus, the museums remain dependent in certain ways on the existence of larger, more traditional sites, which in turn are redefined by their contrasts with the smaller institutions. This interrelationship offers yet another reason why small and local museums are important in American culture.

NOTES

1. Michel Foucault, *The Archaeology of Knowledge* (New York: Pantheon, 1982).

2. "The Museum of Bad Art," www.museumofbadart.org (accessed 29 June 2006).

3. See, for example, Seth Koven, "The Whitechapel Picture Exhibitions and the Politics of Seeing," in *Museum Culture: Histories, Discourse, Spectacle*, ed. Daniel J. Sherman and Irit Rogoff, 22–48 (London: Routledge, 1994).

12

Objects of Dis/Order

Articulating Curiosities and Engaging People at the Freakatorium

LUCIAN GOMOLL

Freaks are simultaneously understood as symbols of the absolute Other and the essential self.

—*Leslie Fiedler,* Tyranny of the Normal

What does one do with a thirty-five-foot-long snake skin? Or a mounted furry fish? Would the American Museum of Natural History display or even store the heads of a two-headed cow? Should a living, anatomically sound two-headed turtle be seen swimming at a zoo? What about photographs of dog-faced women, circus posters of one-legged acrobats, or the world's smallest sculptures? Where should they go? What purposes should they serve?

Museums typically articulate narratives of normativity. As James Clifford indicates, majority museums like the Smithsonian seek out the most exemplary or representative objects of culture and art for their collections, defining normativity and normative ideologies.[1] Even those marked as specialized, such as the National Museum of the American Indian, challenge majority museums in a battle over what is normal, and define their own criteria for group membership and cohesion. Clifford remarks, "This articulation—whether its scope is national, regional, ethnic, or tribal—collects, celebrates, memorializes, values, and sells (directly and indirectly) a way of life. In the process of maintaining an imagined community, it also confronts 'others' and excludes the 'inauthentic.' This is the stuff of contemporary cultural politics."[2] Familiar to many are relatively recent American projects of group visibility and unity, such as the African-American focus on media representation or institutions like El Museo del Barrio,[3] which assert firm group presences. Thus space for the inauthentic, the strangely superlative, the unbelievable, and the anomalous is hard to find. But carefully framed exhibitions do not render incongruities extinct, nor do they prevent imaginations from wandering and wondering. Should the remains of Siamese twins be displayed? If so, how? Some unconventional museums offer spaces for strange objects rejected by the others; if the Dillinger Museum offered insights into outlaw culture, these institutions' curricula present the unique, the weird, the unwanted, and sometimes the unmentionable. Unique like their collections, these museums invent their own standards for displaying curiosities. The choices curators make, often simple or seemingly transparent, are important to recognize, as they are key to museum differences and political rationales. In particular, the act of producing museological frames is a creative process, including choosing a display mode and what Barbara Kirshenblatt-Gimblett calls the *art of excision*, or choosing which parts to show from a nonreplicable whole.[4] A well-known example of a museum that uses the art of excision is the Museum of Jurassic Technology (MJT) in Culver City, which employs strange concepts and theories.[5] Another, more closely resembling the Army Medical Museum, is the Mutter Museum in Philadelphia, a space that coldly displays human anomalies as pathology specimens in jars and drawers. The site functions as a taxonomy of disorder that corroborates scientific and medical definitions of the normative, as it visibly shows us what is "abnormal."

Johnny Fox, the founder and curator of New York City's Freakatorium, possesses many of the objects mentioned in the opening paragraph above. However, Fox explores the agency of his own objects—which could also be found in the MJT and Mutter rooms—in ways very different from the others, generating unique narratives through nontraditional curatorial approaches. With the Freakatorium, Johnny Fox references a specific history of American display and entertainment: he takes P. T. Barnum's American Museum as his museological model and defines the Freakatorium as a contemporary dime museum. Although the site evokes the history Fox targets, which includes freak shows, it would be difficult to imagine Barnum's museum today, because activists would surely criticize it as exploitative and insensitive. As Rosemarie

Thomson states, "Today the notion of a freak show that displays the bodies of disabled people for profit and public entertainment is both repugnant and anachronistic, rejected but nevertheless recent and compelling in memory."[6] Johnny Fox cannot bring Barnum back. Instead, he adds important twists to this "un–politically correct" type of museum, showing how it can effectively convey relevant messages and represent the non-normative *as* non-normative.

The Freakatorium creates a space for the abnormal, including a recuperation of freakishness itself. A collection of anomalies, the Freakatorium is anomalous, too. It is at once a dime museum, a museum of dime museums, a memorial space, and a Freak hall of fame. And since the Freakatorium displays human Freaks, the site directly engages with the discourses of queer and disability politics, as well as constructions of American identities dating back to the nineteenth century.[7] Because of the Freakatorium's own freakishness, Fox is able to exhibit human Freaks—as Barnum once did but differently from him—in an age of identity politics. Johnny Fox is connected to the Freak community, and he sees himself as honoring and remembering Freaks. He rejects the tendency to visualize marginalized groups as cohesive and/or surrogate-normative, and instead celebrates the anomalous as special in its own right. In the same way that Fox attempts to understand productive anomalousness with his Freakatorium, this essay searches for the value and meaning of anomalies as weird and wonderful. The pages that follow explore how, through a creative engagement with the history of displaying curiosities, and by maintaining the dignity of human Freaks, Fox's Freakatorium performs as a site of resonance and mystery, of recuperation and intimate discovery, and of freakishness and new visibility. In this way, it offers its audience a unique but critically important content or curriculum.

A CURIOUS GENEALOGY

Johnny Fox has an active and affectionate relationship with his museum. He is a sword swallower, known to shove swords down his throat during midconversation with an unsuspecting guest. In an interview, Fox told me that his interests began when he participated in a magic act in Florida in 1974: "I had a craving for finding antique magic apparatuses—what was being made at the time was crap." In his search to find higher quality magic show items, Mr. Fox engaged in independent research on the history of magic acts and attended several collectors' conventions. As his collection grew, Johnny Fox explored his affinities for "elements of danger with comic relief" as a street performer, experimenting with various chemicals and fire eating. Gathering magic show props and techniques from the late 1800s and early 1900s led to his discovery of various weird and wonderful acts, and Johnny Fox's collection expanded to include posters, photographs, and more sideshow-related objects. These objects were scattered for over twenty years. Some traveled with him, while he stored others in Colorado, as he continued to perform himself. It was not until his wife passionately persuaded him to "refine the collection" that Johnny Fox decided to share it with the public. He did in 1999, when he opened the Freakatorium.[8]

At that point, Fox made a specific choice to evoke the dime museum mode to display his curiosities in the creation of the Freakatorium, which is unlike the approaches of the MJT or the Mutter Museum. Today, when a visitor to the Freakatorium asks, "What is this place," a well-polished response will follow: "It's basically a present day rendition of a Victorian dime museum—they were very popular in the past." But how is a casual observer supposed to know what that means? One usually doesn't, as dime museums are virtually unknown now. If visitors show confusion, the guides will direct them to a strange display for something more tangible to discuss. Although this is a strategic act to keep a patron's interest, not discussing the history of curiosity displays ignores much of the richness of the Freakatorium's performance as a museum.

In his text, *The Shows of London,* Richard Altick documents early urban amusements and the transitions from cabinets of curiosities to museums between 1600 and 1800.[9] As a general rule, urban attractions ministered to "the desire to be amused or instructed, the indulgence of curiosity and the sheer sense of wonder, sometimes a rudimentary aesthetic sensibility."[10] Paula Findlen describes the early cabinet practices: "Through the choice and juxtaposition of different objects, early modern naturalists formed 'mosaics' that reflected the interpretive process underlying all collecting. Surveying the vast field of knowledge, they selected items that aided them in developing a meaningful understanding of the world."[11] The mosaic display systems, as articulations of ways to possess nature and knowledge, demonstrate the syncretistic tendencies of the ages and cultures in which they were developed. These European projects grew and transformed into more familiar forms, such as art museums and natural history museums. Unlike the earliest cabinets, museums become available to everyone, not only to social elites: "To both the literate and the illiterate, they were a prime means by which the mind and the imagination could be exercised and daily routine experience given occasional welcome patches of variety and color."[12] A distinctly American form of entertainment, the dime museum inherited the cluttered aesthetics of earlier cabinets, often visually represented by drawings, like Imperato's Museum.[13] Uniquely, at the beginning of the nineteenth century, dime museums brought together components of natural history and art museums, freak shows, waxworks, theater, and a variety of performances.

Charles Willson Peale's Philadelphia museum, which he established as an educational site before the rise of dime museums, "operated for nearly sixty years (1786–1845) and during that time was forced to incorporate elements of popular entertainment as part of a larger trend; its owner had to become a showman to survive. When Peale first requested donations, people sent all sorts of bizarre objects."[14] Although Peale's expressed goal was to teach and not to entertain, his need for profit forced him to conform to the increasingly popular dime museum approaches. Thus he displayed oddities, such as a chicken with four legs and four wings, and an 80-pound turnip.[15] Mass interest in dime museums is explained by their unique and seductive exhibits, creating spaces in which both "the mind and the imagination could be exercised," to recall Altick and urban London shows. Along the same lines, Rosemarie Thomson points out that strange exhibits and freak shows "provided dilemmas of classification and definition upon which the throng of spectators could hone the skills needed to tame world and self in the ambitious project of American self-making," in which everyone seemed to participate as the old aristocratic order was systematically rejected and a U.S. identity crisis began.[16]

Underscoring the dime museum's popularity, Andrea Stulman Dennett talks about the diversity and demand for the institutions: "nineteenth-century American dime museums came in all sizes and many types, from grand five-story buildings that contained theaters accommodating three thousand spectators and curio halls parading upwards of ten thousand curiosities to small storefronts that were converted into exhibition rooms displaying old coins, petrified wood, and living anomalies." She continues, "'Dime museum,' however, is a term used to differentiate all of these popular amusement centers from endowed public museums such as New York's American Museum of Natural History (1869) or Boston's Museum of Fine Arts (1876).[17] Clearly, dime museums were of unique and significant importance to Americans of all classes during the nineteenth century. The most popular and influential was P. T. Barnum's American Museum. Dennett asserts that "Barnum not only adopted the early nineteenth-century concept of the proprietary museum, but he popularized and redefined it, transforming it into the dime museum."[18] In her second chapter, "Barnum and the Museum Revolution, 1841–1870," she describes the influence, practices, and philosophies of Barnum's museum. He incorporated the cluttered display aesthetics of earlier cabinets of curiosities, and brought in various modes of performance by displaying Freaks and strange objects as well as offering lectures, all under the roof of one huge five-story building. The American Museum's popularity even reached the global scale as a tourist production: "By the 1850s it was already considered unthinkable to visit New York City without seeing it, and by 1860 the museum was on the itinerary of the well-publicized visit of the Prince of Wales to New York."[19] As a once hugely popular cultural phenomenon, although almost forgotten today, Barnum and the dime museum belong in our collective cultural memory. Aspects of performances still persist in freak show repertoires, such as those at Coney Island. The Freakatorium gives the dime museum an archival place, just as it houses the strange objects that other museums overlook, reject, or show for different purposes.

ANOMALOUS TEMPORALITY AND DISPLAY

As the private curator of the Freakatorium, Johnny Fox appoints himself as a latter-day P. T. Barnum. The history section of the Freakatorium website asserts its intended relationship to the past: "A friend and living link to many of the 20th century's greatest sideshow performers, Johnny has collected stories and objects related to America's entertainment past for nearly thirty years. When he decided to make his collection available to the public, Johnny turned his thoughts to P. T. Barnum and his first great enterprise, the American Museum." The paragraphs that follow offer a summarized textbook history of dime museums, concluding with, "Today, the Freakatorium is New York's only existing dime museum, operating in the very neighborhood where many of its predecessors once stood."[20] How Fox and the Freakatorium evoke this history, however, is more complex than the website suggests; they do not simply replicate Barnum or the dime museum as if no time has passed. Looking closely at an advertisement for the Freakatorium offers some understanding. Underneath the cluttered text on the front of the museum's primary flyer, Johnny Fox welcomes potential patrons into an obscure space. The image is really an appropriation of Charles Peale's famous "The Artist in His Museum" self-portrait, with Fox digitally layered over Peale's body, and the original museum typed over in this freakish pixelized palimpsest. Like Fox assuming the role of a latter-day Barnum, this advertisement asserts the Freakatorium's relationship to museums of the past. In particular, the appropriation is important: it illustrates that the Freakatorium and Johnny Fox perform history with a twist. With Johnny Fox as the focus of the image and the director of our view—Peale's right arm and legs are attached to Fox's face and body—the painting is not the original, just a weird combination of past and present images. Similarly, the Freakatorium cannot act as a genuine dime museum of the nineteenth century.

By filling the Freakatorium's space with curiosities, Johnny Fox invites viewers to engage with objects differently than in most museums. With naked eyes, or mediated through special looking tools, we can view hundreds of unique objects all along a single wall, organized similarly to Imperato's Museum. At the very bottom of a stack is a display of old swords, supporting three glass-enclosed habitats of foreign bugs, all underneath a long showcase-table containing giant rings and other things. Accustomed to the orderly layouts of major museums, we might be quick to judge Johnny Fox's museum as merely a disordered jumble of objects devoid of any aesthetic rationale, to use Huebner's term. Yet taking the historical inspirations into account, we realize that the Freakatorium's ordering is deliberately different. For his suggestive displays, Johnny Fox places formally and thematically similar objects near each other, their relationships rudimentary to complex. Among the many objects in the main table-case are old foot-binding shoes, near the foot carvings of armless wonder Charles Tripp, which command the center. To the left is a Narwhale "unicorn of the sea" horn, echoing the shapes of various nearby penis bones of different sizes. On the wall above the case hang nineteen photos of human Freaks accompanied by detailed biographical captions. Hanging at the right is a protruding stuffed zebra head with other animal heads from far-away lands. The Freakatorium's choice juxtapositions and basic organizational strategies demonstrate how it mimics the mosaic techniques used by dime museums and the older cabinets of curiosities; however, unlike the owners of the cabinets, Fox does not use the mode to assert his possession of the objects. Instead, the Freakatorium is artfully elusive and illusive. An overload of visual stimuli in the small space encourages viewers to take time looking at each object showcased as special, to be discovered by sensitive eyes through the sea of curiosities.

By restoring an old mode of display, the Freakatorium embodies the dime museum as artifact. How the Freakatorium presents art illustrates its dual role as a museum and as a museum of dime museums. At the bottom of a wall is a glass diorama of P. T. Barnum's famous Feejee mermaid. Known as one of the biggest hoaxes of its time, the Feejee mermaid earned Barnum ten thousand dollars in one week—three times his normal revenue. Dennett explains, "He printed enticing stories about the discovery of the Mermaid near the Feejee Islands (Hawaii) by the totally fictitious Dr. J. Griffin from London's 'Lyceum of Natural History.'" She continues, "For weeks the press was filled with Feejee Mermaid anecdotes, and New Yorkers anxiously awaited the false scientist's visit as he supposedly ventured north from Montgomery, Alabama, to New York."[21] Barnum was taken to court for his stories, but the legal process only heightened the exhibit's spectacular quality, bringing him more publicity. In the end, all charges were dropped. According to Dennet, "Barnum found that on their first visit, pleasure-seekers were under the impression that an exhibit was real, but later would return to appease their curiosity and to try to determine how the deception had been achieved. Thus, he made deceit a game and an integral part of his museum exhibits, and he used the press as bait."[22] In contrast, the Freakatorium, existing over a century later, displays the same Feejee hoax at a time when its fraudulent nature is well known. A message hangs on the wall above Johnny Fox's glass-enclosed Feejee mermaid diorama: "We do not expect that our educated patrons believe that the creatures presented here are genuine works of nature. They are however authentic examples of a time-honored art. Animal hoaxes have been exhibited for ages to amaze, perplex and astound—and like the freaks of nature, to make us wonder where the limits of the known world lie. Here are a few of the most remarkable." This note indicates a significant disjunction between the Freakatorium and the predecessors it takes as models. Such a message would never have appeared in Barnum's American museum or another dime museum of the nineteenth century.

The Freakatorium also undermines dime-museum efforts to deceive patrons via visual irony. For example, the museum displays a diorama of El Chupacabra, the notorious "Mexican Goat Sucker." A caption posted on the glass states that the creature was "Captured Alive," like authoritative in-context labels we see in majority museums.[23] However, the legendary creature's exaggerated, fierce pose and the humorous little teal Mexican hat and scarf are manipulations of such in-context label authority. The playful props tacitly ask: was it really captured alive? Can you tell just by looking or relying on the label's claims? If a visitor is not receptive to irony, signs explicitly assert the Freakatorium's intent: the displays are not meant to fool people. And the museum guides will point out hoaxes outright. Johnny Fox presents the Feejee Mermaid-as-hoax, and Chupacabra-as-myth, as time-honored works of art in their own right.

The dis/ordered ways Fox presents curiosities are similar to dime museums and historical cabinets of curiosities; yet undermining his own displays by revealing inauthenticity and questioning his museum's authority suggests a different audience and explores the objects' agency in special, multi-valenced ways. In the Freakatorium, one can look at an object for what it is immediately, perhaps believing it or wondering if it is really true, like someone of the nineteenth century. The visitor may also know the history of the object, with a sense of insider knowledge of the hoax and respect for the object as art. In these ways, the Freakatorium behaves as formally anomalous and complex in relation to museum history and current normative display techniques.

FREAKISHLY EXHIBITING FREAK CULTURE

In the Freakatorium, it is very important that many of the Freaks on display were once alive. The collection features only a few authentic bone displays, but there are many lifelike ones. At left, on the wall displaying pictures of human Freaks, are the mounted heads of a two-headed cow. Like the zebra head, the cow heads are stuffed, and under their chins are bells that echo the humorous props in the Chupacabra diorama. On a table directly below the stuffed cow heads are two attached cow skulls under glass, in the same pose as the pair above it. The displays clearly reference each other, as their spatial layers gesture to the conceptual and contextual layers also at work. The two-headed cow displays represent very different results of the world's curiosity about Freaks: cold, scientific preservation, as opposed to a Freakish posthumous life creating a lingering sense of wonder. The cow skulls display brings the observer's attention primarily to the formal, deviant anatomy of the Freak. They are not picturesque O'Keeffe skulls; the backs of the heads seem smashed together, and their overall shapes appear unhealthy and narrow. Viewers may see into and through parts of the heads they would not be able to perceive if the cow were alive. The scientific approach objectifies, making it readable, as Thomson proposes.[24] On the other hand, the stuffed heads offer a glimpse of what the animal would have looked like when it was alive. It has four wide-open eyes and brown fur, and is posed in a way that makes the creature seem animated, cute, and alive. This display arouses viewers' empathy for the Freak. Playful props like the cowbell, which the Freakatorium staff makes and adds to the displays, insert a sense of life into the motionless heads.

As with the cows, Johnny Fox applies his own animating methods to recuperate the lives of human Freaks—an approach very different from those of

Barnum and past museums. Rosemarie Thomson sharply criticizes Barnum's work in freak shows, arguing that "by highlighting ostensible human anomaly of every sort and combination, Barnum's exhibits challenged audiences not only to classify and explain what they saw, but to relate the performance to themselves, to American individual and collective identity."[25] In other words, Barnum deliberately displayed curiosities in ambiguous ways, seducing spectators into definition and authenticity games of identity and normativity. Such nineteenth-century freak shows encouraged onlookers to define their own identities as *not* disabled, *not* androgynous, *not* monstrous, and so on. Leslie Fiedler also points out that "in his *Autobiography* Barnum refers to human anomalies not as Freaks but as 'curiosities,' lumping them with other attractions which may seem to us of a quite different kind."[26] Johnny Fox is nothing like his model in these ways. He clearly distinguishes Freaks from the other curiosities, and his human displays include in-depth and dignifying biographies. Therefore, the Freakatorium performs as a memorial for Freak performers. Fox himself says, "New York needs a place where people can come see the history of freakdom. People that were born with deformities that were still amazing and sensitive people and they allowed themselves to be viewed and exhibited. They made a good living off doing that. Those people were to be commended for their courageousness and bravery for standing in front of people."[27] Fox's museum displays accomplish just what he says. They are respectable spaces devoted to the lives of amazing people, which foster potential empathy from the visitors—a stark contrast to Freak shows, which directed judgment away from the audience and onto the performers, assuring observers of their own unmarked normalcy.

Stephen Greenblatt's concept of resonance at cultural exhibitions illuminates Fox's displays of Freak culture: "A resonant exhibition often pulls the viewer away from the celebration of isolated objects and toward a series of implied, only half-visible relationships and questions: How did the objects come to be displayed? What is at stake in categorizing them as 'museum quality'? How were they originally used?"[28] The Freakatorium's representations of Tom Thumb, armless wonder Charles Tripp, and the one-legged Brown acrobats cultivate the resonance Greenblatt describes. Once world-famous performers' objects and stories give viewers ideas of the complex people behind the displays and of how Freaks used their now-fragmented belongings. Greenblatt points out "this resonance depends not upon visual stimulation but upon a felt intensity of names, and behind the names, as the very term *resonance* suggests, of voices: the voices of those who chanted, studied, muttered their prayers, wept, and then were forever silenced."[29] A sensitive visitor can *hear* Cheng and Eng, the original Siamese twins, or the Nightingale singer, who are featured in the Freakatorium. We learn about the performers' talents and families, such as General Tom Thumb's songs and the woman he married. We see the enormous jewelry of "giants" like Johann K. Petursson, surrounded by their pictures and biographies containing many superlatives to highlight their extraordinary abilities. Put simply, the Freakatorium renders these people as active and not pathetic. Its curriculum teaches us that Freaks are amazing people—not for overcoming their freakishness and not for the ways in which they might be normal—but for who they are. One of Fox's idols, the late Melvin Burkhart, known as the Human Blockhead because he could hammer nails into his nose, is given a large photographic memorial with a respectful message below it. Facing us on the opposite wall, Lucky Diamond Rich, the most tattooed man, is visibly confident in his own freakish appearance.

Deceased Freaks survive via the vestiges of their lives currently on display. As he accomplishes with such humorous additions to the animal displays as the cowbell and Mexican hat, Fox conjures a posthumous life for human Freaks. However, he is very respectful of the people and does not make jokes about them. Barbara Kirshenblatt-Gimblett indicates that displays of people inherently "teeter-totter on a kind of semiotic seesaw, equipoised between the animate and the inanimate, the living and the dead." She continues, "The semiotic complexity of exhibits of people, particularly those of ethnographic character, may be seen in reciprocities between exhibiting the dead as if they are alive and the living as if they are dead, reciprocities for the art of the undertaker as well as the art of the museum preparatory."[30] Displays in the Freakatorium feature performers in motion, vivid lifelike descriptions, and well-preserved artifacts. And by simply inhabiting the animate Freakatorium space, objects come alive as they interact with one another, on many levels.

Although active, the Freakatorium's objects are inherently partial. Kirshenblatt-Gimblett states that museum collections are condemned to metonyomy. She says, "The art of the metonym is an art that accepts the inherently fragmentary nature of the object. Showing it in all its partiality enhances the aura of its 'realness.'"[31] Viewers thus use their imaginations to fill in the gaps of where a fragmented object came from, how it actually functioned in a different environment, and so on. A Freakish extension of Kirshenblatt-Gimblett's art of the metonym, Fox's objects engage in a sort of theater inside the Freakatorium space: a memory theater staged in the imaginations of visitors. Tom Thumb's shirts and shoes seem to dance with the stories of his performances, giving us a sense of what it would be like to experience his once world-famous repertoire. Fox's memory theater illuminates Diana Taylor's discussions of the haunting nature of performance in *The Archive and the Repertoire*. According to Taylor, figures like Princess Diana and Eva Peron still dance in the different repertoires of that which is here. Indeed, the Freakatorium stages memories of deceased Freaks through haunting displays. Similarly, performers like Tom Thumb dance in our minds, demonstrating and commemorating the resourcefulness and talents of those pushed to the social margins. In a theater that highlights exceptional characters, Freak specters also remind us that they were not always represented in such ways. They haunt those other visualizations of non-normative groups, such as those which attempt to articulate cohesion from essential or common characteristics, or by simply inserting the non-normative into normative display modes.

Most of the Freaks on display at Freakatorium are no longer alive, yet we can imagine what they might have been like because of museum resonance and Fox's memory theater. Greenblatt clarifies what resonance means to him: "I want to avoid the implication that resonance must be necessarily linked to destruction and absence; it can be found as well in unexpected survival. The key is the intimation of a larger community of voices and skills, an imagined ethnographic thickness."[32] Ethnographic thickness is heightened by the fact that Fox continues to perform as a sword swallower and his friends (who include midgets, contortionists, and many other Freaks) are entertainers—survivors who maintain and adapt the traditions of Freaks dating back to the nineteenth century. They are represented in the newer displays scattered throughout the Freakatorium—plaques from sideshow gatherings placed high on the walls and photographs of recent performances.

A recent donation to the Freakatorium is Sammy Davis Junior's glass eye, which rests in its own case near the Feejee Mermaid. An older woman said during a visit, "I can't believe that's Sammy Davis's eye!" The museum guide replied, "It is." The Freak displays are different from hoaxes of the past; their overwhelming humanity makes them real, and we know because the Freakatorium is straightforward about authenticity. The caption for the eye reads: "We've got Sammy Davis's Eye / 'Here's lookin' at you Freaks.'" Interacting with the text, the eye comes alive and at once performs and haunts in this memory theater that showcases the star. The words activate it. It is as if

Sammy Davis can see us inspecting his eye and the other objects in the museum. As at Williamsburg, a visitor might feel on display for a moment, too. Identity and the essential self are questioned and marked. This echoes Fiedler's meditation of seeing a live freak show: "but standing before Siamese Twins, the beholder sees them looking not only at each other, but—both at once—at him. And for an instant it may seem to him that he is a third brother, bound to the pair before him by an invisible bond; so that the distinction between audience and exhibit, we and them, normal and Freaks, is revealed as an illusion, desperately, perhaps even necessarily, defended, but untenable in the end."[33] The "invisible bond" Fiedler suggests might be our shared humanity, our inherited roles as players in the social systems which define us, and/or empathy from similar misfit or on-display experiences. It could be one or more of such possibilities, but acknowledging bonds between the normal and the Freak helps break down the constructed yet inveterate barriers between us. In the Freakatorium, curated liveliness and dignity help establish relationships between the spectator and performer, the living and dead, as well as so-called normal observers and the anomalous wonders it keeps on stage.

CONCLUSION

Johnny Fox's Frik and Frak, a double-headed turtle, is the only live Freak consistently on display at the Freakatorium. When the turtle sits by the side of its tank, which it almost always does, one head peeks above the water and the other stays immersed, never coming up for air. Sometimes, one head sleeps while the other is alert. Despite any questions we may have regarding this creature, Frik and Frak is undoubtedly alive. To have two heads and only one body complicates our very basic concepts of living things. How do the two brains work at once to make up one organism? Does one head perform more of the functions than the other? What about the spirituality of a two-headed creature? Visitors tend to anthropomorphize the animal. Conversely, human Freaks have been severely objectified and animalized throughout history. As Leslie Fiedler puts it, "Only the true Freak challenges the conventional boundaries between male and female, sexed and sexless, animal and human, large and small, self and other, and consequently between reality and illusion, experience and fantasy, fact and myth."[34] Like the Freaks it displays, the Freakatorium itself is exceptionally hybrid.

It is important to note that human Freaks do not perform in the Freakatorium as they did in Barnum's American Museum. However, we can see from the events section of the Freakatorium website that a Freak community surrounds the contemporary museum. For a fee, they will "throw a party your friends and colleagues will *never forget* with 'the Peerless Prodigies and Performers' of the Freakatorium's booking services. Featuring: little people, contortionists, fairies, ballerinas, exotic musicians, snake dancers, stilt-walkers, sword swallowers and fire eaters."[35] Much of the Freakatorium itself is an archive of Freaks who once performed, as well as of nonhuman curiosities like the world's smallest books and a boa constrictor. Outside of the Freakatorium space, too, the history of dime museums and freak shows continues through the body knowledge and reiterated behaviors of Freaks who still perform. In-depth research on Fox's participation in a community of active performers would be valuable to understand the history of freak shows and dime museums even better. In the future, a study of both might be more easily accomplished; in my interview with Johnny, I asked what he plans for the future of his museum. He explained to me, "I hope to make it bigger, grander. I want to get a space somewhere over by Times Square or something, where more tourists can come by. I want to get a larger space so I can have performers featured there. I want to bring them back into it."[36]

The many layers of the Freakatorium teach us new ways to articulate identity and history in a museum space, using a display mode we might dismiss as outdated. The broader issues the museum speaks to, as well as Fox's unique explorations of his objects' agency, reveal that the Freakatorium is not a simple anachronism. A project specifically different from others involved in identity politics, this storefront museum rejects making the anomalous appear normative or unified. It performs aspects of both the history and twisted present of dime museums and memorializes Freak performers, all creatively and Freakishly. Its lovely complexity challenges our very notions of order and disorder, as well as of how narratives can be constructed. As visitors learning about museum history and Freak culture, as well as enjoying an exotic space in the here and now, we are going to leave the Freakatorium with varied impressions. Attending the museum is different from reading Dennett's text or any other, although they are equally important to study. They illuminate and speak to each other. An admiring academic visitor, I hope my essay, my archive, my textual and visual impression of the site, appropriately convey the weird and wonderful aspects of it, in all of its beautiful dis/order. If Johnny Fox achieves his goals, the museum will continue to grow and change. And via his community-oriented projects, the history of dime museums and Freaks will continue through performance, static displays, and blurry areas in between.[37] We can imagine, hear, and see what is so amazing about the anomalous and non-normative. We can also learn much about ourselves, all in a few trips to the Freakatorium.

NOTES

1. James Clifford, *Routes* (Cambridge: Harvard University Press, 1997), 121.

2. Clifford, *Routes*, 218.

3. El Museo del Barrio began as a grassroots Puerto Rican institution in Manhattan. It eventually expanded to include other forms of Latin art, and now favors "universal" Latin forms, such as the arch in its logo, marginalizing the more specific and political forms on which the museum was founded. See Arlene Davila's "Culture in the Battleground: From Nationalist to Pan-Latino Projects," *Museum Anthropology* 23, no. 3 (1999): 26–41, or her book *Barrio Dreams: Puerto Ricans, Latinos, and the Neoliberal City* (Berkeley: University of California Press, 2004).

4. Barbara Kirshenblatt-Gimblett, *Destination Culture* (Berkeley: University of California Press, 1998), 18.

5. See Weschler's creative text, *Mr. Wilson's Cabinet of Wonder* (New York: Vintage, 1995) for an in-depth exploration of the Museum of Jurassic Technology.

6. Rosemarie Thomson, *Extraordinary Bodies* (New York: Columbia University Press, 1996), 58.

7. Queerness and disability exist in the larger context of all non-normative modes, which also include gender, race, class, and so on. Refer to Thomson's theories on how configurations of differences and non-normativity began in the nineteenth century in *Extraordinary Bodies*, 136.

8. All quotations in this paragraph are from the author's interview with Johnny Fox, 6 November 2003.

9. Richard D. Altick, *The Shows of London* (Cambridge: Harvard University Press, 1978), 1–22.

10. Altick, *The Shows of London*, 1.

11. Paula Findlen, *Possessing Nature: Museums, Collecting, and Scientific Culture in Early Modern Italy* (Berkeley: University of California Press, 1996), 50.

12. Altick, *The Shows of London*, 1.

13. Andrea Stulman Dennett, *Weird and Wonderful: The Dime Museum in America* (New York: New York University Press, 1997), 7.

14. Dennett, *Weird and Wonderful*, 17.

15. Dennett, *Weird and Wonderful*, 17.

16. Thomson, *Extraordinary Bodies*, 59.

17. Dennett. *Weird and Wonderful*, 5.

18. Dennett. *Weird and Wonderful*, 43.

19. Dennett. *Weird and Wonderful*, 46.

20. Johnny Fox, "Johnny Fox's Freakatorium," <www.freakatorium.com> (Accessed 7 January 2005).

21. Dennett. *Weird and Wonderful*, 54.

22. Dennett. *Weird and Wonderful*, 56.

23. Kirshenblatt-Gimblett, *Destination Culture*, 21.

24. Thomson, *Extraordinary Bodies*, 57.

25. Thomson, *Extraordinary Bodies*, 58–59.

26. Leslie Fiedler, "Freaks: Myths and Images of the Secret Self," in *The Tyranny of the Normal*, ed. Sheryl Buckley and Carol C. Donley (Kent: Kent State University Press, 1995), 12.

27. Marc Hartzman, "Sword Swallowing, Spike Hammering, and Freaks at Johnny Fox's Freakatorium," *Backwashzine* <www.backwashzine.com/freakatorium.html> (Accessed 7 January 2005).

28. Stephen Greenblatt, "Resonance and Wonder," in *Exhibiting Cultures: The Poetics and Politics of Museum Display*, ed. Ivan Karp and Steven Lavine (Washington, D.C.: Smithsonian Institution Press, 1991), 45.

29. Greenblatt, "Resonance and Wonder," 47.

30. Kirshenblatt-Gimblett, *Destination Culture*, 35.

31. Kirshenblatt-Gimblett, *Destination Culture*, 19–20.

32. Greenblatt, "Resonance and Wonder," 48.

33. Fiedler, "Freaks," 26.

34. Fiedler, "Freaks," 19.

35. Johnny Fox, "Johnny Fox's Freakatorium."

36. Author's interview with Johnny Fox, 6 November 2003.

37. As a result of modern science's ever-advancing technologies, Freaks are in new danger of extinction, perhaps more than ever before. According to Leslie Fiedler, "It is even likely that fewer monsters were denied a chance to live in older 'priest-ridden' societies than in an AMA-controlled age like our own, in which 'therapeutic abortions' are available to mothers expecting monstrous births, and infanticide is practiced under the name of 'removal of life supports from non-viable major terata,'" "Freaks," 17.

13

Cities, Museums, and City Museums

ERIC SANDWEISS

"Cold Beer! Smoking allowed."

Those unfashionably welcoming words greet visitors to Beatnik Bob's Café, a shadowy but comfortable joint that sits beside the railroad tracks. On the nearby train platform, a line of four-foot-tall commuters queues for the next train that will take them in careening circles through the countryside and drop them back where they started. On the wall around the corner, a signed print of R. Crumb's comic "Short History of America" hangs by itself, without label or explanation, as if someone had found a nail sticking out and looked for a picture to cover it with. Welcome to City Museum.

By the time City Museum visitors attain the threshold of Beatnik Bob's, on the third floor of this enormous former warehouse just west of downtown St. Louis, they have already crawled through a reconstructed nineteenth-century farmhouse embedded within a vertiginous outdoor play structure known as MonstroCity; walked nervously beneath a school bus perched over the edge of the roof nine stories above; purchased tickets through a window in the reconstructed terra cotta facade of a well-loved downtown office building; lost their children somewhere in the jaws of a fifty-foot concrete whale or in the maze of imitation Ozark caves to which it leads; climbed the former staircase of the city's early twentieth-century public hospital; watched a twelve-ton granite block being raised and lowered by the world's largest windmill engine; learned how to make shoelaces; and found themselves enlisted as circus performers.

Two miles to the south, the scene appears quite different. Here, on a quiet street at the industrial fringe of St. Louis's Soulard neighborhood, an enormous flatbed trailer neatly marked with the words "St. Louis Architectural Art Company" idles outside an unremarkable nineteenth-century industrial building. A tall, thin man, dressed in pressed khakis and flannels and sporting a gray Errol Flynn moustache, swings the wooden stable doors open, revealing a scene to rival the final moments of *Raiders of the Lost Ark*: row upon row of stacked wooden crates with stenciled notations painted on their slats, stretching back into the gloom as far as the eye can see. Around the crates, intruding into the carefully swept aisles, stand stained-glass windows, baptismal fonts, iron rails, elevator cages, enormous metal signs, stacks of molded bricks, and pieces of steam engines. A spiral iron staircase and an oversized freight elevator lead up to a second story where, one rightly suspects, more treasure awaits.

Someday, this, too, will be a museum. Like Bob Cassilly, proprietor of the City Museum, Larry Giles has watched a city being wrenched apart, brick by brick. Like Cassilly, Giles dreams of a place where he can reconstruct that history in new and unexpected ways—for those who still remember it and for their children who never will. But the difference between the two projects—the first already a noisy reality, the second still a quiet dream—remains as vast as the tracts of empty land that separate the clustered remnants of St. Louis's once densely settled inner-city landscape. Somewhere in that wide gap lies the question of how our urban museums will look in the coming century and, with it, the larger question of how we want to memorialize the great material legacy of two centuries of urban growth.

CITY MUSEUM

If City Museum is any indication, St. Louisans are more than ready—even eager—to entertain unconventional answers to those questions. Despite an admissions tariff that has doubled from its original six dollars per person, City Museum's annual attendance has remained at roughly 300,000 since its opening in 1997. What draws these audiences in such steady numbers is an opportunity to enjoy precisely the sense of uncertainty and overstimulation that accredited, established museums have traditionally worked so hard to have their visitors avoid. Better than most attempts within traditional museum contexts at reworking the content and technique of the exhibition medium,

City Museum has succeeded in questioning the foundations of the museum experience and substituting for them a variety of as-yet unassimilated possibilities for future directions in the profession.

Presiding initially over the project was a team of creative, energetic artists, builders, craftspeople, and collectors headed by the then husband and wife team of Gail and Bob Cassilly. It was the Cassillys who, in 1993, purchased the landmark International Shoe Company building on Washington Avenue in the city's garment district and the adjacent 600,000-square-foot warehouse in which a young Tom "Tennessee" Williams once struggled to hold a respectable job (an experience he would later attribute to his namesake character in his play, *The Glass Menagerie*).

St. Louisans were already somewhat familiar with Cassilly's career as an architectural salvager (exacting but steady work in this demolition-friendly city, which diminished in its population from more than 800,000 in 1950 to just under 350,000 by the turn of the century), and as the creator of some fanciful environmental sculptures scattered around the region. Gail, an artist, was reputed to be the business end of the operation. The purchase and rehabilitation of the International Shoe complex seemed a bid for respectability—a shrewd real estate move at a time when this downtown-fringe neighborhood was well-poised for a comeback.

But if the Cassillys proved smart, they soon laid to rest any fears that they might also have gone straight. Instead, what they revealed to curious St. Louisans when they opened City Museum's doors in October 1997 was a funhouse of industrial proportions. Concrete slab floors, where they seemed to be in the way, had been cut clean through; massive elements from demolished local buildings had been resurrected; one whole floor had been transformed with enough caves, ropes, hollow trees, and tunnels to lose a whole class of school children; a third-floor wall was adorned by what were quite plausibly described as the world's largest pair of underpants.

The common element in this startling menagerie was its reassemblage of once familiar fragments of our industrial and commercial culture into a new and sometimes unrecognizable context. Cast-off materials made up not only the content of many of the museum's displays—such as the St. Louis Architectural Museum, a display of building fragments from the collection of Cassilly's fellow salvager, Bruce Gerrie—but also the structure of the museum itself, its curriculum. Titanium debris from the factory floor at McDonnell-Douglas adorned the columns of the Lizard Lounge; a staircase banister revealed itself on closer inspection to be crafted from dozens of conveyor belt rollers; stacked rows of metal steam-table warming trays made up the walls of the first floor restrooms. Elsewhere, inlaid mosaics across the walls and floors turned bits and pieces of broken objects into a tropical fantasy of lizards, fish, and jungle flora. Gail, interviewed for a video that documented the making of the museum, explained matter-of-factly that "Bob's always had a close relationship with junk," while Cassilly himself offered that "if you can buy it in a store, we don't want it."[1]

City Museum, as St. Louisans experience it, is one museum and many. In some ways, it resembles the Daughters of Utah Pioneers collections. It orders the world through chaos, and it edifies through silliness. Its early exhibitions seldom added up to a single, clear "take-home message." Its interpretive labels—sometimes typed pages taped to the wall—are grammatically erratic. With the possible exception of a temporary exhibition space on the top floor (itself the site of exhibits on topics ranging from Russian dinosaurs to shoe collectors to birdcages), no portion of the museum seems likely to meet American Association of Museum standards for traveling exhibit sites.

The institution's title of "museum" suggests a certain level of ambiguity in a city long blessed with substantial and publicly sanctioned museums of science, art, and history, not to mention with lesser-known institutions dedicated to, among other subjects, Jesuit missionaries, dogs, bowling, and Elvis's second coming (Beeny's museum described earlier in this book). If the appellation lends an air of credibility to the operation, it functions simultaneously as a splendid joke. This is a museum of museums, a display of displays, and the kind of place that bored children might fantasize about on a class field trip to the art museum. Its unconventional pedagogy challenges Schwab's commonplaces. If some of its temporary exhibitions, such as the "Sullivan in the City" architectural exhibit in the temporary gallery in 1999, attempt to impart serious historical content, there are just as many whose sole purpose is only as serious as getting us to understand the history of the corn dog in American culture. City Museum has managed to shake up familiar formulas and send them cascading in a delightful mess back to the ground. Following the Cassillys' bitter and much-publicized divorce in 2002, Cassilly purchased the museum from its board and converted it from a nonprofit corporation to a private business, opening it still further to change, surprise, and unpredictability.[2] Today, he has begun working on an enormous rooftop water park; the space once devoted to temporary exhibitions has found new life as a skateless skateboard park, and the second floor has been given over to the World Aquarium, which Cassilly helped to rescue from its obscure existence in a suburban industrial park in 2004.

THE NATIONAL ARCHITECTURAL ARTS CENTER

"Where did it all go?" The question is not an uncommon one for St. Louisans to hear as they shepherd first-time visitors from the city's well-heeled suburbs toward one or another of its considerable but often isolated urban cultural attractions. On the city's north side, in particular, the loss of over one-half of St. Louis's 1950 population is glaringly evident in vacant and deteriorating buildings as well as in empty blocks disconcertingly well-maintained by city grounds crews. While the number of people dwelling in the greater metropolitan area, as opposed to those within the city limits, has grown slowly and continuously, the effect of this growth and of the accompanying desertion of urban neighborhoods has manifested itself in a spreading suburban fringe that is often more densely settled than the heart of the city.

Yet in St. Louis, unlike in Detroit, Cleveland, or other cities similarly affected by the postwar decline of urban and industrial America, the visitor's question invites more than a pro forma answer. For thirty years, many of the most significant pieces of "it" have in fact gone somewhere quite specific—into one of two inconspicuous south St. Louis buildings, the one described at the beginning of this chapter, or a converted supermarket two miles further west, both owned by self-described "architectural recovery" specialist Larry Giles.[3]

Giles himself has never been a wrecker, but by contracting with firms already engaged in the process of demolishing local buildings, he has secured for himself significant pieces (including cornices, storefronts, entryways, window spandrels, decorative stone and ironwork, and other examples of what he has often called, in informal conversations and business presentations, "building systems") of hundreds of nineteenth- and twentieth-century structures, ranging from nameless cast iron storefronts to celebrated skyscrapers. Like Cassilly and Bruce Gerrie, Giles has made money from the sale of parts of his collection (in Giles's case, primarily brick and clay tile). But to an extent greater than other St. Louis salvagers, and perhaps more than any other person in the country, Giles has obsessively documented and preserved his pieces in the hope of someday bringing them before the public. Most of his "systems" are represented in detailed photographs and architectural drawings prepared before demolition, their pieces carefully numbered for future reassembly. When the scaffolding comes down and the pieces have been lowered to the ground, Giles piles them onto a long black flatbed and trucks them off to his warehouses, where, placed in enormous, custom-built crates, they patiently await their reappearance before the public. In a basement room beside one of the warehouses, he keeps his books, magazines, trade journals, postcards, and office correspondence, comprising one of the finest private architecture and construction libraries in the nation.

In recent years Giles's quixotic mission has been aided by the formation of a nonprofit corporation, the St. Louis Building Arts Foundation, and the development of an increasingly refined proposal for a National Architectural Arts Center in which to house and display the collection. Local developer Steve Trampe, who employed him to help refurbish the Art Deco Continental Building in midtown St. Louis, stepped in with financial and organizational assistance in 2003; with Trampe's help, the foundation has entered preliminary negotiations for a donated site on the long-vacant East St. Louis, Illinois, riverfront, across from the Gateway Arch and downtown St. Louis. The site, if it comes to pass, will at last make possible the task of taking the pieces of St. Louis's past out of their shadowy hiding places and back into the eye of the public. Along with the basic goal of displaying and organizing the pieces, the foundation's board has developed a program for public education, vocational training, and civic advocacy that would bring life and activity to the museum's exhibitions. This plan would embrace Schwab's commonplaces of education as well as Huebner's rationales.

CITY MUSEUMS AND CITY HISTORY

Both Cassilly and Giles bring a larger-than-life quality to their missions—one through his anything-goes energy, the other through a quiet tenacity that has persisted over several decades' worth of work in an unremunerative pursuit. The two know one another well, but if the idea of joining forces in their singular quests was ever entertained, it quickly disappeared in the chasm that divides their personalities and visions from one another. Cassilly looks out at the detritus of St. Louis's late twentieth-century urban decay and sees toys for his sandbox; Giles sees sacraments awaiting their shrine. The museums' rationales are radically different. Each man, in his utterly distinctive way, proposes to recontextualize the fragments of his city within a new whole, to re-present a vanished world upon the site of its own disappearance. What, then, do their disparate visions suggest about cities, museums, and the relations between the two?

In the wake of a century's continuous refinement and standardization of museum practice, the public's favorable response to City Museum's well-practiced anarchy is reflected in visitation numbers that have yet to show the customary decline that attends most new museums. This circumstance suggests a desire on the part of museum makers and museum goers alike for an experience less predictable, possibly more troubling, but ultimately more uplifting, than those to which they have grown accustomed in the American museum. Ironically, this reaction is in its own way embedded in history; City Museum's jumble of useful information and shameless novelty resembles not too remotely the fare offered by the small, entrepreneurial museums that popped up more than 150 years ago in frontier cities across the United States, including several that stood, at different times, on the St. Louis waterfront just a mile east of this site.[4]

Like Johnny Fox's Freakatorium, Cassilly's museum taps more broadly into the well of surprise and spectacle that characterized earlier cabinets of curiosities and that continued in this country both in P. T. Barnum's legendary American Museum and the seemingly higher-minded efforts of polymath Charles Willson Peale, who sought to provide his audience with a display of "rational amuseuments" (and whose collection was later divided and sold, in part, to Barnum himself).[5] The ideal of the museum as laboratory, or theater, as a place in which to amass knowledge through unmediated experience, has never completely disappeared from American museums—the prevalence of period rooms and dioramas after the turn of the twentieth century attests to its continued popularity in even the most respectable museums. But the countervailing influence of the trend that began with the Smithsonian Institution's George Brown Goode's call in 1888 for "a collection of instructive labels each illustrated by a well-selected specimen,"[6] and continues today in the careful scholarship standards of the National Endowment for the Humanities, has been stronger. It is the rare history exhibition in a major museum that succeeds in being more than a subspecies of what museum professionals refer to disparagingly as the "book on the wall," more than a display of artifacts serving simply as illustrations or evidence of intellectual conclusions whose transmittal remains the primary object of the show. One suspects that, were City Museum staff asked to create such an exhibition, they would respond successfully with a display of books on the wall. Conceptual art has nothing to do with it; novelty, surprise, and sensation do. Moreover, such goals have precedents in the history of American museums.

Giles's project has an even more specific historical precedent and, with it, a sense of mission particular to St. Louis. The notion of a museum of American architecture achieved its first full articulation in this city in the 1930s, when architect and historian Charles E. Peterson, dispatched by the National Park Service to oversee landscape planning for the newly designated Jefferson National Expansion Memorial, began to conceive of alternate uses for the memorial's site, a thirty-seven-block swath of St. Louis's central waterfront. Here, at the city's historic heart, civic officials long concerned with declining property values, constrained traffic, and obsolete structures seized upon the opportunity presented by New Deal–era federal funding. The crowded waterfront blocks, envisioned for decades as cleared land serving a higher and better use as a site for high-speed transit, automobile parking, or truck-oriented warehousing, coincided almost completely with the original plat of the city as it was laid out by French traders early in 1764. By declaring the blocks to be of historic importance, local officials positioned themselves to receive the government funding they needed to proceed with their dream of destroying every trace of them.

Peterson, sent to help the government prepare a site plan for its newly acquired property, seized on the less destructive idea of an architectural museum—an open-air site, not unlike those underway at Greenfield Village and Colonial Williamsburg, in which fragments and facades from the colonial and nineteenth-century commercial structures facing the wrecking ball might form the core of a collection devoted to highlighting the entire history of American buildings. Writing for the American Institute of Architects' journal, *The Octagon*, he pleaded that "the field of American architecture is a vast one and can be investigated thoroughly only by a permanent institution with ample resources of personnel and finance."[7] Three years later, Peterson persuaded the Swiss architect Sigfried Giedion to travel to the city during his temporary residence in the United States for a detailed tour of the waterfront in the days before demolition began. Giedion returned the favor shortly thereafter, making the case for the value of the St. Louis buildings and for Peterson's endangered project in part of his influential work, *Space, Time, and Architecture*. In one passage, he cast the waterfront as an important contributor to the hitherto anonymous line of engineering and architectural forebears of the Modernist movement.[8] By 1941, with demolition underway, Peterson noted in the

Journal of the Society of Architectural Historians that he had successfully salvaged important pieces of the hundreds of architectural casualties and was storing them for future display. Perhaps under the influence of Giedion's singular view, Peterson by this time presented the premodernist argument and specifically cited the waterfront structures' ample use of iron and glass as one of his most important justifications for pushing the museum idea.[9]

Idea never became reality. The plan eventually drafted for the national design competition for the Jefferson National Expansion Memorial in 1947 called for the preservation of only a handful of landmark buildings and made no provision for Peterson's proposed museum. Eero Saarinen's Gateway Arch plan featured an uncompromising landscape (ultimately designed by Dan Kiley) of grass, water, and trees at the base of his totalizing, modernist monument. The pieces so assiduously catalogued by Peterson were scattered among several sites, many of them allegedly disappearing underneath the landfill required for the Arch itself.[10] Today, in much the same way as Arthurdale has risen again from a New Deal vision, Giles frames his efforts in reference to the failed project of the 1930s, a project that descended not only from the contemporary examples of Ford and Rockefeller but also from a longer line of architectural museum development.[11]

CITY MUSEUMS AND CITY FUTURES

If each of the St. Louis projects can thus claim connection to a longer historical legacy, they also obtain a good part of their power from their situation in contemporary St. Louis. In the case of City Museum, just as the word *museum* makes a subversive appeal to people's desires to overturn the pious authority of mainstream museums, so does the word *city* provide a key to the young institution's success. St. Louisans, like other citizens of our largely suburban nation, share a simultaneous loathing and desire for the city neighborhoods from which their parents and grandparents fled, and through which today they run just as quickly, searching for the right highway off-ramp, the stadium parking garage, or the lot to which their car has been towed. Museums have been part of this trend. Many urban museums, such as the Philadelphia Art Museum or the New York and Chicago Historical Societies, not to mention St. Louis's own history and art museums, migrated a century or so ago to park-like settings well removed from downtown businesses. While now subject to the suspicion and wariness of suburban audiences, such locations have remained largely well-recognized sites for the staging of public culture. Even the much-touted addition, in the last two decades, of downtown satellites to such respected institutions as the High and Guggenheim Museums has taken place within blocks safely sanctified as sites of white-collar respectability.

On the contrary, City Museum has offered St. Louisans a chance to return to what was ten years ago an unreconstructed corner of the city center—not into the preplanned islands of the festival marketplace, the sports stadium, or the office tower, but into a historically messy and unpredictable place. Here, even in the wake of subsequent high-end reinvestment spurred in part by Cassilly's success, bridal-gown merchants and upholsterers still operate out of aged storefronts or upstairs lofts; bums wander over from the nearby public library; and trucks lumber along with their freight. Once inside the museum, visitors witness a density of sight, sound, and experience that can only be described as urban, but that is distinctly not urbane. The noises of pinball compete with those of the train whistle, the circus performers, the giant bucket dumping water into an artificial stream, and above all, kids' laughter. Here is one preserve—accessible, fun, and often, though not always, entirely safe—where the palimpsest of the urban landscape is still tangible.

If City Museum has conspicuously inserted itself into the urban landscape, the National Architectural Arts Center remains, at the time of this writing, an intangible presence. In terms strictly of its counterpoint to the existing cityscape, leaving aside the considerable fact that it remains essentially a private storehouse, Giles's collection actually functions quite effectively. The contrast between the inconspicuous exteriors of his two warehouses and the incalculable value of what hides within is itself astonishing; more delightful still is their location upon streets and within neighborhoods where the brick, clay, and iron of nineteenth-century St. Louis itself still holds together, however tenuously, streets where the molded bricks, terra cotta ornaments, and cast-iron storefronts must somehow feel at home. What will happen once this material leaves its obscurity for the limelight of a well-designed, publicly accessible museum structure? The effort to place the hoped-for museum upon the East St. Louis waterfront on land already sanctified for tourist development and well removed from the messy realities both of that impoverished city and of St. Louis itself may bring with it all sorts of financial advantages and an increased likelihood for visitation.[12] But the price exacted by those advantages may be a loss of the kind of ironic connection that City Museum maintains between its inner elements and the world outside of its walls. Will it lose an opportunity to reenter, to redefine, and to revitalize some extant piece of the streetscape (say, in some distressed but still potentially salvageable area of the city's north or south sides) from which its pieces are drawn? The trade-off is not an easy one, and its consequences are impossible to foresee.

It is ironic that we look to museums to offer us a rich experience of discovery in the American city. Largely shorn of their original character as sites of densely packed, face-to-face, commercial exchange, most downtowns have successfully marginalized small-scale retail, wholesale, and manufacturing activities, as well as the accidental human dramas that go with them, to suburban malls, carefully zoned industrial parks, or foreign lands. Today, in place of the structures and streetscapes that once supported these various, and not altogether predictable, processes, a few well-lacquered historic structures typically punctuate the prevailing downtown landscape of office plazas, hotels, and convention centers.[13] Washington Avenue is not immune to the syndrome. City Museum's success has already hastened the development of a loft, restaurant, and nightlife district along the street, and with it, an infusion of comforting bohemian commercialism to draw suburban revelers to the domain of milliners and hosiers. On the other hand, unlike such literal recreations of the urban landscape as one finds in Los Angeles's Universal City Walk or Las Vegas's New York-New York Hotel and Casino (and even, for that matter, in New York's Times Square), City Museum and, to some extent, its surrounding neighborhood, remains an unpredictable place. In a manner not dissimilar to that of the process of urban planning in the streets outside, City Museum seems constantly at war within itself between a need for greater administrative oversight and fiscal responsibility, on the one hand, and the desire, on the other, to remain true to Bob Cassilly's restless vision of the place as a constantly evolving funhouse.

Meanwhile, Washington Avenue landlords up and down the street lobby for the public improvements, police presence, and signage design standards they deem—with no sense of irony—necessary for maintaining their neighborhood's cachet as the hip place to be. Across the river, the East St. Louis waterfront remains a cleared and seldom-visited site with little besides a casino boat and a view of the Arch to draw visitors. Here, the effort to secure development through government partnerships and official planning processes trumps any expectation of spontaneous commercial development and mirrors, in a sense, the methodical care with which Giles, Trampe, and their colleagues (including, at times, myself) are seeking to build a stable and respected institution around the piecemeal treasures of Giles's collection.

CHALLENGES FOR THE FUTURE

City Museum's challenges are, first, to stay afloat, and then to stay fresh—to reinvent itself in such a way that the jokes don't get old or the surprises mundane. If it succeeds, the institution seems as though it might through sheer magnetic energy reverse the traditional, post–Progressive Era relationship of city to museum: the longstanding presumption that the museum provides a haven of order and logic, wherein the disorderly realm of the surrounding streets gives way to systematic display and controlled learning. At a time in which we have become ever more adept at controlling what happens on the street, perhaps it is the museum that can now be the keeper of the old urban alchemy, an incubator for the accidental, the felicitous, and the happy ordinariness of human contact that has become increasingly hard to come by in public. There may even come a time when the museum becomes, once again, a reflection of the "novelties of the town," as P.T. Barnum once described his own museum.[14] The Architectural Arts Center, which actually contains a collection far more reflective of urban novelties, faces a quite different challenge: to avoid framing that collection (through its program, its design, its site) in ways that endanger its capacity for surprise and delight. If the theater facades and church pews, terra cotta cornices and electric signs of late nineteenth- and early twentieth-century St. Louis are to find a home in the twenty-first, they need to be put back to work, to effect change, surprise, activity, at some level comparable to what they possessed upon their initial appearance in the city. The key to doing so need not be through silliness or frivolity, as at City Museum and other city museums; however, its most important task may be to preserve the spirit of surprise that we have so successfully removed from other realms of our daily lives. Every now and then, a cold beer hits the spot.

NOTES

1. Gail Cassilly, interviewed in a City Museum orientation video, displayed in 1998. As of the time of writing, the museum no longer displays the film.

2. "Protest Blocks City Museum Parking: Museum's Board Threatens Legal Action Against Its Creator and Landlord," *St. Louis Post-Dispatch*, 13 April, 2001; Linda Tucci, "Cassilly Gets Back What He Created: City Museum Would Switch to For-Profit Status after the Sale," *St. Louis Business Journal* (22 February 2002).

3. Giles has long favored "recovery," rather than "salvage," as an apt term for his efforts. See the St. Louis Building Arts Foundation website, www.buildingmuseum.org/recovery.htm (accessed 26 June 2006).

4. On contemporary directions in museum practice, see for example, Thomas J. Schlereth, *Cultural History and Material Culture: Everyday Life, Landscapes, Museums* (Ann Arbor: UMI Research Press, 1990); Reesa Greenberg, Bruce W. Ferguson, and Sandy Nairne., eds., *Thinking about Exhibitions* (London, New York: Routledge, 1996); Ivan Karp and Steven D. Lavine, eds., *Exhibiting Cultures: The Poetics and Politics of Museum Display* (Washington, D.C., Smithsonian Institution Press, 1991); and Gaynor Kavanagh, ed., *Museum Provision and Professionalism* (London: Routledge, 1994). On early Western museums, see Michael Long, "Enterprise and Exchange: The Growth of Research in Henry Shaw's St. Louis," in *Beyond the Garden Wall: St. Louis in the Century of Henry Shaw*, ed. Eric Sandweiss (Columbia: University of Missouri Press, 2003), 136–66; John C. Ewers, "William Clark's Indian Museum in St. Louis," in *A Cabinet of Curiosities: Five Episodes in the Evolution of the American Museums*, Whitfield J. Bell, Jr., ed. (Charlottesville, VA: University Press of Virginia, 1967), 49–72; and John F. McDermott, "Museums in Early St. Louis," *Missouri Historical Society Bulletin* 4, no. 3 (April 1948): 129–38.

5. Peale quoted in David R. Brigham, *Public Culture in the Early Republic: Peale's Museum and Its Audience* (Washington, D.C.: Smithsonian Institution Press, 1995). On Barnum, see P. T. Barnum, *Struggles and Triumphs, or Forty Years' Recollections* (1889; New York: Penguin, 1987); Neil Harris, *Humbug: The Art of P. T. Barnum* (Boston: Little, Brown, 1973).

6. Quoted in Kenneth Hudson, *A Social History of Museums: What the Visitors Thought* (London: Macmillan, 1975), 68.

7. Charles E. Peterson, "A Museum of American Architecture: A Proposed Institution of Research and Public Education," *The Octagon: A Journal of the American Institute of Architects*, November 1936 (unpaginated offprint in possession of the author).

8. Sigfried Giedion, *Space, Time, and Architecture: The Growth of a New Tradition* (Cambridge: Harvard University Press, 1941), 134–38.

9. Peterson, "The Museum of American Architecture: A Progress Report," *Journal of the Society of Architectural Historians* 1, no. 3–4 (July-October 1941), 24–26.

10. W. Arthur Mehrhoff, *The Gateway Arch: Fact and Symbol* (Bowling Green, OH: Bowling Green University Popular Press, 1992); Robert J. Moore, *The Gateway Arch: An Architectural Dream* (St. Louis: Jefferson National Parks Association, 2005); Charles Van Ravensway, *The Jefferson National Expansion Memorial: A Brief History of an Important Project* (St. Louis: Missouri Historical Society, 1948).

11. Edward N. Kaufman, "A History of the Architectural Museum: From Napoleon through Henry Ford," in *Fragments of Chicago's Past: The Collection of Architectural Fragments at the Art Institute of Chicago*, ed. Pauline A. Saliga and Robert Bruegmann (Chicago: Art Institute of Chicago, 1990), 16–51.

12. On plans for the East St. Louis waterfront, see Abt Associates, Inc., "East St. Louis Riverfront Master Plan: Implementation Plan Final Report," prepared for the city and released 15 March 2004.

13. Among the many books to shed more light on these trends, see Larry Bennett, *Fragments of Cities: The New American Downtowns and Neighborhoods* (Columbus: Ohio State University Press, 1990), M. Christine Boyer, *The City of Collective Memory: Its Historical Imagery and Architectural Entertainments* (Cambridge: MIT Press, 1994); and Robert M. Fogelson, *Downtown: Its Rise and Fall* (New Haven: Yale University Press, 2001).

14. Barnum, *Struggles and Triumphs,* 136.

NO BUSINESS LIKE SHOW BUSINESS

The Freakatorium and the City Museum of St. Louis, like the Old State Capitol Museum in Baton Rouge and many of the other institutions described in this book, are concerned with theatricality as well as with education. This circumstance has been true of American museums since the earliest days of the republic. Their theatricality is apparent in the kind of script performed at Historic Arthurdale, in the Hollywood-influenced design of Old Cowtown, and in the multimedia messages conveyed at the Dillinger Museum. Even the simplicity of the Daughters of Utah Pioneers (DUP) exhibits could be considered a kind of presentation.

The shows in local museums are also very much about business; they may succeed or fail in terms that can be tracked by technical measures, such as attendance, visitor demographics, or shop revenue. This point is nowhere more evident than in and around New York, a city more often cited for its major museums. Tourists from every part of the globe visit New York's most visible institutions, the Metropolitan Museum of Art, the American Museum of Natural History, the Guggenheim, the Whitney, and the Museum of Modern Art. They line up to take the ferry to the Statue of Liberty and flock to see the latest Broadway musicals. Fewer individuals plan trips to lesser-known sites, such as the Lower East Side Tenement Museum or the Museum of Chinese in the Americas, missing moving, informative, and at times quirky views of Manhattan and its residents. Significantly, those who do visit such sites often have a personal connection to the neighborhood, perhaps a grandparent who sold clothes out of the Jewish tenements on Orchard Street or an Asian-born uncle who was unable to find a job in a white-owned company and ultimately sold tea out of a small storefront. Thus, in addition to commemorating the former residents of their neighborhoods, such museums teach children and adults about the kinds of stores that prospered there. High museum attendance and revenues reflect neighborhood pride and interest, but the success of these museums also reflects a political rationale for the appeal of their subject matter. In addition, the museums' popularity reflects the aesthetic success of their exhibitions' design and the quality of the experiences they offer.

Just as local museums display information about neighborhood businesses, they may be supported by them, and when they focus on a particular subject, local museums may also be endowed by corporations outside the region with an interest in that subject. An alarm company might sponsor a firefighters' museum; a munitions factory might underwrite a military museum; and a health insurance corporation might lend its name, funds, and prestige to an exhibit on human anatomy. Such sponsorships are taken for granted by American civic institutions, many of which would be unable to survive without them. In return, the institutions contribute to the public's positive perceptions of the businesses. For example, when Sara Lee contributes to the DuSable Museum of African-American History in Chicago, the grant pays dividends because it indicates to shoppers that the firm is committed to African Americans. But what happens when a liquor company is a major donor to a police museum staffed in part by some of the city's "finest"? What perspectives on labor strife or government regulations might we expect at a museum on business that is sponsored by a Fortune 500 corporation? How do such relationships affect the shows put on by museums?

To the extent that museums are businesses, too, how does their need to survive financially affect what they show and how they show it? The DUP museums are not part of the Mormon church, but it would be unlikely (and perhaps unwise) if a Utah DUP museum were to present a highly derogatory view of the church. The Smithsonian depends in part on government appropriations, a circumstance that carried considerable political weight when members of Congress and their constituents objected to the original plans for an exhibit on the Enola Gay, the plane that launched the first atomic attack on

Hiroshima. On a more positive note, the New York City Police Museum added several graphic and moving displays about police involvement on 9/11 and the ensuing cleanup. These shows are appropriate to the museum's mission and have garnered positive reviews in the New York media; at the same time, they have drawn additional visitors to the museum, making it more financially viable. While any museum would welcome a successful exhibit, local museums, which may have less access to funding than major institutions, benefit particularly from increased visitor numbers.

A final connection between museums and commerce is evident in the ubiquitous bookstore. Some gift shops have become so popular that they have branches outside their museums. Customers at Denver's chic Cherry Creek shopping center, for example, may drop into a branch of the Metropolitan Museum of Art's store. Gifts from this shop signal that the giver is a cultured and thoughtful person, definitely not poor, and the equally cultured recipient might be expected to notice certain trademarks of the museum, such as its enlarged *M* logo or the ubiquitous image of the medieval unicorn. Thus, a purchase from the gift shop can impart the same kind of social capital as a visit to the museum's collection. Yet perhaps the best proof of the importance of museum gift shops may be found north of Manhattan in the Hudson River Museum in Yonkers. The Hudson River Museum is proud to feature a special storefront by contemporary artist Red Grooms, which was commissioned in the late 1970s by Richard Koshalek, the museum's director at the time. The store itself is one of the objects on display, and its painted entrance challenges visitors to consider the way the value of art is linked to commerce.

With these multiple connections between museums and businesses in mind, I have written the last two chapters of this book about smaller institutions in lower Manhattan. The contrasts among the institutions reveal fascinating insights into the workings of race and class in our nation. These institutions are the New York City Police Museum, the Museum of American Financial History, and the Heye Center of the National Museum of the American Indian, part of the Smithsonian Institution. Some might argue that the latter is not a local institution. However, close to the site where the island of Manhattan was sold to Peter Minuit, the museum is a vital and visible reminder of a key part of New York's history.

The following chapter focuses on these institutions prior to 9/11 and outlines the complicated interrelationships between the museums and American business. The concluding chapter of this book, on the other hand, analyzes how the museums changed as a result of 9/11, when they were literally steps away from Ground Zero. Now, the three museums stand as examples of ways in which local museums can face the political and ethical challenges of the new century and continue to carve out distinctive niches for themselves in America's cultural landscape. In doing so, they bring together the themes discussed in the preceding chapters, preparing readers for future museum explorations of their own.

14

Business as Usual

Can Museums Be Bought?

AMY K. LEVIN

Museums are big business. They always have been in this country, from the time when Rembrandt and Raphaelle Peale opened their museum of oddities in Philadelphia. The openings of major urban museums such as the Metropolitan Museum of Art in New York and the Boston Museum of Fine Arts depended on funding from wealthy patrons, as do this week's art museum openings. Many critics of contemporary museums (including, at times, myself) have deplored the commercialization of museums, citing everything from tacky store paraphernalia to cozy relationships with donors that affect exhibit content. Yet the issue is more about how the connections between museums and money have evolved rather than whether they exist at all. More importantly, in an era when museums are increasingly viewed as essential to achieving political and cultural goals of social inclusiveness in the United States, it is crucial to examine the narratives created by museums' links to business, industry, or special interests to ensure that they reflect America's diversity instead of perpetuating a white upper-middle-class hegemony.

Inevitably, museums are implicated in national and international discussions of ethics as well, particularly those concerning stolen objects and their repatriation. These connections occur on two levels: first, as the market in art and antiquities creates an environment in which individuals can profit from the illegal transfer of objects, and second, as individuals and corporations sponsoring exhibits find themselves sucked into controversies regarding the ownership and display of the objects. The vagaries of the art market with regard to works from developing nations have been documented at length in Mari Carmen Ramirez's astute article, "Brokering Identities: Art Curators and the Politics of Cultural Representation." At the core of Ramirez's argument is the assertion that careful manipulations of the art market can create particular images of nations and their politics, and that in turn, perceptions about certain countries can affect the value of art objects originating from them.[1]

Perceptions of countries that have hoarded antiquities from indigenous peoples are changing as well. Not long ago, Pre-Columbian art collector Leo Harris scoffed, "Suffice it to say that there is little legal risk to concern the collector of Pre-Columbian art or artifacts, if he or she is willing to suffer port-of-entry indignities from the Customs Service." Now, such justifications that objects were knowingly sold to foreigners are exposed as self-serving remnants of colonialism, as are arguments such as Douglas Ewing's diatribe in an article opposing the Customs Service's enforcement of rules about the ownership of cultural artifacts from abroad. It is increasingly difficult for museums to justify their holdings in terms of old rules about the spoils of war belonging to the victors or patronizing attitudes about the superior preservation of objects in Western museums. For example, even though Gillett G. Griffin argues that so-called third world museums are not "reliable custodians" of objects, Electa Draper and others have noted that the collections amassed by dominant white groups in the United States are not necessarily cared for well, either.[2] A spate of recent books and articles suggest that the tide of public opinion is turning against powerful nations' ownership of other countries' cultural heritage. Philosopher Karen Warren questions the concept of ownership altogether, noting that among certain Native American peoples, cultural artifacts are not considered property. She argues convincingly that the very notion of "cultural heritage" is embedded in Western culture with its "male-biased language of patrimony."[3] Such arguments are for the most part more compelling than those defending white collectors' hoards of Pre-Columbian and Native American artifacts.

Repatriation is raising increasingly complex ethical issues. Many developing countries want cultural items repatriated, claiming that Westerners can visit them *in situ*, where the originating peoples have access to the objects. In *The International Trade in Art*, Paul Bator discusses the intricacies of this matter, even as he reminds readers that there are legitimate reasons why nations should allow some of their art out of their countries, primarily to promote international cultural understanding and appreciation, but also to inhibit smuggling by making a certain number of objects available openly and legally[4].

If any discussion of museums and business is associated with concerns about power relations and ethics, then such conversations are inevitably marked by questions of class and privilege as well. These issues are implicit in analyses of the disposition of the cultural heritage of indigenous peoples as well as in the struggle for the return of art stolen from Jews by the Nazis in World War II. The indigenous people of many nations, including the United States, have a hard time persuading the world that they have a right to their own cultural products. In contrast, the necessity of returning art stolen by the Nazis to its rightful owners is a well-publicized international cause, even though the issues are incredibly complicated. For instance, the Nazis claimed that they took art as "prepayment and advance for war reparations";[5] the Russians looted German collections as reparations for World War II damages and to an extent continue to refuse to repatriate their takings;[6] and American forces siphoned off numerous artworks as well in the aftermath of the war.[7] Supposedly neutral, Switzerland also ended up as a conduit for Jewish art during World War II.[8] Now, the United States, together with many European nations, is at the forefront of those seeking a return of the art and antiquities.

Corporations and donors can easily get sucked into these ethical quagmires concerning art ownership, as when Coca-Cola trumpeted its involvement in the conservation of works at the Hermitage museum in Leningrad, one of the institutions that have refused to return World War II loot.[9] In 2001, the Hermitage partnered with the Guggenheim in opening a museum in the Venetian casino in Las Vegas, reifying many people's stereotypes of the city and of Russian émigrés' involvement in organized crime. Similarly, a large donation may make museum curators feel compromised. For instance, "In return for a recent $38 million gift from entrepreneur Catherine Reynolds, Small [then head of the Smithsonian] agreed to create a 10,000-square-foot 'hall of achievers,'" with Reynolds's foundation having "control of the nominations of those to be honored, though final approval lies with the Smithsonian."[10] Curators, together with members of the public, objected so strenuously that the gift was revoked. Significantly, another gift that has raised eyebrows at the Smithsonian comes from one of the vice presidents of the Reynolds Foundation, Kenneth Behring.

A triad of museums in lower Manhattan illustrates the myriad kinds of entanglements introduced above; instead of taking a somewhat humorous approach to the issues, as the Freakatorium does, these institutions offer possible solutions to their difficulties. Moreover, all three institutions—the New York City Police Museum, the Museum of American Financial History, and the National Museum of the American Indian—are relatively new to their sites and therefore represent recent approaches and attitudes to their subjects and the city's history. Their curricula are more likely to reflect current practice than those of some other institutions discussed in this work. At the same time, because the museums focus on disparate topics, they allow us to consider different aspects of the relationships of museums to commerce. All three museums were also at Ground Zero for the terrorist attacks in Manhattan on September 11, 2001, so they serve as examples of how museums can work with and teach their communities in times of crisis. Since the changes in the museums as a result of the terrorist destruction will prove a major focal point of the next chapter, this essay will concentrate primarily on the collections in the summer of 2001, as they existed immediately before the disaster.

The former site of the New York City Police Museum on Broadway offers an excellent example of the complicated and sometimes awkward links between museums, governmental bodies, and private companies, while the Museum of American Financial History embodies an entity devoted to business as its subject, one that focuses primarily on the upper echelons of society. Finally, in its setting in the former U.S. Customs House, the National Museum of the American Indian demonstrates how through the use of irony and careful installation techniques, an institution can at once signify on the oppression of those who have been excluded from the mainstream economy and present the richness of their cultural products. These three museums have various institutional connections: the police museum is linked to the city, the financial history museum is an affiliate of the Smithsonian Institution, and the Native American galleries are part of the Smithsonian itself.

The entire area at the tip of Manhattan is becoming a center for museums, including not only the sites discussed in this article, but also the Fraunces Tavern Museum, the Museum of Jewish Heritage, the Skyscraper Museum, as well as ferry access to the Statue of Liberty and Ellis Island historic site. Just north of these sites, tourists visit still other museums, such as the Freakatorium, the Lower East Side Tenement Museum and the Museum of Chinese in the Americas. All of this tourist activity indicates that the area embodies an alternative to New York's "museums of influence," such as the Metropolitan Museum of Art, lining the patrician stretches of Museum Mile on Fifth Avenue.

Although this is not necessarily or deliberately part of their ethical and political rationales, the cluster of museums in lower Manhattan reveals the world of upper Fifth Avenue with gloves off, the sources of its money and power exposed. According to the mission statement posted on the New York Police Museum's website, the institution "captures the history of the NYPD as well as a present-day look at the world of law enforcement through the eyes of its officers."[11] Indeed, at its former site, the institution unabashedly glorified New York's finest, incorporating a Wall of Honor displaying the badges of officers killed in the line of duty; portraits of all the (white male) police commissioners; a history of the police force; weapons and vehicles; explanations of legal terms such as *arraignment*; and examples of forensic techniques with some hands-on activities for children. While the galleries contained sections on famous criminals, cases involving police corruption or brutality were given little or no mention. The "world of law enforcement through the eyes" of minority communities was for the most part absent as well. The narrative in many ways resembled the message or curriculum of the Dillinger Museum.

This is not to say that the museum's administration was unaware of the city's diversity. The mission statement at the time explicitly referred to the "melting pot" of people in the area: "The New York City Police Department has reflected the history of the City, both through its service to the City's many communities and through the diversity of the Department's personnel."[12] Small exhibits informed visitors about the roles of women and minorities in the force throughout its history. Yet, in many ways the museum reflected the history of mingled prejudice and privilege in the city through its exclusions. The contradictions underlying the museum's mission statement were revealed to visitors, who might perceive that the perspectives in the exhibits were primarily those of historically dominant forces within the police force, and not entirely reflective of the viewpoints of all of the city's neighborhoods.

Significantly, the wall of badges was sponsored not only by the Police Relief Fund, but also by the New York Stock Exchange. This installation was only one of clues that a "hidden" mission of the museum was to present the mutually supportive relationships between commerce and government. The list of donors included the City of New York itself as well as realty corporations (such as Tishman-Speyer), individuals (David Rockefeller), entertainment organizations (the Nederlander Organization, Shubert Organization, Sony Music), the liquor industry (Joseph E. Segram and Sons), investment firms and banks (Chase Manhattan, Merrill Lynch, Bear Stearns), drug companies (the

Pfizer Foundation), and the media (Hachette and Filipacchie Magazines, Reuters America). Not surprisingly, safety industries were represented, too, including the Federal Drug Agents Foundation and Belrose Fire Suppression. Even the tobacco market was visible through the support of Philip Morris.

The broad base of support garnered by the museum was impressive, although citizens might have been surprised to find an institution linked to the Police Department (and staffed twenty-four hours a day by at least two officers in uniform) proudly displaying its connection to the liquor industry when one of the force's charges is to curb excessive drinking. It seemed ironic, too, that the museum was sponsored by a cigarette company in an era when increasing numbers of Americans shunned tobacco as a dangerous, addictive substance.

The "selling" of the institution raised the danger that the museum would become a version of the proverbial policemen's ball, tickets or sponsorships traded with a wink for leniency or other favors. In fact, *Newsday* reporter Leonard Levitt suggested that a golf game to benefit the museum and other fund-raising efforts put the police force in an ambiguous position. He quoted Sheldon Leffler, chairman of the City Council's Public Safety Committee, saying that such behavior "creates the impression that money buys access" to the force.[13] And, significantly, the museum's website stopped proudly listing major donors, although their names were posted at the museum.

Depending on one's perspective, one of the museum's major donors through its transition, Canadian Mark Nathanson, embodies the problematic intricacies and political consequences of accepting donations from so many sources. Nathanson has been prominent in two industries: gold mining and forensic investigations. As director of IAMGOLD (International African Mining Gold), Nathanson has been involved in exploration and development of mines in South America[14] as well as Africa. A 1996 article from the *Financial Times* of London offered a narrative in which a heroic Nathanson, part detective and part adventurer, performed feats similar to those of his nineteenth-century precursors: "His researches took him to museums in Spain to study ancient maps and many times to talk with tribesmen in Mali. . . . During one visit to Sadiola [in Mali] he learned of an area close by where it was forbidden for the villagers to go—many years before, several hundred had been buried by falling ground he was told. Obviously, they had been mining, probably for gold. After using all his persuasion, and the sacrifice of a cow, Mr. Nathanson was permitted to go to this forbidden area. Today it is the site of the Sadiola Hill gold project."[15]

The above account reproduces narratives of Europeans conquering ignorance and superstition in their quest to "open" Africa, a controversial project in itself. Nathanson and IAMGOLD were also involved in legal disputes and business relationships that raised questions about whether they would be ideal sponsors for a police museum. In May 1999, Ontario courts found against IAMGOLD in a suit brought by Kinbauri Gold Corporation because IAMGOLD pulled out of an amalgamation plan for the two companies. George Hervey-Bathurst, another investor, brought suit against Nathanson's company after a Nathanson mining venture failed.[16] Others, including Canadian journalist Bruce Livesey, questioned the relationships between Nathanson's company and oppressive governments in some of the countries in which IAMGOLD operates.[17]

Nathanson's forensic enterprises can be viewed from radically disparate perspectives as well. He was lauded as the founding benefactor of the Nathanson Centre for Organized Crime and Corruption at York University in Canada. As Chairman of International FIA (Forensic Investigative Associates), he has also worked in national and international security and investigations for large corporations and governments, including some in Africa. Yet FIA's investigative activities also raised questions, in particular regarding a study of Canadian cigarette smuggling. According to Bruce Livesey, the report investigating tobacco smuggling was funded by the tobacco industry itself and served its legislative needs.[18] FIA was named in connection with a mining scandal in Indonesia, too, where it was claimed that FIA's report ultimately shielded company executives in "the fraudulent manipulation of ore samples."[19]

This research has drawn readers quite far from the New York City Police Museum, not to promote guilt by association, or to rely overly heavily on allegations published in a single media outlet, but to demonstrate how what appears to be a legitimate and welcome donation can bring an institution into controversial territory and questionable associations. Local museums are not equipped financially or otherwise to "follow the money" that comes in, and many perfectly legitimate donors would be put off if they felt that their generosity would simultaneously subject them to full investigation. These questions of the relationships of museums to their donors will bear further study in the next decade, as new corporate accounting rules may affect museums' policies for accepting donations.

The NYC Police Museum garnered media attention on its own as well. Former New York Police Commissioner Howard Safir made the museum one of his special projects and appointed his wife to the board. Controversies surrounding his tenure involved the lease arrangement for the museum and the number of full-time police officers assigned duty at the museum (originally 22).[20] The next commissioner, Bernard Kerik, appointed Safir to the museum's board and in May 2001 fired the museum's executive director and another employee for "alleged mismanagement,"[21] which involved leases of expensive cars. Part of the difficulty in untangling the ethics of the matter is the fact that the museum, while technically a private, nonprofit institution, was until recently largely staffed by police force employees, who must function under stricter regulations than the general public.

The New York City Police Museum at its former site could be said to have provided an example of the workings of American financial history, but the institution devoted to that subject across the street offers a fuller perspective on the issue. The museum, founded in 1988, is appropriately located in the building that once housed Alexander Hamilton's law office and later the main office of Rockefeller's Standard Oil Company. Like its companion, the Museum of American Financial History offers a primarily positive perspective; as its brochure says, the institution is "dedicated to celebrating the capital markets." Elsewhere, the leaflet advertises "the American Dream on Display," referring to the "economic miracle" of investors' markets and "communicating an empowering message: how a democratic free-market economy creates growth and opportunity."[22] For visitors during the 2001–2003 economic downturn, these words may have seemed ironic; not that the museum ignores the Depression of the 1920s and 1930s, but its overwhelming emphasis is on the history of *successful* finances.

For all its emphasis on largeness and success, the museum itself occupies a small, crowded suite of rooms. The institution's curriculum demonstrates how a local emphasis, the importance of New York as a financial center, can be intertwined with a subject of national interest. For example, a prominent sign notes that the museum's designation as a Smithsonian affiliate occurred at the same time as the inauguration of after-hours trading in New York: "This designation recognizes Wall Street's history—and the Museum's role—on the landscape of American storytelling." Although the museum did offer a temporary exhibit on African currency, the museum's story is primarily that of America's rich and famous. In early summer of 2001, visitors had an opportunity to view a proof of age affidavit for Carole Lombard, signed by her then husband, Clark Gable. A letter from Frank Lloyd Wright was on display as well. Earlier special exhibits focused on New York financial giants John Rockefeller and J. P. Morgan, the latter containing such trivial items as his cigar and a bottle of his claret. Such display objects created a sense of atmosphere and intimations of the true wealth of the possessors, even as they appealed to the celebrity-hungry.

Education occurred in other parts of the display. In a section on printing and engraving, visitors could see an example of a mortgage bond or use an old-fashioned embossing seal. The museum displayed stocks, checks, and other legal documents, including examples of stock certificates from popular companies such as Disney, Ringling Brothers, and Lionel. In another area, people could lift flaps with financial terms such as "exchange" written on them to discover their meaning. Such educational materials promoted economic opportunity in ways that the rest of the displays did not by offering visitors familiarity with the vocabulary and procedures of high finance. Other items on display included large busts of Hamilton and Rockefeller as well as an interactive computer sponsored by CNN, reifying the museum's image as a shrine to major corporations. In the shop, tourists could purchase pricey money-related paraphernalia, ranging from a tie with an Indian penny design to cuff links decorated like stock shares. Significantly, most of these gift items were designed for men, reflecting the continuing dominance of money markets by males.

A review of newspaper articles suggests that the museum garnered little of the negative attention that has surrounded the police museum, despite or because of this institution's affiliation with the national museum powerhouse, the Smithsonian. In part, this might have been due to the museum's setting in the financial district, as opposed to, say, in a disadvantaged neighborhood. On the other hand, one might argue that a different setting would dispel the elitist aura surrounding the site. The press silence regarding the museum may also have been due to its relative obscurity (although the same might be said by non–New Yorkers regarding the police museum). Or perhaps the gaps and omissions in the museum's narrative of financial history were so obvious that they needed no direct utterance. The ethical and political rationales were self-evident.

While the police and the financial museums tended to focus on mainstream and generally local history, the Heye Center of the National Museum of the American Indian (installed in 1994), just south of them, took—and still takes—an entirely different approach. The Heye Center is one section of a tripartite institution, with a research center in Maryland and a museum on the Mall in Washington. Like the Museum of American Financial History, the Heye Center is located in a historically and commercially significant building—the former Alexander Hamilton U.S. Customs House. All of Schwab's commonplaces come into play in a discussion of the institution's innovations.

This setting almost inevitably invokes remarks about the Indians taking back Manhattan, since it was near this site that Manhattan Island was "purchased" by Peter Minuit in 1626.[23] Senator Daniel Patrick Moynihan of New York commented at the institution's opening that the Heye Center is located on the site that initiated the "longstanding Wall Street tradition of selling things that don't belong to you."[24] The *Rocky Mountain News* found the site "jarring,"[25] but according to Susanna Sirefman, a critic of museum architecture, "A more resonant location could not have been chosen for a celebratory venue of the American Indian. The disparate juxtaposition between program and building is wonderfully ironic. It is bizarre and remarkable that such an imposing, politically incorrect capitalist monument is now the haven for Native American artifacts. The result is an extraordinary example of lateral and literal potency in architectural narrative."[26] *Baltimore Sun* art critic John Dorsey disagreed, arguing that the "facility doesn't fit with complete comfort in the building it occupies."[27] However, the discomfort aroused by recurring traces of the building's previous use is exactly what creates a conversation in viewers' minds about the museum's ethical rationale and the relationships between America's first peoples and white latecomers.

The building's classical colonnaded exterior suggests that the interior will reflect the Greek tradition, and statues by Daniel Chester French around the base of the building remain as examples of Westerners' patronizing and colonial views of other continents. Again, Sirefman provided apt commentary:

> The four seated figures represent America, Asia, Europe, and Africa. America sits proudly on her throne, a sheaf of Indian corn in her lap. Her foot rests on the ruins of the head of the Aztec deity Quetzalcoatl. A Native American wearing full headdress crouches behind her, unmistakably depicted as a second-class citizen. This antiquated, prejudiced work symbolizes the victory of America over the continent's indigenous civilizations. The hooded Africa is asleep; Asia represents the conquest and superiority of Christianity over paganism; and, of course, Europe proclaims the eternal moral superiority of its culture, traditions, and judicial system. How ironically symbolic that today the interior of this building is dedicated to celebrating the culture of the Native American.[28]

Not surprisingly, similar effects occur on the interior of the building. For instance, the resource center is in a room still marked as the cashier's territory, and visitors pass another door marked with the sign, "Collector's Office." In the building's Great Rotunda, occupied by a circle of desks where individuals brought their customs documents for examination, visitors are greeted with a vast empty space, surrounded by frescoes of ships and New York, alternating with pictures of European explorers of the American continents—Vespucius, Hudson, Verrazzano, and Columbus. Light, clear, and clean, the space rings hollow. One feels as if one is visiting a carefully restored ruin of a past civilization. Lower on the walls are some signs about the museum, and from the rotunda one may enter the three smaller exhibition spaces which are dedicated to presenting past and present works by native peoples of all the Americas. Indeed, one of the principal tenets of the museum is the continuity and enduring presence of Native American cultures, which renders the silent excess of European culture in the Grand Rotunda all the more ironic.

What is most remarkable about these galleries is their *transparency*, that is, the way the names of those involved and their perspectives are rendered absolutely explicit. In many mainstream institutions, the displays convey a sense of permanence and authority, almost even of destiny, because their creators are hidden, often to bolster claims that the exhibit shows truth, pure and impersonal, untainted by ideology. In contrast, every show at the Heye Center credits all those involved in its presentation, not only the artists. The reasons for selecting particular works are explained as well, so that visitors need not feel that mysterious and elitist mechanisms of aesthetic judgment are at work.

A 2001 exhibit on Plains Indian shirts was prefaced by a sign listing the names of the curator, exhibit manager, and museum staff, as well as "tribal elders and others." Labels named the shirt maker (when known) as well as his or her tribal affiliation and often related information that offered viewers a sense of the culture; for instance, a note by one shirt indicated that it was made for Alonzo Spang's graduation from his doctoral program. Although this personal touch derived from a contemporary desire to provide multicultural education, it was reminiscent of the contents of the labels at the DUP museums in Utah. In another exhibit, titled "All Roads Are Good: Native Voices on Life and Culture," twenty-three Native Americans chose the objects to be displayed. Next to the objects were plaques by the selectors explaining why the pieces were chosen. Although the dates of the shirts were marked in the former exhibit, in this display, the ages of objects were not consistently marked, presumably to signal cultural continuity and a non-European sense of time. The third display that summer focused on childhood and children's cradle boards, its respective parts being appropriately titled, "newborn ancestors" and "gifts of pride and love." Displays have covered other important themes as well. For instance, a 1998 exhibit at the Heye Center focused on Native American humor. Recurrent motifs included the importance of humor as a survival tool and the fact that humor can be exclusive as well as inclusive.[29]

Susan Sirefman has noted that for the most part the museum's purpose is "celebratory,"[30] and Julia Klein criticizes the opening displays for their "uncritical blandness." Klein has also commented of the "All Roads Are Good" display that "visitors come away without any master narrative to help organize their impressions," and she notes that another inaugural exhibit was "cacophonous and muddled."[31] Yet the exhibit, with its twenty-three selectors, is in fact multivocal, and it includes a wide range of different kinds of objects. No master narrative or monologic curriculum controls visitors, in part because the notion of a strict chronological narrative is counter to some tribal beliefs. Moreover, the museum's multiplicity of voices is designed at once to empower the array of different native cultures and to counter white monologic histories of America's indigenous peoples. Thus, Steven Dubin finds the display methods successful: "The meaning of objects is magnified by native interpretations. The sensation of the objects themselves is enhanced by recorded voices and authentic music. The galleries are seen as places for dialogue. They are also seen as places where viewpoints may clash."[32] Clearly, disparate cultural values are at work.

Some of these arguments resemble those raised about the police museum; however, we must remember the different context of these displays in a building that everywhere reminds viewers of white oppression. The difficulties with meeting varied cultural expectations are apparent in some of the initial reviews of the Heye Center. David Zimmerman of *USA Today* praised the museum for its "series of exhibits that virtually live and breathe. Some objects are touchable; one gallery has a traditional salmon scent (supplied by modern chemistry)."[33] The salmon scent disappeared, but other 2001 activities were designed to engage a range of audiences. For instance, in the exhibit on childhood, there was a small table where children could sit and write on index cards, "How do you show love for a child?" The exhibit also included a book and flash cards so children could learn some Comanche words. At the same time, John Dorsey of the *Baltimore Sun* found the inaugural displays crowded and overloaded with information, and he repeatedly voiced concerns about the intrusion of the video sound.[34] Nevertheless, the multimedia displays at

NMAI were far fewer and subtler than in many mainstream institutions such as the Field Museum in Chicago.[35]

Surprisingly, the Heye Center was not—and still is not—as direct about one aspect of its collection as it is about others, and this aspect would contribute considerably to dialogue. The center carries the name of George Gustav Heye, and its literature makes clear that much of the museum's collection comes from Heye's vast accumulations. However, there is little reference to the irony that Heye was in fact one of the white collectors who specialized in acquiring grave objects and sacred items. The main museum brochure notes simply that the collection was "assembled" by Heye, obscuring his methods. John Dorsey is particularly critical of this omission, noting that "the new museum's desire to be sensitive to the opinions of Indian communities extends to an almost total silence about the man responsible for the museum's collection. . . . he barely gets a mention in the thirty-two page press kit prepared for the museum's opening."[36] Under Cheyenne director Richard West, the institution repatriated many items, but nevertheless, visitors' experiences lose something by the elision of many objects' provenance, especially since that provenance tells so much about the economic differences among Americans of different races and ethnicities.

While the museum largely evaded one source of potential controversy, there were some conflicts in its creation focusing primarily around Native American traditions. For instance, some tribes were unwilling for certain sacred objects to be on display and reluctant to explain their uses. Others simply did not trust a federal institution.[37] Significantly, the museum's own goals acknowledged this difficulty, rendering the exhibitions in some ways the opposite of mainstream ones, from whose cultural perspectives nonwhites might feel excluded. Others questioned the ability of the institution to answer at once to a variety of governments, ranging from the federal bureaucracy with its troubling history regarding indigenous peoples, to elders, for many of whom the "notion of the museum is itself foreign."[38]

As with the other museums discussed in this chapter, some of the controversy ultimately revolved around funding and financial constraints. According to the *Denver Post*, the NMAI is the "first [branch of the Smithsonian] that Congress has declined to finance in full; one-third of the $110 million goal must be raised from non-federal funds."[39] This decision largely reflected changing attitudes regarding federal funding for the arts. Nevertheless, the glaring inequity in the way this museum was funded creates the impression that America's first peoples were yet again being treated as second-class citizens. By 1996, much of the match had been raised by corporations and individuals (more than 71,000 people); West indicated that "almost half of the money raised so far is from the native tribes." The largest donation at that point was $10 million from the Mashantucket Pequot Tribal Nation with funds raised from the 320-people nation's casino in Connecticut. The $10 million donation was also at the top of the Smithsonian's list of single contributions throughout its entire history.[40] This impressive achievement did much to counter stereotypes of Indians as cartoon characters or poverty-stricken alcoholics.

Yet among certain circles, these contributions, together with Rick West's 2000 presentation for the National Indian Gaming Association, raised questions similar to those posed by Mark Nathanson's connection to the New York City Police Museum. Some Native peoples, such as the Navajo, have refused to participate in gaming, claiming that it is counter to their beliefs. Other critics of Native American casinos range from those who fear increased gambling addiction to those who claim that casinos are linked to organized crime, benefit non-Indians, and are involved in other fraudulent activities. In December 2000, the *Boston Globe* published a series of articles on the subject, and follow-up reports have appeared regularly in the newspaper.[41] Rick Hill, head of the National Indian Gaming Association, issued a rebuttal, available on its web page, indicating that many of the disputes arose from different perceptions of sovereignty, claiming that the *Globe*'s coverage perpetuates white racist attitudes toward native government.[42] The charges and countercharges will no doubt continue for a long time, but for the purposes of this essay, the question remains whether donations from gaming reflect positively on the Heye Center and the Smithsonian Institution.

Indeed, some might consider the very triad of museums at the tip of Manhattan rather cacophonous, given the vast differences among the institutions. Yet, situated in the midst of the financial district, the voices of these museums reveal a great deal about business, power, and representation in America's cultural sites. Together and apart, they create an appropriately complicated picture of lower Manhattan and instigate a dialogue regarding our nation's values. Most of all, they indicate the extent to which museums can no longer be viewed from a perspective that treats them as separate from and purer than the "real" world. Their very survival is embedded in the machinations of business, and many of the intricacies of business are worked out in conjunction with museums, which are frequent sites for business parties and promotions. At the same time, there is no clear resolution to the question of whether all these relationships are beneficial (and to whom). What we can learn from these three institutions, however, is that much is to be gained from careful study of individual cases, tracing relevant history, donations, government appropriations, and other factors.

NOTES

1. Mari Carmen Ramirez, "Brokering Identities: Art Curators and the Politics of Cultural Representation," in *Thinking About Exhibitions*, ed. Reesa Greenberg, Bruce W. Ferguson, Sandy Nairne, 21–38 (New York: Routledge, 1996).

2. Leo J. Harris, "From the Collector's Perspective: The Legality of Importing Pre-Columbian Art and Artifacts," in *The Ethics of Collecting Cultural Property*, 2d. ed., ed. Phyllis Mauch Messenger (Albuquerque: University of New Mexico Press, 1999), 169; Douglas Ewing, "What Is 'Stolen'? The McClain Case Revisited," in *The Ethics of Collecting Cultural Property*, ed. Messenger, 177–83; Gillett G. Griffin, "Collecting Pre-Columbian Art," in *The Ethics of Collecting Cultural Property*, ed. Messenger, 110; Electa Draper, "Park's Artifact Storage an Anachronism," *Denver Post*, 25 July 2001.

3. Karen Warren, "Introduction. A Philosophical Perspective on the Ethics and Resolution of Cultural Property Issues," in *The Ethics of Collecting Cultural Property*, ed. Messenger, 15.

4. Paul Bator, *The International Trade in Art* (Chicago: University of Chicago Press, 1981), 46 and passim.

5. Hector Feliciano, *The Lost Museum: The Nazi Conspiracy to Steal the World's Greatest Works of Art* (New York: Basic Books, 1997), 35.

6. "Nazi 'Trophy Art' Returned to Russia," *Chicago Tribune*, 30 April 2001.

7. Kenneth D. Alford, *The Spoils of World War II: The American Military's Role in the Stealing of Europe's Art Treasures* (New York: Birch Lane Press, 1994), ix–x.

8. Feliciano, *The Lost Museum*, 196–221.

9. For information on Coca Cola's involvement with the Hermitage, see www.hermitagemuseum.org/html_En/11/b2003/hm11_1_101.html (accessed 27 June 2006); for information on the Hermitage's reluctance to return "trophy art," see, for instance, Rachel Katz, "Hermitage to Display More World War II Loot," *St. Petersburg Times* (Russia) 5 August 1998; rpt. www.dhh-3.de/biblio/news/1998/0508a (accessed 27 June 2006).

10. Michael Kilian, "National Museum's Direction Scrutinized," *Chicago Tribune*, 30 June 2001.

11. See http://nycpolicemuseum.org/html/museum-mission.html (accessed 27 June 2006).

12. See http://nycpolicemuseum.org/html/museum-mission.html.

13. Leonard Levitt, "One Police Plaza/Confidential/Safir Tees Off For Cop Museum," *Newsday*, 16 October 2000.

14. In some places, Nathanson is referred to as Dr. Nathanson. According to Bruce Livesey in "The Privatization of Rodney Stamler," www.eye.net/eye/issue/issue10.21.99/news/stamler.html (accessed 10 December 2002), Nathanson adopted the title in the 1970s without earning a Ph.D. or M.D. degree. I have found him referred to with the title in only one source, under a description of IAMGOLD at www.denvergold.org/members/iamgold.htm (accessed 10 December 2002).

15. Kenneth Gooding, "Sadiola—Nathanson's Luckiest Strike," *Financial Times* (London), 9 February 1996.

16. John Mason, "Solicitor Jailed over Conspiracy," *Financial Times* (London), 4 March 1997.

17. See, for instance, Gooding, "Sadiola—Nathanson's Luckiest Strike," and Livesey, "The Privatization of Rodney Stamler."

18. Livesey, "The Privatization of Rodney Stamler."

19. Livesey, "The Privatization of Rodney Stamler"; William Marsden, "Tobacco Firms Behind Tax Protest," *Montreal Gazette*, 17 January 2000.

20. William Rashbaum, "Police Museum Has Its Staff Overhauled," *New York Times*, 21 April 2001.

21. John Marzulli, "Kerik Will Name Safir to Museum Board," *Daily News* (New York), 2 May 2001.

22. *Museum of American Financial History* (museum leaflet).

23. Susanna Sirefman, "Formed and Forming: Contemporary Museum Architecture," *Daedalus* 128, no. 3 (Summer 1999): 306.

24. Quoted in David Zimmerman, "Native Americans Have Their Say in New Museum," *USA Today*, 27 October 1994.

25. Mary Voelz Chandler, "Indians Return to Manhattan: Native American Art Finds Home Near Wall Street," *Rocky Mountain News*, 14 March 1995.

26. Sirefman, "Formed and Forming," 306.

27. John Dorsey, "Museum of the American Indian Tries to Do Too Much, Too Noisily," *Baltimore Sun*, 6 November 1994.

28. Sirefman, "Formed and Forming," 307.

29. Suzan Shown Harjo, "Without Reservation," *Native Peoples Magazine* (Spring 1998), www.nativepeoples.com/article/categories/%3E-Archives/1998/Spring (accessed 27 June 2006).

30. Sirefman, "Formed and Forming," 306.

31. Julia Klein, "Native Americans in Museums: Lost in Translation?" *APF* (Alicia Patterson Foundation) *Reporter* 19, no. 4 (2001), www.aliciapatterson.org/APF1904/Klein/Klein.html (accessed 27 June 2006).

32. Steven C. Dubin, *Displays of Power: Memory and Amnesia in the American Museum* (New York: New York University Press, 1999), 244.

33. David Zimmerman, "Native Americans Have Their Say in New Museum."

34. John Dorsey, "Museum of the American Indian Tries to Do Too Much, Too Noisily."

35. For more information on this double standard, see Amy Levin, "The Family Camping Hall of Fame and Other Wonders: Local Museums and Local History," *Studies in Popular Culture* 19, no. 3 (1997): 86.

36. John Dorsey, "Museum of the American Indian Tries to Do Too Much, Too Noisily."

37. Julia Klein, "Native Americans in Museums: Lost in Translation?"

38. Klein, "Native Americans in Museums."

39. Joanne Ditmer, "Native American History Gains Four-Fold Home: DC Mall Site Part of National Museum," *Denver Post*, 4 April 1996.

40. Ditmer, "Native American History Gains Four-Fold Home."

41. "Tribal Gamble: The Series." *Boston Globe*, 10–13 December 2000, www.boston.com/globe/nation/packages/gaming (accessed 10 December 2002).

42. Rick Hill, Letter to the *Boston Globe*, 12 December 2000, http://indiangaming.org/info/bostonglobe.shtml (accessed 12 December 2002).

15

Conclusion

Museums and the American Imagination

AMY K. LEVIN

The museums discussed in the previous chapter offer an excellent example of the way institutions may capture—or be captured by—a particular time as well as place. The chapter was originally completed over Labor Day weekend, 2001, which is why the section on the New York City Police Museum focuses on its Broadway site, instead of its current location a few blocks away. We all know what happened ten days later, on September 11, 2001. As a result of the terrorist attacks, the three museums I had just finished writing about were suddenly at Ground Zero in one of the worst human calamities in history. For a long time, no one was entirely sure how the collections had fared or how long the museums would be closed. Compared to the number of deaths that occurred on and shortly after September 11, the fate of the museums in the vicinity seems a footnote to history. Nevertheless, there is much to be learned from these museums' experiences. The ways in which they handled the transition from life pre-9/11 to post-9/11 sums up many of the themes of this book. In addition, the survival and transformations of these museums indicate future directions for other local museums.

To the visitor, the Heye Center collection appears unscathed and there is little change in the exhibition methods or in the attention to the lived experiences of Native Americans. Staff reports on the American Association of Museums

(AAM) website after the disaster indicate that the main problem the museum faced after 9/11 was piles of dust. According to Scott Merritt, Research Branch Manager, "The building is covered in a few inches of ash. But it was completely closed, as were intake vents, resulting in little if any impact on the collection." Because many of the museum's objects are considered sacred and had to be installed with special rituals, they also had to be cleaned and treated in a way that respected tribal traditions and ceremonies. As a result, the cleaning task was more complicated than one might initially imagine. Indeed, a second staff report on the AAM website indicated that the building would reopen to staff on September 19, 2001, with "a full Native American ceremonial blessing."[1]

Another change at the Heye Center is the addition of a wall display on Native American art in New York, giving the institution a more local character. This display includes a photo of George Gustav Heye, the white collector after whom the institution is named. In a sense, the display is a meta-exhibit about installation methods and museum interpretation. Crammed in a hallway, it consists almost entirely of photographs and text. The exhibit begins in 1918 and features prominently a 1919 display at the American Museum of Natural History, the "Exhibition of Industrial Art in Textiles and Costumes." Such early museum shows did not feature Native American work as *art*. This was typical of the early display methods of the works of colonized peoples in American and European museums; for instance, African objects were long displayed as curiosities or primitive remains similar to those shown in the early days of the Dickson Mounds Museum, regardless of their age. The wall display at the NMAI records a change in this attitude in a 1927 exhibit from the National Gallery of Canada, a landmark because it presented the works as art first and ethnologic objects second. The exhibit ends with the 1984 primitivism show at the Museum of Modern Art in New York, which encouraged viewers to see connections between the creations of twentieth-century artists such as Picasso and the works of so-called primitive peoples, including Africans, Native Americans, and Australian aborigines.

The inclusion of this exhibit at the Heye Center is significant for several reasons. First, it ties the institution more closely to its location at a time when residents, neighborhood workers, and tourists see the area as a symbol of American sorrow and courage. Second, the exhibit contextualizes the rest of the museum by explaining why a museum dedicated to Native American art as art is such an important development. The display also demonstrates for viewers how the museum's insistence on identifying all "voices" behind exhibits is a response to more directive museum scripts such as the ones at the primitivism exhibit. But as useful as the display might be to those unaware of the history of exhibitions of Native American art, it does guide or teach viewers and implicitly asks them to accept the museum's rationales. We are expected to perceive the Heye Center as "good" (ethically, politically, and aesthetically) and prior exhibitions as inadequate, laughable, demeaning, or racist. In doing so, it takes away from some of the openness of other Heye Center exhibits; it "tells" rather than "shows."

The Museum of American Financial History shows few effects of 9/11 as well, and, in fact, was not listed in the AAM report on museums in the area. Gift store staff report that the collection was not damaged, but that the museum's business suffered along with the entire financial district. Given the museum's focus, this circumstance seems oddly if sadly appropriate.

In May 2004, one exhibit, held over from 2003, celebrated "Pan Am and the Golden Age of Air Travel." This display was mostly a paean to the now defunct airline, the information it contained imbued with nostalgia. The exhibit included posters, promotional items, pins, a pilot's jacket, and a display case on the first Air Force One plane. The implicit message, that flying isn't what it used to be, replaced any mention of the role of aircraft in the 9/11 disaster with a longing for a dream life at some imaginary, unspecified time in the twentieth century. Or, if not a dream life, a life in film. Like Wichita's Old Cowtown, the Financial History Museum based its presentation on flying in part on the glamorous images in old movies and newsreels. The connection to Hollywood is further emphasized in a museum brochure article on the building, which lists the blockbusters that have featured shots of the building.[2]

"Do It Yourself," another 2004 exhibit, concentrated on the Small Business Administration or SBA, and was a notable shift from the institution's primary emphasis on big business. The exhibit focused on a group of well-known businesses that received SBA assistance in their early days, such as Panera Bread, Tom's of Maine, and Ben and Jerry's ice cream. A small part of the exhibit was set aside for each corporation. The mini-displays included examples of the companies' products in addition to listing the names of their owners, the dates of SBA loans, and their amounts. They also incorporated a short history of each business. This exhibit had a more populist emphasis than the display on J. P. Morgan, with prominent signs that announced, "Small businesses employ half of America's private work force," and "Small business brings economic opportunity within the reach of millions of Americans." Yet only a smaller board emphasized diversity, "The agency has special programs in place to assist women, Native Americans and other minorities." The El Monterey corporation appeared to be the token Latino business in the exhibit.

In fact, despite all the efforts to indicate that the SBA helps all Americans, the script reified my original conception of the museum as an institution that glorified the American dream of business success. The bold headline on one sign virtually shouted, "The Story of Small Business Is the Story of the American Dream." A test question for visitors asked where Fred Smith, the founder of FedEx, went to college, and the answer was the Ivy League school Yale. Finally, the museum flyer on the exhibit proclaimed, "We're proud to host the official exhibition celebrating SBA's fiftieth anniversary. We salute them—and the millions of enterprising Americans they serve every day."[3]

The SBA exhibit did nod to the effects of the 9/11 disaster, but not in terms of the museum itself. Instead, part of the exhibit's praise song for the government agency was a comment that since the day of the terrorist attacks on Manhattan, the agency "provided over $235 million in disaster relief to assist small businesses here in lower Manhattan."[4] In this way, the museum was able to reassert its ties to the city and to indicate that it was concerned about the events of 2001.

The exhibit following the SBA show focused on migrant farm workers in the Northeast and appeared to be another effort to diversify the exhibition schedule. In this case, the brochure advertised, "In the Museum's efforts to examine all aspects of the nation's economy, we are pleased to be the first Wall Street venue to present this exhibit."[5] This show appeared to take its populist mission more seriously, since it was bilingual, with information in English and Spanish. Clearly, then, even though its efforts have been somewhat limited, since 9/11 the Museum of American Financial History has strived to be more inclusive in terms of race and class and to reflect the financial history of all Americans. These efforts play a role in the image of America that is presented to the public, thus shaping the institution's curriculum.

The New York City Police Museum was shut on 9/11 in preparation for a move, so in some ways it was least affected by the destruction, even though its collection was covered with ash and debris. Yet its current exhibits are more reflective of the disasters than those at the Heye Center and Museum of American Financial History, perhaps because the museum's subject—the police—played the most visible role on 9/11 and in the following months. Moreover, the changes tend to alter the museum's curricular message from one similar to that of the Dillinger Museum, "Crime does not pay," to one that humanizes members of the force and emphasizes their rescue mission as well as their crime-fighting responsibilities. At the same time, the museum has become more inclusive of race and gender.

The displays on the ground floor of the museum continue to depict crime-fighting methods and the history of the police force. Cases contain myriad objects, such as guns, regulation books, badges, and related paraphernalia. The early parts of the narrative focus on informal kinds of police, for instance the watchmen of the 1690s, with increasing detail about police work in the nineteenth and twentieth centuries. Women are mentioned briefly, for instance, in an 1845 rule book, but the emphasis is on the police force as an example of the power of the city's white males. Another section focuses on the notorious 1930s Italian Squad, which aimed to eliminate gangs of Italian immigrants. This section features a book significantly titled *One Must Be Rough*, written in 1930 by Michael Fischetti. Theodore Roosevelt is also featured in his role as president of the Board of Police Commissioners.

The signs in this section are invariably sympathetic to the police. Describing the life of officers in the 1870s, one text reads as it might about police today: "The career of a policeman during this period was a mixed experience. . . . It seemed no matter what action they took the police would anger a number of citizens." Other signs sound defensive. A description of the 1863 Draft Riots informs visitors that "many observers **praised the police** for their courageous efforts in putting down the riot." Negatives are elided; signs discuss the "sweeping changes" of the 1990s but not any problems that might have precipitated those alterations:

> These changes led to the reduction of street crimes, the seizure of illegal weapons, narcotics and marijuana, and a decrease in the number of stolen automobiles. At the same time, new initiatives and a philosophy of **Courtesy, Professionalism, and Respect** strengthened the ties between the police and New York City's citizens.

Displays upstairs supplement this depiction of the force and give visitors opportunities to learn about forensics, DNA, notorious criminals, and the police academy. These exhibits, too, tend to be celebratory of the skills of New York's "finest." Those seeking an experiential opportunity may visit a jail cell, which is a more monitory offering.

Another room on the ground floor, displaying uniforms, raises the question of why such displays are so frequently found at police and military museums. While uniforms and their accoutrements are evidence of the kind of work done by their wearers, the mannequins depersonalize displays, creating a sense of the police as anonymous, sometimes faceless, personifications of authority. Whereas guns, regulation books, and other objects more visible in the previous area give a sense of the police's activities and responsibilities, the uniforms create a more passive view of the police, as people who walk around in a kind of costume, observing what happens.

The ground floor also contains an extensive exhibit about women in policing, which covers the walls of a room whose center is filled with examples of police vehicles. In one sense, this leaves the impression that women remain marginal or peripheral; however, the display is detailed and balanced enough to dispel this image somewhat. For instance, one sign notes that the first women's police precinct was concerned primarily with welfare work, which at the time was presumed to be more suited to women's nurturing capacities. Another quotes a patrolman's disgust at the notion of a woman driving a police vehicle. Other signs inform readers of women's progress within the force, but note that in 2002, women still comprised only 16.5 percent of the force. Objects, too, record the at times quirky and uneven progress of women in the force, such as the fact that policewomen were required to wear high heels as late as 1968. One case contains everything from a copy of a trial exam for women to a special lipstick, similar to one issued with a revolver in a special gun case cum makeup kit for policewomen, circa 1943. The tone of the displays and narratives is one of bemused nostalgia, which works to forestall or minimize anger at the treatment of women in the force.

The museum's shift in political rationale is evident elsewhere, too. One of the two upper floors includes a room dedicated to Samuel Battle, the first African-American New York City policeman. This narrative is presented as an all-American success story, beginning, "As the son of former slaves, Samuel Battle was determined to make the most of what his country had to offer. Overcoming what seemed to be insurmountable obstacles in his great quest for equality, he became the first African American hired by the consolidated NYPD in 1911."[6] Later parts of the narrative describe the racism and other difficulties he faced in entering the force and gaining promotions before he was appointed Commissioner of the New York City Parole Commission. A tape plays excerpts of Battle's oral history and shows images of his life. The room sends visitors a clear message that African Americans and other minorities are parts of the force; however, because Battle retired in 1951, there is little discussion of the fate of minorities on the force in more recent years.

One of the museum's proud sponsors is Steven Bochco Productions, the television powerhouse that created such hits as *LA Law* and, more significantly, *NYPD Blue.* It comes as little surprise then, that one of the upstairs rooms focuses on how the police force is dramatized on television. The display concentrates primarily on action shows that depict the police solving cases, rather than on documentaries that might provide a more in-depth view of the force's work. Like Wichita's Old Cowtown, this exhibit suggests the interrelationships of popular culture and museums, the ways in which media images fictionalize reality and in turn affect that reality. It also reminds visitors that police work gains the most public recognition when it is dramatic and morally clear, and at the same time, that police work is always in the process of being translated into a media product, through press releases, television shows, and film.

The exhibits described above have a mixed success in overcoming some of the difficulties posed by the monologic narrative at the previous site of the museum. The room on the media raises questions about how images of the police are created and perpetuated among the public. But it is the very presence of dramatic media that makes the "9.11 Remembered" exhibit so compelling. "The Pile" shows the detritus that NYPD sifted for evidence, which included a gun encased in concrete by the heat. The room also contains twin towers of stacked monitors, each showing photos of the attacks and police in action. The monitors turn black as the towers are struck down. Reminders that twenty-three police officers died are prominent as well.

While the main room contains graphic descriptions of the event, a side room is quiet, a memorial to the police who received a posthumous medal of honor for their work. A message book in the room contains mostly congratulatory comments, thanks to the police, and religious messages. The room serves as a shrine for police officers visiting from other places, many of whom have signed the guest book with such comments as "I love all you american hero's [sic] you make me feel safe." One page provides an oppositional message, however: "Fuck the cops." The exhibit spills over into the adjoining room on forensics, with information on how the police sifted debris from the World Trade Center site. Samples of wreckage provide a moving testament to the gruesome task facing those sorting ash and other remnants at the Fresh Kills landfill.

The "9.11 Remembered" display effectively conveys the hard work and losses suffered by the force on America's saddest day. The date is also memorialized repeatedly throughout the upper floors of the museum. A small hallway shows badges and gifts given by other police forces as well as letters from children on the force's role in 9/11. Visitors can add to the display on a board provided for that purpose. The "Hall of Heroes," another shrine-like space, displays the badges of all police who died while on duty in a somber room with dark blue walls. It also includes another memorial to those who died on 9/11. An audio tape plays the names of the dead, the dates on which they died, and bagpipes. The room is set off by blue velvet curtains at the entrance.

The reconfigured New York City Police Museum thus brings together many of the themes introduced in previous chapters. Certain exhibits offer the kind of guided, one-sided narrative of history and "look at me" inclusion of women and minorities evident in the museums described in the "Rebirth of a Nation" section as well as those in the chapters focusing on nostalgia as epistemology. But the new displays on 9/11 take the techniques evident in the museums described in the articles about City Museum and the DUP collections to extremes, incorporating debris, fragments, photos, and celebratory displays, while hinting at the voices lost in the tragedy. Together with the message books and walls inviting additional comments, the displays create a multivocal narrative that can be constantly reimagined through visitors' responses. The museum offers a model for how local institutions can mix contemporary multimedia with more traditional display methods in communicating both the local and global significance of events in their vicinity. As at the Museum of American Financial History, these exhibitions signal a renewed commitment to the importance of diversity, because it is critical to the survival of the nation and to its businesses.

Most of all, the New York City Police Museum's emphasis on 9/11 shows us why and how local museums can play crucial roles in teaching America's history, and why they will continue to offer important images of our nation in coming years. The articles in this collection have taken us beyond New York on a tour of the United States, even as they have offered vistas into significant points in its history. We have explored sites in New England, the Deep South, the Rocky Mountain West, and the Midwest, finding how institutions deal with the unique features of their locations and how they face common concerns about depicting an area. We have noted how local museums often focus on transitional periods in American or local history—the colonial era, the New Deal, the beginnings of settlement in the West, and the end of the cowboys. In fact, as with the New York City Police Museum, we can argue that the power of many of these museums' instruction comes from their temporal location as well as their spatial location. Their appeal is drawn largely from the fact that they at once record the end of one era and the beginning of a new one. In doing so, they grapple with the inherent contradictions and shifts in attitudes accompanying such changes.

The significance of such collections lies not only in the way they show us, for instance, how New Deal policies were designed to transform a poverty-stricken region into an ideal of a self-sufficient agrarian community, but also in how the museums themselves have recorded continuing change, most recently after 9/11. In creating new visions of the past, these museums have faced many of the challenges described in the introduction to this book. For instance, the comparisons of tour scripts for the *House of the Seven Gables* in Tami Christopher's article exemplify particularly well how a museum's educational staff will tell only the stories citizens are prepared to hear. The simultaneous embrace of new technology and an anticrime message at the Dillinger Museum is yet another example of how local museums adapt to meet the needs of different audiences. Old Cowtown, the Museum of American Financial History, and the New York Police Museum exemplify how museums may perpetuate media stereotypes. And, of course, these changes are attended by their own controversies.

Social transitions have also brought about shifts in the problems faced by local museums. Technology has altered the role of the U.S. Army Medical Museum. Historic society collections, such as the Daughters of Utah Pioneers exhibits, face questions of survival as the members of the community who founded and staffed the museums retire or pass away. If such museums decide to expand their focus to include newcomers to the community, then they have an opportunity to draw more diverse audiences and fresh volunteers who are crucial to their continuation. Or, if these museums are able to establish the centrality of their narrative to the community as a whole, they will also be likely to survive. When Arthurdale, West Virginia, recast itself to emphasize collaboration among its citizens instead of homesteading, it found a new popularity. Now that the Museum of American Financial History offers more displays on the disadvantaged, it, too, will reflect and draw a better cross-section of the American public.

Finances remain a recurrent theme and source of contradictions in the stories of local museums, too. Funding determines whether a museum will be able to employ sufficiently contemporary display techniques to appeal to audiences glutted on videos, the internet, and digital imagery. When such media is available, there is always the danger that the means of presentation will overshadow the objects in a collection. In some cases, such as the John Dillinger Museum and the New York City Police Museum, new technologies help situate objects within a narrative that supports dominant ideologies, for instance, about crime and punishment.

Funding also affects the extent to which a museum can encompass cultural diversity. As we have seen, the institution at Dickson Mounds struggled and changed ownership in its efforts to deal appropriately with native remains. In contrast, the richer Heye Center of the National Museum of the American Indian has been able to mount comprehensive exhibits with artifacts from various groups of America's first peoples. The irony of its setting in the old Customs House and close to the site of the sale of Manhattan to Peter Minuit imbues the museum with a tension and immediacy that is not evident in the relationship between more general museums and their locations, such as the Metropolitan Museum of Art.

Cultural diversity is dependent on the relative homogeneity or heterogeneity of a population over time as well. Because Arthurdale was initially designed to exclude African Americans and most recent immigrants, stories of its past and remaining artifacts reveal little about these minorities. Similarly, since the Daughters of Utah Pioneers define their membership according to the time when certain Mormons settled in the state, groups that arrived with or after the railroad are excluded from their exhibits. DUP museums have come to represent a smaller and smaller percentage of the state's population and an increasingly distant time in the state's history. It could be argued that their major remaining purpose is to warm the hearts of DUP descendants and to educate youngsters about an early part in the state's history. Yet, as Embry and Nelson note, one irony of their existence is that their minimal labels have come to reflect modernist thinking. Small museums often demonstrate gaps in our knowledge by including what larger museums might store as excessive specimens, but in doing so, they tell us stories which other museums cannot. And sometimes, as in the case of the 9/11 exhibit at the NYC Police Museum, the fragmentation becomes, ironically, an accurate reflection of our times.

Moreover, in her article that opens this collection, Elizabeth Vallance has emphasized the importance of educating young people in local museums. She reminds us that a primary goal of such institutions is to teach history (or, more accurately, histories), whether they include accounts of famous historical sites such as Williamsburg or are found in less attractive neighborhoods like the City Museum in Saint Louis. Other authors in the collection, such as Stuart Patterson, Eric Gable, and Richard Handler, argue that even more than teaching histories, museums contribute to the creation of a collective memory, either of individuals' pleasurable experiences at the site, or of nostalgic communal images of a locale. They may add to personal memories of defining events, such as 9/11, as well. As the Freakatorium illustrates, the desire to combine entertainment, experience, and education goes back to P. T. Barnum and the Peale family galleries of the early republic and is critical to our understanding of the functions of local museums.

Without bits and pieces, quirky dreams, and odd obsessions, America would not possess the marvelous variety of local museums that dot its landscape; without the pioneering and entrepreneurial spirit of those who set out to represent their communities, without individuals' grandiose or petty dreams, we would be bereft of the array of institutions described in this book. America without its local museums would resemble a supermarket carrying only major brands, impoverished and impoverishing for those who value choice and eclecticism, who seek variety not merely for its own sake but because it is likely to reflect a wider segment of the population.

Finally, local museums allow us to work through and imagine ways to represent the divergent voices and uncertainties of our own times. The evolving nature of the exhibits at Dickson Mounds, for example, reminds us of persistent arguments about the ownership of culture. The glorious accumulations at the Freakatorium and the City Museum in St. Louis recall at once the weirdness of our cultural products and their closeness to being trash. The difficulties of the DUP museums in Utah illustrate the effects of shifting demographics in our smaller towns, while the removal from display of items at Dickson Mounds offers an example of the way cultural differences constantly need to be renegotiated. In contrast, the Heye Center witnesses a growing valuation of Native American cultures through the voices of their people. The stories of these institutions offer above all evidence that communities survive and grow through change and tension. Educational goals shift to reflect these changes.

Steven Lavine once argued that "the task of recognizing and responding to the diversity represented in museum audiences may require smaller institutions rooted in specific communities."[7] The articles in this book confirm the vitality of local museums, and even more, their continuing importance in the larger debates about culture, power, imagination, and voice that define American society today.

NOTES

1. American Association of Museums, "Status of Museums in the Affected Areas," www.aam-us.org/helpnyc/updates.htm (accessed 8 October 2001).

2. "About 26 Broadway," *About the Museum* [museum brochure] (New York: Museum of American Financial History, n.d.), 4.

3. Meg Ventrudo, *Do It Yourself* [museum flyer] (New York: Museum of American Financial History, 2003).

4. Ventrudo, *Do It Yourself.*

5. Meg Ventrudo, *Coming Up on the Season: Migrant Farmworkers in the Northeast*" [brochure] (New York: Museum of American Financial History, 2004).

6. New York City Police Museum, *On the Job with Lt. Samuel Jesse Battle* [leaflet] (New York: New York City Police Museum, n.d.), 2.

7. Steven D. Lavine, "Audience, Ownership, and Authority," in *Museums and Communities: The Politics of Public Culture*, ed., Ivan Karp, Christine Mullen Kreamer, and Steven D. Lavine (Washington, D.C., Smithsonian Institution Press, 1992), 147.

Selected Bibliography

BOOKS

Altick, Richard D. *The Shows of London.* Cambridge: Harvard University Press, 1978.

Anderson, Benedict. *Imagined Communities: Reflections on the Origin and Spread of Nationalism.* London: Verso, 1983.

Barthel, Diane. *Historic Preservation: Collective Memory and Historical Identity.* New Brunswick: Rutgers University Press, 1996.

Bator, Paul. *The International Trade in Art.* Chicago: University of Chicago Press, 1981.

Becker, Carl. *Everyman His Own Historian.* Chicago: Quadrangle Paperbacks, 1966.

Bell, Whitfield J., Jr., ed. *A Cabinet of Curiosities: Five Episodes in the Evolution of the American Museums.* Charlottesville: University Press of Virginia, 1967.

Bennett, Tony. *The Birth of the Museum.* New York: Routledge, 1995.

Benson, Susan P., Stephen Brier, and Roy Rosenzweig, eds. *Presenting the Past: Essays on History and the Public.* Philadelphia: Temple University Press, 1986.

Bodnar, John. *Remaking America: Public Memory, Commemoration, and Patriotism.* Princeton, NJ: Princeton University Press, 1992.

Brigham, David R. *Public Culture in the Early Republic: Peale's Museum and Its Audience.* Washington, D.C.: Smithsonian Institution Press, 1995.

Brown, Julie K. *Making Culture Visible: Photography and Its Display at Industrial Fairs, International Exhibitions and Institutional Exhibitions in the United States, 1847–1900.* Amsterdam: Harwood Academic Press, 2001.

Clifford, James. *Routes.* Cambridge: Harvard University Press, 1997.

Connerton, Paul. *How Societies Remember.* Cambridge: Cambridge University Press, 1989.

Crane, Susan. *Museums and Memory.* Palo Alto, CA: Stanford University Press, 2000.

Dennett, Andrea Stulman. *Weird and Wonderful: The Dime Museum in America.* New York: New York University Press, 1997.

Dubin, Steven C. *Displays of Power: Memory and Amnesia in the American Museum.* New York: New York University Press, 1999.

Falk, John, and Lynne Dierking. *The Museum Experience.* Washington, D.C.: Whalesback Books, 1992.

Foucault, Michel. *The Archaeology of Knowledge.* New York: Pantheon, 1982.

Green, Ernestine, ed. *Ethics and Values in Archaeology.* New York: Free Press MAC, 1984.

Greenberg, Reesa, Bruce W. Ferguson, and Sandy Nairne, eds. *Thinking about Exhibitions.* London, New York: Routledge, 1996.

Halbwachs, Maurice. *On Collective Memory.* Chicago: University of Chicago Press, 1994.

Handler, Richard, and Eric Gable. *The New History in an Old Museum.* Durham, NC: Duke University Press, 1997.

Hudson, Kenneth. *Museums of Influence.* Cambridge: Cambridge University Press, 1987.

———. *A Social History of Museums: What the Visitors Thought.* London: Macmillan, 1975.

Jameson, John H., ed. *The Reconstructed Past: Reconstructions in the Public Interpretation of Archaeology and History.* Walnut Creek, CA: AltaMira Press, 2004.

Kammen, Carol. *On Doing Local History.* New York: AltaMira Press, 2003.

Kammen, Michael. *The Mystic Chords of Memory: The Transformation of Tradition in American Culture.* New York: Alfred A. Knopf, 1991.

Karp, Ivan, and Steven Lavine, eds. *Exhibiting Cultures: The Poetics and Politics of Museum Display.* Washington, D.C.: Smithsonian Institution Press, 1991.

Karp, Ivan, Christine Mullen Kreamer, and Steven D. Lavine, eds. *Museums and Communities: The Politics of Public Culture.* Washington, D.C.: Smithsonian Institution Press, 1992.

Kavanagh, Gaynor. *History Curatorship.* Leicester: Leicester University Press, 1990.

———, ed. *Making Histories in Museums.* London and New York: Leicester University Press, 1996.

———. *Museum Provision and Professionalism.* London: Routledge, 1994.

Kirshenblatt-Gimblett, Barbara. *Destination Culture: Tourism, Museums and Heritage.* Berkeley: University of California Press, 1998.

Lowenthal, David. *The Past Is a Foreign Country.* Cambridge: Cambridge University Press, 1985.

———. *Possessed by the Past: The Heritage Crusade and the Spoils of History.* New York: Free Press, 1996.

Lumley, Robert, ed. *The Museum Time Machine.* London: Routledge, 1988.

Messenger, Phyllis, ed. *The Ethics of Collecting Property: Whose Culture? Whose Property?* 2d. ed. (Albuquerque: University of New Mexico Press, 1999).

Roberts, Lisa. *From Knowledge to Narrative: Educators and the Changing Museum.* Washington, D.C.: Smithsonian Institution Press, 1997.

Rosenzweig, Roy, and David Thelen. *The Presence of the Past: Popular Uses of History in American Life.* New York: Columbia University Press, 1998.

Schlereth, Thomas J. *Cultural History and Material Culture: Everyday Life, Landscapes, Museums.* Ann Arbor: UMI Research Press, 1990.

Sherman, Daniel and Irit Rogoff, eds. *Museum Culture: Histories, Discourses, Spectacles.* Minneapolis: University of Minnesota Press, 1994.

Wallace, Michael. *Mickey Mouse History and Other Essays on American Memory.* Philadelphia: Temple University Press, 1996.

Wechsler, Lawrence. *Mr. Wilson's Cabinet of Wonders.* New York: Vintage, 1996.

ARTICLES

Chew, Ron. "In Praise of the Small Museum." *Museum News* 81, no. 2 (March/April 2002): 36–41.

Davila, Arlene. "Culture in the Battleground: From Nationalist to Pan-Latino Projects." *Museum Anthropology* 23, no. 3 (1999): 26–41.

Gable, Eric. "Maintaining Boundaries, or 'Mainstreaming' Black History into a White Museum." In *Museum Theory,* edited by Sharon Macdonald and Gordon Fyfe, 177–202. Oxford: Blackwell, 1996.

Graubard, Stephen R., ed. *America's Museums,* special issue of *Daedalus* 128, no. 3 (Summer 1999).

Handler, Richard, and William Saxton. "Dyssimulation: Reflexivity, Narrative, and the Quest for Authenticity in 'Living History.'" *Cultural Anthropology* 3 (August 1988): 242–61.

Huebner, Dwayne "Curricular Language and Classroom Meanings." In *Language and Meaning,* edited by J. B. Macdonald and R. R. Leeper, 8–26. Washington, D.C.: Association for Supervision and Curriculum Development, 1966.

Levin, Amy. "The Family Camping Hall of Fame and Other Wonders: Local Museums and Local History." *Studies in Popular Culture* 29, no. 3 (1997): 77–90.

Schwab, Joseph. "The Practical: A Language for Curriculum." *School Review* 78, no.1 (November 1969): 1-23.

Vallance, Elizabeth. "The Public Curriculum of Orderly Images." *Educational Researcher* 24, no. 2 (March 1995): 4–13.

WEBSITES

American Association of Museums. "Museum Accreditation: Criteria and Concerns." www.aam-us.org/programs/accreditation/webc&c.cfn (accessed 27 June 2006).

Index

About the Contributors

Tami Christopher earned her M.A. in American and New England Studies from the University of Southern Maine and a B.A. in English from Central Connecticut State University. She specializes in nineteenth-century American social and literary history. Christopher has worked for several New England historical and cultural institutions, including the Maine State Museum, the Connecticut Historical Society, and the Antiquarian and Landmarks Society. She is currently teaching online for Axia College. Her publications include contributions to the *Louisa May Alcott Encyclopedia* and *American Literature Archive* online (2001).

James T. H. Connor is assistant director in charge of the five anatomical and historical collections at the National Museum of Health and Sciences. He was former director of the Hannah Institute for the History of Medicine in Toronto and curator/archivist of the Medical Museum and Archives at University Hospital, London, Ontario. He is currently an associated scholar with the Institute for the History and Philosophy of Science and Technology at the University of Toronto and coeditor of McGill-Queen University Press's History of Medicine, Health, and Society Series. Connor has written two books, *Doing Good: The Life of Toronto's General Hospital* (Toronto: University of Toronto Press, 2000), which has received numerous awards, and *A Heritage of*

Healing: The London Health Association and Its Hospitals (London, Ontario: London Health Association, 1990). After receiving his doctorate in history from the University of Waterloo in Ontario, he also held faculty appointments at the University of Toronto and the University of Western Ontario.

J. Daniel d'Oney recently joined the faculty of the Albany College of Pharmacy as associate professor in the Arts and Humanities division. A native of Louisiana, d'Oney interned with the Louisiana Old State Capitol as its historian and still conducts contract work for the museum through his consulting firm, Honeythorn Historical Research and Consulting.

Jessie L. Embry is assistant director of the Charles Redd Center for Western Studies and instructor of history at Brigham Young University. She received a B.A. and M.A. in American history from B.Y.U. and has worked at the Charles Redd Center since 1979. She is the author of six books and over seventy articles on the history of Mormons, women, Utah, and Western America. She has also written on oral history. Embry is a volunteer docent at the Latter-day Saints Museum of Church History and Art.

Eric Gable is associate professor at Mary Washington College. Together with Richard Handler, he has written *The New History in an Old Museum: Creating the Past at Colonial Williamsburg* and numerous articles on Colonial Williamsburg. He has also written several articles based on fieldwork on political and religious conflicts in Guinea-Bissau and in highland Sulawesi.

Lucian Gomoll is currently a Ph.D. candidate and Eugene Cota-Robles fellow in the History of Consciousness program at the University of California, Santa Cruz. He holds an M.A. in Performance Studies from New York University. Gomoll is primarily interested in cultural representations and political experimentations with form, particularly in museum spaces. He is a feminist who has taught courses and guest lectured in women's studies at the University of Michigan, Ann Arbor. He is also a visual artist and performer, who composed and performed in "Acting the Other," produced by Anna Deveare Smith.

Richard Handler received his B.A. in English literature from Columbia University in 1972 and his Ph.D. in anthropology from the University of Chicago in 1979. His books include *Nationalism and the Politics of Culture in*

Quebec and, with Eric Gable, *The New History in an Old Museum: Creating the Past at Colonial Williamsburg*. He has taught at the University of Virginia since 1986, where he is currently professor of anthropology and associate dean for academic programs in the College of Arts and Sciences. He is editor of *History of Anthropology* and is completing *Critics Against Culture*, a collection of essays on anthropology and cultural criticism.

David E. Kyvig is Distinguished Research Professor and professor of history at Northern Illinois University. He is the coauthor, with Myron Marty, of *Nearby History: Exploring the Past Around You*, as well as the editor of ten research guides to topics in nearby history. His 1996 book, *Explicit and Authentic Acts: Amending the U.S. Constitution, 1776–1995*, won the Bancroft Prize, and he is currently writing a book to be called *The Age of Impeachment*.

Donna Langford is the curator at Tinker Swiss Cottage Museum in Rockford, Illinois. She received a Master of Arts in Anthropology from Northern Illinois University, specializing in human skeletal analysis.

Amy K. Levin is director of women's studies and professor of English at Northern Illinois University. She is also chair of the Museum Studies Steering Committee, which administers the museum studies graduate certificate program. Levin has published two books of literary criticism, *The Suppressed Sister* and *Africanism and Authenticity in African-American Women's Novels*. Levin has considerable experience teaching in museums and is completing a monograph titled "The Museum of Museums and Other Wonders: Museums, Narrative, and Culture."

Mauri Liljenquist Nelson graduated from Brigham Young University with an M.A. in American history with an emphasis in museum studies. Her thesis, "The Commodification of Twentieth-Century Hopi Kachina Dolls," examined how the commercial market affected the Hopi people and the style of their kachina dolls in the twentieth century. Nelson has worked in several Utah museums, including DUP sites and the Museum of Peoples and Cultures at Brigham Young University. She was curator for an exhibit titled "Kachinas and the Hopi Worlds," which highlighted her research and Hopi oral tradition. She also served as assistant editor of *Relics Revisited: A Twentieth-Century Look at a Turn of the Century Collection (The Pectol-Lee Collection from Capitol Reef)*.

Stuart Patterson is assistant professor of liberal arts at Shimer College in Chicago, Illinois. His dissertation focuses on two New Deal "subsistence homesteads" communities—Arthurdale, West Virginia, and Aberdeen Gardens, Virginia. The study compares both the towns' histories and current residents' museums of the communities' origins in the 1930s. His publications include a history of a third New Deal community, Cumberland Homesteads in Tennessee. Patterson is currently planning an oral history and documentary history of Shimer College and its 150 years in Illinois.

Heather R. Perry is assistant professor in the history department at the University of North Carolina at Charlotte. She received her Ph.D. from Indiana University in 2005. She is currently working on a book on medicine, masculinity, and the male body in World War I Germany. She has also served as a research fellow at the Center for Interdisciplinary Research on Women and Gender (ZiF) at the Christian-Albrechts-University of Kiel, Germany, and as an editorial assistant at the *American Historical Review.* Her publications include "Re-Arming the Disabled Veteran: Artificially Rebuilding State and Society in WWI Germany," in *Artificial Parts and Practical Lives*, ed. Katherine Ott, David Serlin and Stephen Mihm.

Jay Price directs the public history program at Wichita State University. He is a native of Santa Fe, New Mexico, and has degrees from the University of New Mexico, the College of William and Mary, and Arizona State University. At Wichita State, he teaches classes on public history, the American West, religion in America, and U.S. popular culture. His research interest is in how communities shape and promote their identity through monuments, parks, roadside attractions, and architecture. His most recent publication is a photo history of early Wichita, and he is in the process of having another book, on Arizona's state park system, published.

Michael G. Rhode has been chief archivist of the Otis Historical Archives at the National Museum of Health and Medicine since 1989. Prior to that, he was an archives technician at the National Archives and Records Administration. Rhode has authored numerous papers and articles in addition to making many presentations on medical history. Exhibits he has curated include "American Angels of Mercy: Dr. Anita Newcomb McGee's Pictorial Record of the Russo-Japanese War, 1904" and "Battlefield Surgery 101: From the Civil War to Vietnam." He coauthored the catalogs for both exhibits as well.

Eric Sandweiss is Carmony Chair and associate professor of history at Indiana University, as well as editor of the *Indiana Magazine of History*. For ten years, he served as director of research at the Missouri Historical Society in St. Louis. He is author of *St. Louis: The Evolution of an American Urban Landscape* and editor of *St. Louis in the Century of Henry Shaw: A View Beyond the Garden Wall.*

Elizabeth Vallance is associate professor of art education at Indiana University, Bloomington. She taught art education and museum studies at Northern Illinois University, 2001–2006, chairing NIU's Museum Studies Steering Committee. She was director of education at The Saint Louis Art Museum for fifteen years before that. Her publications focus on aesthetic education, museum education, the hidden curriculum, and applications of curriculum theory to nonschool settings. She is active in the American Association of Museums, the National Art Education Association, the Association of Midwest Museums, and the American Educational Research Association.